What The
THE M

"It is with great _____ ___ ___g
revelations that Ni__ _____ ___ci-
pants in *THE MESSENGERS* act as messengers themselves, clearing our collective spiritual
path of the cumulative misunderstandings that
centuries have wrought, showing us that angels
are alive and well in everyone's life."

—*The New Times*

"The verbatim transcripts . . . are absorbing.
There is much food for thought in the unfolding
story of the relationship between Jesus and Paul,
a relationship that rings with firsthand knowledge."

—*NAPRA ReView*

"*THE MESSENGERS* sheds light on some
very controversial doctrine. . . . Nick Bunick's
stories are deeply moving and compelling. . . ."

—*The Light Connection*

*Nick Bunick gives back to us an ageless message spo-
ken 2,000 years ago when Jesus walked the earth.
That message is as true today as it was then:
Within every one of us is a part of God. It is that
which gives us life and it is that which is everlasting.
If we but look within, our own love will fashion a
new and compassionate world. That message is the
gateway into our next millennium.*

The MESSENGERS

—— *A* ——

True Story of

Angelic Presence

and the

Return to the

Age of Miracles

Julia Ingram
and G.W. Hardin

POCKET STAR BOOKS
New York   London   Toronto   Sydney   Tokyo   Singapore

A Pocket Star Book published by
POCKET BOOKS, a division of Simon & Schuster Inc.
1230 Avenue of the Americas, New York, NY 10020

Copyright © 1996 by Skywin

Published by arrangement with Skywin

Published in hardcover in 1997 by Pocket Books

ISBN: 0-671-01687-3

First Pocket Books paperback printing August 1998

10 9 8 7 6 5 4 3 2 1

POCKET STAR BOOKS and colophon are registered
trademarks of Simon & Schuster Inc.

Cover art by Stanley Martucci

Printed in the U.S.A.

This is a true story. Sara's actual name has been changed at
her request. In Book II, exact wording was used from tape
transcriptions of the dialog, except where noted.

Testimony of Truth

*I*f *The Messengers* were fiction, it still would be an outstanding story for the emotions it will generate, for its overwhelming inspiration, and for the wisdom and love contained within these pages.

The Messengers is not fiction. The story is true. For that reason it is one of the most extraordinary chronicles written during the 20th century. The message in *The Messengers* is the gateway into our next millennium.

This book is dedicated to those who were unknowingly involved in the angelic plan to bring this book forward. To them we give our thanks for their fortitude and their trust.

"Each one of us whose name appears below was brought into Nick Bunick's life in a different way. Each one of us played a different role in confirming to Nick that angels are intervening in his life by the angelic experiences we personally had. We humorously refer to this experience as having come 'underneath the angelic umbrella.' Come join us."

Mary Jo Avery	Boris Lopatin
Beth Ayres	Laurie McQuary
Rick Eckard	Abe Pauls
Gary Hardin	Thomas Tsoi
Julia Ingram	Mark Wagner
Beth Jarman	Paul White

Acknowledgments

No project of this magnitude is accomplished by a few individuals. Many have contributed in ways deserving recognition beyond mere thanks. It is to those nameless many that we acknowledge the power of loving free will and generosity, working in harmony with the power of the angels, in bringing this book to print.

Special thanks is warmly extended to Beth Ayres, whose groundedness and patience kindly served those unexpectedly dazed by the wonder of angels coming into their lives.

Several professionals trusted in this project when conventionalism might have dictated they invest their time and professionalism in more traditional areas. We offer our appreciation to Joanna Hurley, Ciaran Mercier, Duane Warren, David VonDerLinn, Susi Henderson, and Jennifer Lauck. And a special thank you to our editor, Jane Cavolina, who joined with us both in spirit and effort in making *The Messengers* available to the national market.

Finally, we offer our eternal gratitude to those who have witnessed these angelic events, whose names appear in the Testimony of Truth. In an era of skepticism and judgment, we recognize the courage it takes to stand up before the world and publicly acknowledge that the heavenly has touched one's life. Some of these people did not even believe in angels or spiritual phenomena at the time. May their personal stories and the story told within these pages give hope to the world, ever reminding us that we are indeed returning to the Age of Miracles.

Contents

BOOK I
GATHERING OF ANGELS

BOOK II
HE WALKED WITH THE MASTER: THE MANUSCRIPT

Contents

Book I

GATHERING OF ANGELS

Chapter 1

THE MANUSCRIPT

*F*rom the time he was a little boy, Nick knew he was somehow different. It was not a feeling he understood, nor a topic he discussed with others. He recognized the disparities of life at an early age but chose to stand above them. Though Nick had risen from the poor streets of Boston, he did not look upon those streets with disdain. He had learned great truths on those streets, great compassion, unexpected sharing among those who had little, and most important, simple respect on those streets.

He was born to hard-working Russian immigrants who knew the value of a dollar and also understood the values a dollar could not buy. It was with silent admiration that Nick had witnessed his father give food to neighbors who had gone without eating, when his own family had little to eat. Nick would never lose this respect for his mother and father. They had fostered in Nick a wealth that money could not touch.

As a boy, he never walked the streets of his neighborhood with his head hung down. Nick's eyes saw far. And to see far, one had to look far. It wasn't just his being a high-

3

school football star and a scholar that had made him stand out in his early years, nor was it his ability to get a university education on an athletic scholarship. It was something else—perhaps his compassion, his capacity to make friends with anyone in the neighborhood. Some of those friends would end up in prison, some would leave the streets to become doctors and engineers. To Nick, they were all just friends; status simply did not matter. He wasn't afraid to take chances with people, nor was he afraid to take risks in business. It was as if he could occupy two different worlds simultaneously.

Now in his fifties, Nick found those two worlds colliding. His heart was troubled because he fit in so easily with the rich and powerful while those who also mattered to him sometimes went hungry or wanting. But now he felt more troubled than ever. No longer did he wander the poor streets of Boston. No longer did his differentness linger about him like an unknown, shadowy figure. His was now a world few, if any, could ever imagine.

The evening air was heavy with moisture as he jogged along the lakeside path. His head bowed forward as he watched one foot blur in front of the other. January's coolness calmed him with its misty, blanketing feeling as he seemed to drift along the path and through the evergreens of Lake Oswego. This was his neighborhood, his "digs," his creation. Nick was pleased with the land development he had fostered at this end of the lake. Here the homes were an integral part of the forest, unlike the jumbled edifices to wealth on other parts of the lake. Nature's richness interwove with the elegance of well-designed dwellings, creating a tapestry of primeval firs and hemlocks interspersed with young oaks and maple trees and civilized rhododendrons embracing homes: one esthetic balancing another. Nick liked this harmony, especially since it seemed to elude him now.

As he ran, a mood of spiritual peacefulness teetered

against the thoughts racing in his mind as the birds overhead echoed their cries across the steep Oregon hills surrounding this end of the lake. He wanted to call back at them, but their wings reminded him of the phone conversation earlier in the day, the source of this wonderment that captured his thoughts. As wet patches of dead fir needles, decayed oak and maple leaves rhythmically squished beneath his running shoes, Nick's attention once more turned to digest the significance of all that had happened this day. What was he to do about it? Perhaps there was nothing to do but run.

His thoughts stopped, his feet stopped. With his hands on the waist of his jogging shorts, Nick stared out across the length of the lake to its opposite end, which peeked into downtown Lake Oswego. The evening shadows were tucking the lake to sleep. Reflected clouds softened the black surface of the water. To the north, the city lights of Portland were beginning to dominate the edge of the sky. Nick's labored breathing was the only sound to be heard. Even the birds had departed for their nightly havens. "Why don't I just enjoy this for now?" he gasped between breaths. "After all, how often do you get to speak to your angels?" He glanced up into the trees, half expecting an answer.

The pronouncement seemed to end the struggle between head and heart. Yes, some things should just be enjoyed. Nick continued his jog, taking the last leg of the outing up the hill and back to his house. As he rounded the turn into the cul-de-sac, the street lamp next to his house flickered to life.

As dusk eased into night, Nick found himself gazing out through the glass French doors, which opened onto the high deck suspended above the lakeside escarpment. The few lights across the lake twinkled on the waters below.

The phone rang, stirring him from his euphoria. The voice on the other end seemed hesitant. "Nick?"

"Yes, this is Nick."

"Are you all right? Is anything wrong?"

It was Abe Pauls calling from his hotel room in Switzerland. "Everything's fine, Abe. Why?" There was a short pause. It was obvious that Abe seemed a bit unsettled, perhaps confused. His sleepy voice hung in the air as he tried to begin his next sentence.

"Nick. I have absolutely no idea why I am calling you. In fact, I am embarrassed." Abe cleared his throat. "I was fast asleep. It's the middle of the night here in Geneva. Something woke me up from my sleep. I looked at the clock, it was 4:44 a.m. and something told me, 'Call Nick right away. You must call Nick.' I have absolutely no idea why I am calling you."

Both men were silent, each for different reasons. Nick knew right away what was going on, he just couldn't believe it was already starting. How was he going to explain this to Abe? After all, Abe was a business colleague, not an old friend. He did not want to lose credibility with this man. Nick pondered the possibility of losing Abe as a business associate. Would he be able to understand? Should he be told? Of course he should be told. Why else would he be waking up in the middle of the night in Geneva, Switzerland, compelled to make a phone call he had absolutely no reason for making? Nick knew the reason for the call. But how could he tell Abe?

Nick decided to break the silence, beginning slowly yet deliberately. "Abe, do you remember the copy of my personal manuscript I gave to you?" Because Abe had not mentioned a word about the document since being handed a copy a while ago, even this route of conversation could prove costly. The manuscript was a chronicle of events that had surrounded Nick two years earlier. Few had been allowed to read the document since its completion. And with good reason. The contents could destroy Nick's career, maybe even threaten his entire financial domain. It was a chance Nick took in yielding a copy to Abe. He was fond of Abe and trusted him. Knew Abe to have a good heart, a good soul. But perhaps the information in the story conflicted with Abe's own spiritual beliefs.

"Do I remember it?" Abe croaked with incredulity, the sleepiness still hanging in his throat. "I've read it three times. In fact, it's sitting on the nightstand next to my bed here. Why?"

A half-smile crept across Nick's face as he began. "Rather than tell you why, let me explain what has happened." Nick sat down as he tried to figure out where to start. A brightness eased across his face as he began collecting parts of the story in his head to share with Abe. In moments like this, Nick appeared ageless, one might even say innocent.

"A little more than a week ago, I received a phone call from my daughter, Kim. She had been down in Southern California to see the University of Oregon play in the Rose Bowl against Penn State. One week after the game, Kim returned to Oregon and called me." Nick wasn't sure why he was giving such detail, but it somehow seemed necessary. He wanted Abe to fully appreciate the broad picture.

Nick continued, "Kim asked if she could come over and talk to me. She said she had something very important she wanted to share with me." He described for Abe how his daughter had driven right over, breezed through the front door and presented him with a cassette tape. How he had asked what it was for, and how she had insisted he play it to find out. While getting the cassette deck ready, Kim informed him how her girlfriend had told her about a gifted lady who lived in the Los Angeles area—a lady who could speak with angels. Nick paused a bit at this point in his story to see if Abe had any reaction—then continued.

"So after the Rose Bowl, Kim made an appointment to see this angel lady. Kim told me that the lady revealed to her information of the most personal nature, information that was impossible for this lady to know." The information had struck Kim profoundly. This angel lady described details regarding Kim's private life and told her that she was speaking to Kim's angels, sharing information that Kim's angels were telling her.

"So I listened to the tape. And I have to tell you that I was equally amazed. The angel lady went into information regarding Kim's medical problems that would be absolutely impossible for her to know."

Nick explained to Abe how Kim appeared to be an extremely healthy woman in her twenties, very attractive and full of energy and life—on the surface. Nonetheless, this angel lady had been able to diagnose internal problems Kim was having, as well as give Kim remedies for the illness. On the tape, the lady had stated several times that she was not a psychic. The information she was sharing with Kim was coming from Kim's angels.

Once again Nick waited to hear any objections or questions from Abe, and once again there was only silence. It was too late to back out now. Nick took a deep breath and resumed the story.

"I didn't quite know what to think about this, Abe. I know my daughter. She's a pretty grounded person. Listening to her and listening to the tape was amazing. I wondered how this lady could be speaking with angels. I had never seriously believed there was any such thing as angels —just a pleasant tale to comfort children."

Nick went on to explain how he thought this woman must be a psychic of extraordinary talent who was pretending to speak with angels, and how no person could have had that kind of psychic ability. "Abe, she wasn't speaking in generalities. This lady was giving details to Kim even though there weren't any specific questions from Kim for her to cue off of. Nor did she ask any questions so she could determine what direction to go with any of the information she gave to Kim."

Nick paused briefly, once again surmising how he must be sounding. "I know of no source or skill that any person could possibly have to be able to give that kind of personal detail. In fact, some of the information was so esoteric only to Kim, that even I didn't know about it."

Abe's own religious upbringing allowed him to be open-minded about such things. He had not only heard stories about angels throughout his childhood, he had been through experiences just as unlikely as the one Nick was describing. Events had occurred in Abe's life that left him wondering why he was alive today. Rather than question Nick's story, Abe was intrigued by it. The manuscript resting on his nightstand contained a story others might find unbelievable, but Abe was warmed by it. It filled in gaps regarding events ages ago, when miracles were the topic of everyday conversation.

Though he came from a strong religious background, Abe had been a spiritual rebel. He had posed questions, serious questions to his church elders that never seemed to get answered. He had been so persistent in his questions about God and Jesus that he ultimately was asked not to come back to church. He was "too disruptive," as the minister had put it.

What Nick was bringing into Abe's life was not more questions, but answers—answers that had long waited to be heard. The silence on the other end of the phone was not coming out of doubt, but quite the opposite. Abe's ears had long wanted to hear the kinds of stories Nick was bringing into his life. But Nick didn't know this as he wondered if he should just shut up and leave the rest of the tale untold.

"Wow," was all Abe said after a while. "You know, I'm not that surprised to hear of such things. I've had some rather extraordinary events happen to me that made me feel that someone was watching over me. I wanted to believe it was angels watching over me. But how do you really know? You don't, until you hear something like this. What happened next?"

Nick relaxed, knowing Abe wanted to hear the rest. "Well, after Kim and I discussed the tape at great length, Kim said I ought to call the angel lady and get a reading."

Kim had explained how this delightful lady could talk to Nick's angels while he was talking to her over the phone. All he had to do was write down the questions he wanted answered and give his angels permission to talk to her. He didn't even have to tell her what the questions were.

Nick explained to Abe how incredible Kim felt it would be for him to call this gifted woman, particularly because of his past experiences. Kim was referring to the story in the manuscript, and Abe knew it. They were extraordinary experiences, indeed.

With the skill of a medieval storyteller, Nick continued to lead Abe through the accounts with the angel lady—how he had called the number his daughter had given him the next day, how the voice on the other end had come from an answering machine, asking the caller to leave a message.

Nick had left his phone number and received a call back two days later. The woman's voice was sweet and polite, almost the voice one would expect from a child. She had told Nick she could give a reading in the latter part of the week, Saturday, January 14. Her instructions had been the same as Kim's: to write down on a piece of paper the questions that Nick wanted answered; also to write down permission to his angels to talk to her so they could provide the answers to his questions.

Early Saturday afternoon, Nick had sat with a sheet of paper at the kitchen table writing three questions he wished answered. The first had dealt with his unborn son, who was three months from term. He wanted reassurance that his son would be healthy, and he wanted information regarding the boy's future. His second question had related to business matters. Would Abe Pauls, the Canadian, and Abe's partner, Thomas Tsoi, the gentleman from Hong Kong, be able to complete the business transactions many people were relying on? Or, would the opportunities not become reality?

Abe broke into a full grin at hearing this, raking his fingers through his light-brown hair in a kind of nervous appreciation. Nick was so much like himself, Abe thought: a businessman who cared about the forthrightness of others. Like Nick, Abe put great stock in integrity and honesty, not only in his business dealings but throughout his whole life. He knew, as Nick did, that the business transactions were subject to Thomas' ability and his own ability to pull through on the financial end. Nick wanted to know if they were going to be successful. For that matter, so did Abe. He hung onto every word to find out what the angel lady, whose name was Sara, would say as Nick enthusiastically continued his narrative.

The third question Nick had written down related to the manuscript. Nick had wanted to know if the manuscript would ever be published as a book. Did it have a future? What meaning and significance would the book have to Nick this year, 1995?

Abe interrupted. "Were you able to ask only three questions?"

"No, I could ask as many as I wanted, but those were the only questions I wanted answered."

"I see," was Abe's reply. He was sorry he had interrupted. He wanted to hear more. Nick picked up on the silence.

"After I finished writing the three questions, I proceeded to tell my 'angels' that they had my permission to speak with the woman in Los Angeles, who claimed to listen to the angels, and for them to share the answers with her." Nick went off on a tangent telling Abe how skeptical he was about all this. First of all, Nick didn't really believe angels actually existed. He thought they were the creation of poets and myth-makers. No adult would take such stories seriously.

This surprised Abe. For he had felt the guardianship of these protectors throughout his years. They may have been the subjects of stories from his mother and favorite aunt, but they were stories he chose to give credence to. His own rebellious lifestyle was a testimony to having been watched over by forces certainly beyond himself. Rather than engage Nick in a discussion as to whether angels did or did not exist, Abe sat stonelike on his bed wanting to hear the remainder of the story.

Nick rattled on. "Every book I have ever read, every documentary I have ever seen, every article I have ever been exposed to in which angels were supposedly involved have always included the same scenario. There was absolutely no proof. The stories were always based exclusively on the word of one individual. There were no witnesses who could authenticate or verify the incident. I had always assumed it was either honest imagination of the individual or a totally fabricated story. I knew that there were no such things as angels."

However, at 2 o'clock on Saturday afternoon, January 14, 1995, Nick would discover he was wrong. It was the first of many encounters that not only he but also many of his colleagues would experience during the next several months.

Abe knew Nick had a matter-of-fact way of looking at life. It didn't surprise him to hear Nick's skepticism about whether angels really existed. However, the thought did cross his mind that angels just might be a little put off about being thought of that way—maybe even put off enough not to engage such a doubter. And what did all of this have to do with his being awakened at 4:44 in the morning? He listened intently as Nick began describing the phone call.

"I hooked up my telephone to a device that would tape-record the phone conversation, and I placed the questions I had written in front of me. I also had a pad of paper and pencils on the table so I could scribble notes as we talked, just in case the recorder didn't work."

At exactly 2 p.m., Nick had dialed Sara's phone number, having no idea what to expect. He had prayed for seven or eight minutes. He was now ready. He was calm.

Sara had answered the phone and wasted no time with small talk. "Your angels are already here," she had said. "I have already gotten a lot of information which they have given me. I cannot believe the energy in this room. It's incredible. I am very excited and am ready to begin. First I would like to start with a prayer."

Her somewhat childlike voice had seemed even more innocent as she began to ask for guidance, protection and worthiness to speak to Nick's angels. Sara's voice was very soft and the prayer was deliberate, as if she had been reading the prayer off a card or saying it from memory. She then asked Nick to say his full name.

"What happened after that can only be described as miraculous," Nick related in an almost reverent voice.

Although the questions on the paper in front of him had been listed in order of Nick's priorities—first wanting to know about his coming son, then information regarding his business ventures and, lastly, information about the manuscript becoming a book—the response did not follow that order.

"Nick," she had begun, "they are telling me something about work you are doing with a person from Canada and his Asian partner. It is very good and very important, and it is going to be tremendously successful. You will be getting letters or documents from them that will indicate how things are moving forward. This will represent confirmation that it is all going to be very successful. They are telling me the man from Canada has a very high forehead, pale blue eyes and light brown hair. Also, that he is short of stature."

She had described Abe to a tee. Nick had been astounded to hear this. As Abe listened to this part of the phone conversation, the muscles in his aging, athletic body tightened. The angels had talked about him, Abe Pauls? What for?

"Abe, I have been around psychics before, even great ones, but never has a person been able to do something like that."

"Didn't she say she wasn't a psychic?" reminded Abe.

"True, she doesn't represent herself that way. She told me, as she had told Kim, that her information is coming exclusively from the angels. In fact, she made a point of telling me that she doesn't have psychic abilities." Nick paused a few moments to let the notion of talking angels sink in. "She had more to say about you.

"She said, 'This Canadian man is actually in Europe. However, I see them moving their offices to other places and expanding. He has an Asian partner with whom you will be very much involved. I am being told that they are going to increase the line of their product—whatever it is—which might be financial. The angels are saying that the business is going to be large and will involve many international dealings, that it will have positive impact on people all over the world.' "

There was no way in the world Sara or any other source on earth would have knowledge of what Abe and his partner, Thomas, were doing with Nick. Also, all three were bound by a nondisclosure agreement. Any leak of information could be disastrous. Abe's rising eyebrows pulled the sleep out of his eyes. The thought that he might be in league with the angels was almost amusing. It was true that their business dealings involved making a better world. So maybe it wasn't so farfetched to think that angels were trying to help out.

"Abe, this lady was using financial terms that had no

meaning to her. She had to ask me if I knew the meaning of certain words that the angels were telling her because she didn't understand them. She'd have to have been very experienced in the world of international finance to understand some of the words she was using. There was no way in the world she could have known about you and Thomas and our dealings."

Abe was now in full grin. *Wait till Thomas wakes up and hears this story*, he thought. Though Thomas was Asian and lived in Hong Kong, he was also a Christian, and a man of deep spiritual conviction. Abe wanted to charge down the hotel hallway to Thomas' room and rouse him from his sleep. But no, there was obviously more to the story.

"And it didn't stop there," Nick warned. "She then said, 'They are also showing me the letters of a company whose last letter is W and the first letter is H, which is a business transaction that is very, very good. In fact, it is going to work out wonderfully for you. You have been putting a lot of energy and time into this company, but it is all going to pay off. Wonderful things will come as a result of it. This company is going to be tremendously successful.' "

Abe's fingers brushed playfully against his receding hairline as he smilingly recognized the initials matching one of six companies Nick had brought into the negotiations. This company had developed significant new medical technology that would enable detection of certain diseases many years before a patient would otherwise be diagnosed. Nick had thought so much of the company that not only had the partnership signed an agreement to provide substantial investment funds, but Nick went so far as to invest his own money into the company. That Sara knew about this company was simply astonishing.

It was Nick's turn to grin as he listened to Abe take in a deep breath. Master presenter that he was, Nick let his tale sink in a bit longer before revealing more. "And then...," he said, adding another deliberate pause, "Sara proceeded to tell me that the Canadian man and his Asian partner would soon be creating office space in the Portland area.

"She told me that the angels are bringing us together because of my reluctance to have the manuscript published." Again, Nick waited.

Abe's eyes immediately went to the neatly bound document on his nightstand. He had been awestruck by the information it contained. He had read it three times because it had made such a deep impact on him. And now angels were conveying a message that he, Abe Pauls, would somehow be connected to its story? Just thinking about it evoked a sense of wonder. *What if this is all true? What did it all mean?*

"She said the angels are bringing us together for a purpose," Nick continued. "That the angels are going to make what we are doing successful beyond our greatest expectations. The reason is that I am supposed to move ahead and have the manuscript published as a book. She told me I had been holding back in allowing publication because of my concerns about how it would affect me financially as well as personally."

Nick was now speaking in *largo*, holding on to each word to make sure it could be heard. He wanted Abe to absorb the implications of this information. If the manuscript's being made public had concerned someone like Nick, then surely Abe would find it even more disturbing, more threatening.

But Abe was a different kind of player than Nick. Sure, he could play his part in harmony with others around him, but he was also the kind of man who had no trouble playing solo. Nick was, indeed, the type of businessman who enjoyed orchestrating business. Abe was the kind of entrepreneur capable of juggling business demands like a street musician. He wasn't afraid of tin cups, nor was he afraid of business suits. He wasn't afraid of what others might say of him, and he wasn't afraid of losing business or going it alone if others disapproved. In fact, he felt warmed by the thought of somehow being involved with the striking implications in that manuscript. The manuscript implied a return to the Age of Miracles. And that was just fine with Abe.

Nick continued, "The angels say it is important that I move ahead with getting the book published, and they will provide me with the security I need so that I'm comfortable in making sure its message is heard."

There was a long pause. Abe decided it was time for Nick to know where he, Abe, personally stood. He told Nick about some of his own background and his spiritual convictions, as opposed to religious convictions. The two of them also talked about business, and the business of business. They talked philosophies and attitudes, personal histories and concerns. Abe's affable character brought a charm to an otherwise bizarre discussion. Nick now felt as if he were talking to a friend, a man who could not only understand the recent turn of events but appreciate the intimidating truths buried in the manuscript. Abe was a man who walked with peace. Nothing in life could threaten him, and there was nothing in life he chose to threaten. He had no use for negativity, and it showed.

A rapport was developing between the two men over the thousands of miles. Both felt it and welcomed it. As anecdotes and jokes were swapped, the conversation ambled back to the lady who spoke with angels. Abe wanted to hear more about what the angels had to say. And Nick, comforted by the ease he now felt with Abe, wanted to tell him.

"Well, she went on to answer the other question on my piece of paper, which was about my son, Nicholas. Though I never told her a word about him, she knew he was going to be born in April, that I would have a son, and that his name would be Nicholas. But what really cinched it was when she said, 'The angels are telling me that Nicholas is going to be very healthy and that you don't have to worry anymore.' The truth of the matter was that both Mary Jo and I had been concerned because of some minor complications during the pregnancy. When I heard Nicholas was going to be fine, I couldn't have been more thrilled." Emotions rose in Nick's heart as he recalled the moment. When a man has such rapid change come to him in so short a moment, emotions become strong memories. And this had been a moment that Nick would never forget. He continued, "I felt with complete conviction that I was talking with the messengers of God. And shortly before this, I had believed they didn't even exist."

Though Sara had passed on more information about his future son, Nick didn't feel it necessary to tell Abe everything. It was quite personal, something he and his wife would remember for years to come.

After exchanging a few more comments with Abe, Nick returned to what the angels had revealed about Thomas. "Sara asked me if I had any more questions, and I said I did not. So then she asked, 'Who is the man with the glasses who is involved with your spiritual being? Oh, I know, he is the Asian man. Although you haven't met him yet, you have known each other before. You have been together before. He is very spiritual, and the two of you are very close together.' Then she said, 'Somehow, the man with the glasses was also there in that past lifetime with Jesus. And they are telling me that he is going to be involved in the future also, not only in this lifetime, but in future lifetimes.' "

Hearing this sent electricity through Abe. Thomas Tsoi? His closest friend? Connected to Nick and the revelations in the manuscript? Abe's mind began to spin, goose bumps erupted on his arms. *What if all of this were true?* he asked himself again. And why was he, Abe Pauls, involved? Why hadn't Thomas been awakened at 4:44 in the morning, instead of himself? He needed to think, but now wasn't the time.

The notion of time began to disappear as the two men discussed the implications of the angelic information regarding business, as well as the apparent connection to the manuscript. They wished each other well as they hung up the phone, Nick going back to his window view of the lake, Abe pulling on his clothes to go for a much-needed walk.

As he left the empty lobby of the Noga Hilton, Lake Geneva seemed to invite Abe for a stroll along her ancient shores. The night air of Switzerland was crisp with anticipation of the coming dawn. The empty streets of Geneva hushed themselves against Abe's raging thoughts. With his hands stuffed stiffly in his trench coat pockets, he scuffed along toward the bridge spanning the waters of the grandmotherly lake. There were few answers to the many questions racing around in his head, and Abe knew he had to go along with what was happening. Something deep within told him whatever his role was, he would fulfill it.

The bridge behind him, Abe veered from the roadway onto a lakeside path. The waves calmly voiced soothing approval as they lapped against the silent shore. Abe knew that what lay ahead was not to be feared. He knew he was not only ready for the strange events surrounding him, he was meant for them. Questions continued to plague him with each succeeding turn along the path. And the lake seemed to caress away each concern with the rhythm of her waters. The Noga Hilton was once more coming into view. As traffic began crawling along the streets, Abe headed back toward the hotel. Thomas had to hear about this!

Nick contemplated the information he had decided not to share with Abe at this time. There was more, much more that the angels had communicated, but they had also been careful to warn Nick not to alarm others. What was coming was of great benefit to humankind. But some might not see it that way. Even though Abe had read the manuscript three times, Nick decided not to make known to Abe what the angels had told Sara about Nick and his history in the manuscript. Nick, himself, still had to wrestle with the information. Sara's words echoed in his mind.

"My God, Nick, you are a brilliant soul! I am honored to be able to talk to you as well as your angels. I am really honored. Your angels are also telling me that your energies are holding the manuscript back from being published because you are concerned for your family and your financial structure. It is OK to release it now and move ahead. The angels are saying that the book will be contracted for in the next six months."

Sara had then revealed what the angels had to say about major events about to happen to the world, mentioning the manuscript again. He remembered how deeply he felt about hearing all this. "It is very important that the book be published before these events happen," the angels had urged. "There is information in the manuscript that is coded, and people who have the correct spiritual DNA will be moved by the book and understand it and love it."

Spiritual DNA? He had never heard the term before. What did the manuscript have to do with spiritual DNA? The only DNA Nick knew of was the kind his researchers used to investigate diseases and their cures. Certainly, no one had ever assumed there was also DNA that described one's soul and spirituality. But Sara had said even more about this:

"They are saying to me, Nick, that just as people have different DNA in their cells, people also have different spiritual DNA. There are some people who will criticize you and the book. You should not concern yourself with them. They do not have the proper spiritual DNA, and there is nothing that you can do about it. You should concentrate on giving the information to people who have the proper spiritual DNA, for they are the ones who will understand and benefit from your book, and who will be prepared when these special events take place in the world. The information in your book is related to the collective event, but I can't explain it exactly."

What could possibly be in the manuscript that would connect with this coming special event? he wondered. Were the events themselves the purpose for getting the manuscript published? Or was it more a matter of spiritually preparing people for what was to come? Certainly, others he let see the manuscript, such as Abe, had expressed profound reactions to it. It made him feel good to hear that. But was spiritual DNA the reason? Had he not tried to get the manuscript published already? Had not four of the top publishers in the United States said they had wanted to publish it, only to turn it down later? Sara had said that he, Nick, was to blame. It was true he had felt strong concern for his family and the embarrassment he could face from financial colleagues if the book were released. Sara had said that kind of concern was what stopped the book from getting published. Could he have that much influence on the actions of others? he asked himself.

Sara had said, "After you came back from meeting with the publishers in New York, the reason it got turned down was because of you, because your energy was not ready. The angels are saying that one of the other publishing companies has now had a change of personnel. They say there is a new person who will play a very important role in having the book published." The angels even told Sara her name.

The idea of angels intervening to get his manuscript published struck Nick as strange. *Could angels actually get certain people hired to make sure the book would see the light of day?* He would have to check with his agent to see if this person actually existed. If this person was now working for one of the New York publishers that had turned down the manuscript, then Nick had no choice but to try once again to get that specific publishing house to turn the manuscript into a book. After all, Sara had said to Nick that the angels were always with him and were going to make things move ahead very quickly.

What a gift this woman has, thought Nick. He felt honored and blessed to have had this opportunity. And for the first time in his life, he felt the company of constant companions: his angels. Sometimes Nick took some real convincing, and this was one of these occasions. But the truth of the matter was that he was, indeed, convinced. But what to do about it? As he continued staring out across the lake, he remembered one last thing the angels had said: that his special number was a series of fours. It seemed rather important to Sara, as if the angels were making a big deal out of it. But why? It mildly puzzled Nick. Hadn't Abe said he was awakened at 4:44 a.m.? He thought twice about whether he should have said something to Abe about the fours. *Nahhh*, he thought. *Probably just a coincidence.*

Chapter 2

THE 444S

Throughout history, sacred beings have acted as if some divine comedian were secretly running Heaven. Paradoxes have cascaded down upon Earth from generation to generation. First Nation traditions abound with lore about Raven, Coyote, and other divine tricksters. These sacred archetypes were constantly testing, stealing, tricking, and teaching humans the folly of their mortal world of expectations, disharmony, and illusion. Stories from every known religion are replete with paradox, parody, and playfulness visited upon humanity by the heavens.

Not only shall the first be last, but the meek will inherit the earth. A simple carpenter, "the stone which the builders have rejected," becomes the cornerstone of Christianity. A stutterer is sent before Pharaoh to speak on behalf of a nation—Moses is his name. A peaceful farmer is approached by an angel of the Lord telling him to raise up an army. Gideon doesn't trust this calling. He wants proof. Three times he asks for proof that it is Yahweh who is asking him to do this. How reluctant can a man be? Providence might suggest that the heavens would at least interview a few generals for the job, or find someone more accommodating. But no, a farmer has been chosen, and a farmer it's going to be.

Even today, in our everyday lives, it seems inevitable that the least likely of us is called on by Heaven for the strangest of tasks. And so it was with Rick Eckard. Rick's passion was sports, so much so that he spent his working life setting up scholarship programs for promising high-school athletes. He was a kind man, to be sure, a man of the earth who loved the excitement of the game: excellence and skill against strength and brute force—a pride that sports brought to him and those with whom he worked. Though a good-hearted man, Rick pooh-poohed religion, especially the idea of people talking with angels.

Perhaps it was because he was a "jock" or the way he took teasing so well. Yes, that must have been what attracted the playful eye of Heaven. Or maybe it was simply that Rick occupied one of the offices in the third floor suite leased by Nick Bunick. In fact, Rick's office was right next to Nick's office. If he had known what was to befall him, he might never have accepted Nick's generous offer to use the space, free of charge, as long as it wasn't needed by the corporation. Nick so admired Rick's work with young athletes that it seemed the right thing to do. Yes, the heavenly humorist must have thought, *This is too perfect; this is too good to pass up*.

And so it happened that this man, who always slept like death, was awakened in the middle of the night in the same way as Abe Pauls, half a world away. It was as if someone had come into his bedroom and shaken him out of his sound sleep. Rick woke with such a start he almost roused his wife, sleeping next to him. His eyes searched the darkness for an intruder. The strangest feeling of urgency came over him. He had to write something down. Why? He had no idea.

With pencil and paper in hand, he sat down at the

desk in the family room and began to write. What he was writing was beyond him. But instead of being panicked by his incomprehension of what was happening, Rick felt strangely assured, as if some friendly hand were on his shoulder letting him know how important this message was. A wave of contentment and peacefulness flowed through him. Words and images seemed to flow from some great sea of knowledge. The images were not like those of a daydream but more like images in a vivid dream that seems so real you wonder if you are still dreaming when you wake up.

For some reason, he had to write down the time. The digital clock in the bedroom had been the first thing he saw when he was awakened. He scribbled down 4:44 a.m. In the upper left-hand corner he wrote "Nick." Why was he writing "Nick"? What did this have to do with Nick? More lines of scribble came from the pencil. It made no sense to him. Only later would he discover that what he was writing had special significance regarding a manuscript. In the middle of the page he now wrote, "The number four is very important to you." His present reverie would turn to awe when he found out later that this was a direct quote from the angels, given to Nick by the lady who could speak to them.

A triangle appeared in his vision, and his hand drew it on the sheet of paper. His hand wrote "Trinity" above the figure, underlining the word with a sense of profound importance, and then continued writing, "is confused in Bible or changed in modern writing." With deliberateness, his pencil pressed hard against the sheet as he wrote "The Father" on the top of the triangle; "Son" on the lower left corner of the triangle; and "Holy Ghost" on the right-hand vertex. Below that he felt compelled to write, "Leaves out—the future + light people + guardian angels." On a logical level, what this meant was totally baffling to him. But at some other level it all seemed right, even magnificent.

Rick reached for another sheet of paper. The scribbling continued. A new image appeared in his mind's eye, some kind of diamond shape. As he tried to draw the figure, his reasoning mind felt incapable of the task. It was as if two separate realities were flashing through him. What he could see in his mind seemed so simple, beautiful and awesome. But translating this into a sketch was like trying to speak Greek. His hand mutinied against his thoughts, scrawling with a confidence beyond him.

A two-dimensional diamondlike shape was now on the paper. To the left of the diamond his hand wrote, "They complete things." *What things?* he thought. *Complete what things?* His hand took off again. "Father, Son, Holy Spirit (in man) and angels or spirit guides." At the top of the diamond he had written the letter "F," the letter "S" to the left, "HS" (for Holy Spirit) to the right, and an "A" at the bottom point of the diamond, standing for the angels. Below the diamond was written another direct quote from Nick's angels. But Rick would only find that out later from Nick.

His hand began again, sketching another diamond, this one with an eye in the middle of it. He didn't know why. Then words came through again. He didn't know what they meant, but he wrote them nonetheless: "Symbol = third eye, mind's eye." *What is a third eye?* "Mind's eye" he could understand, but what is this third eye stuff about? One part of his mind could see all of this as if it were the most rational thing in all the world. But his thinking mind was almost totally baffled if it tried to make sense of it. He continued writing, this time underneath the diamond figure, and in small letters, "or three dimensional. That's why we don't understand."

That's an understatement, he thought. Yet his mind continued to struggle with the presence of two realities: one that felt as right as rain, the other as wild as a thunderstorm. Rick now saw himself writing in large block letters that took up the rest of the second sheet of paper, "THIS REP-

RESENTS THE COMPLETE SPIRITUAL NETWORK FOR MAN TO FULLY EVOLVE—THE SPIRITUAL PATH FOR SPIRIT GUIDES MUST EXIST." He felt as if he were taking dictation. And at the bottom of the sheet of paper came an even more mysterious line of words, "SPIRITUAL DNA = EXISTENCE OF PATH FOR SPIRITUAL GUIDES TO WORK—SOME ARE BLESSED WITH THIS POWER!"

Again, Rick's logical mind was puzzled but did not question why he felt so compelled to write this nonsensical verbiage. Whatever force was at hand, Rick knew this information was from it for Nick. Who "it" was, he could not imagine. He just knew it was imperative to convey these messages to Nick. He reached for a new sheet of paper. More was coming through.

Strange figures began appearing. He found himself struggling to draw a tetrahedron, a three-dimensional pyramid made up of four equilateral triangles. Another kind of tetrahedron took shape. How could he possibly draw this figure? It was as if it were a three-dimensional star made up of one triangular pyramid sitting upside-down intersecting the other. Next to it he tried to draw a two-dimensional representation. It appeared to be the Mogen David, the Star of David, with lines going throughout the figure, as if something were being connected. Again, the name of the biblical figure was written, as it was on the first sheet, once again referring to Nick's manuscript. After the name, he wrote "New Testament." More geometric figures appeared, one page of nothing but tetrahedrons. One had an eye in the center. Rick tried to understand why he was drawing these figures. They seemed important, quite important. But why? How could these star figures that resembled crystal shapes be important? He didn't know, he just knew he had to draw them.

As suddenly as it had all begun, it ended. The sensations left him wonder-struck. Five sheets of paper lay in front of him with scribblings that might as well have come from the moon. He knew he had to give this stuff to Nick. But why? How? And why this inexplicable feeling of great contentment, fulfillment, rightness? Logically, it didn't make sense. But in his heart this seemed correct, even necessary, to Rick. He shook his head, shuffling through the papers once again to see if anything made sense. What gave him the most comfort was his knowledge of Nick's strong spiritual side. And this weirdness in front of him appeared related to the spiritual—except the geometric figures. They seemed to have nothing to do with anything. Before he gathered up the scrawlings, he wrote at the top of the first sheet, "Woke up at 4:44 in the morning, and by 4:50 this was completed." He swirled a large circle around the sentence, got up from the table and headed back to bed, his body humming with a calm ecstasy. *I can hardly wait to see the look on Nick's face,* he said to himself. He didn't know why, but he knew this must be given to Nick.

❧

As Rick peered out the glass divider into the reception area, he could see Nick talking to his assistant, Beth. Rick didn't know Nick's business very well, but he did know that once Nick started his day, it was usually nonstop. If he were going to talk to Nick, it would have to be now. With anticipation, he grappled with the papers from the night before and parked himself patiently at Nick's office door.

"Rick! Good morning." Nick studied the queer look on Rick's face as he approached. Rick looked shyly apprehensive, almost as if he were going to explode.

"Nick, I have something very important to tell you. Can I meet with you?" There. He had done it. Now the feeling inside him would go away, leave him alone.

Nick studied his unexpected guest once more. "I'm

sorry, Rick. I have to leave immediately for a business appointment. But I can talk to you later in the day. Would that be OK?" Nick had never seen Rick this way. He hoped it wasn't some kind of family problem, or something personal. Nick had to get to his meeting.

"Sure, Nick. That'll work. I'll catch you later."

As he ambled back into his office, Rick became increasingly aware of the returning humming sensation within him. *How odd,* he mused, realizing how upbeat and confident he felt about getting together with Nick. One might have expected disappointment over Nick's busy schedule. But like the night before, Rick felt an invisible hand on his shoulder reassuring him that he was doing the right thing. As he sank into his chair, staring through his glass partition, watching Nick bustle out the door, a pleased look played on his big, kind face. What had happened last night seemed to have come from a place without time. Yes, this could wait until Nick was ready.

At 5:30 in the afternoon, Rick stuck his head into Nick's office. "Nick. Are you able to meet with me?"

"Sure," was Nick's only reply. Rick returned to his desk to retrieve the "weirdo papers" and marched back into Nick's office. He planted himself in the padded chair in front of Nick's executive desk. Nick apologized for not being able to meet with him earlier in the morning, Rick only half-hearing him.

"Nick, something happened to me last night. I was awakened in the middle of the night, and that has never happened to me. Not only did I wake up, but something compelled me to grab a pencil and some paper and go downstairs to my desk to write information down. I don't understand it, and I don't know why I did it. All I know is that I was compelled to write down this information, and that I am supposed to give it to you. I don't understand it, Nick. Maybe you will."

Nick stared at the papers handed him. His eyes immediately went to the time written in the upper-left corner: 4:44 a.m. A warm grin flowed across his face. The angels, again. With businesslike precision, Nick scanned the scribblings on the rest of the sheets, once again looking up at Rick. His eyes looked as big as softballs. Nick wanted to chuckle but thought better of it. He realized that Rick, like Abe, didn't have a clue what was going on. And like Abe, Rick was probably feeling embarrassed, if not confused. It seemed to Nick that the angels were not only making their presence known to him but were also helping him to trust in all that Sara had conveyed. Why else would Rick have been awakened at 4:44 in the morning, just like Abe?

Nick's eyes fell on the diamond figure with the word "angels" at the bottom of the sketch. His smile broadened. As Nick continued to peruse quickly through the writings, his eyes froze on the message below the diamond figure with the eye. "Spiritual DNA" stood out like a neon sign. There it was again! He had never even heard of the term until three days ago. Here was confirmation on a topic Nick never knew existed, written by a casual friend, using exactly the same expressions that had come through Sara. Although Nick received this information quietly, inside he was emotionally moved. Before this moment, the only world these two men had in common was football. The humor of it all—how these angels must have a joyful sense of the comical! When heaven and earth meet, it is not with trumpets and bolts of lightning, it's with peals of laughter. Nick and Rick ... sitting there ... each wondering what was going to happen next.

As Nick contemplated the geometric drawings, he remembered Rick's aversion to religious topics. Yet, across from him sat a man gladdened to be giving him sheets full of what must have seemed to be sacred gibberish. Nick wasn't aware of what all the messages meant. Neither man knew what they meant, but both would find out weeks later.

The figures were from an ancient Jewish mystical tradition known as Qabalism.[1] And within this tradition existed a "science" known as the Sacred Geometry. The figures on the sheet of paper were nothing less than excerpts from these ancient secrets of the sacred. But most curious of all was the figure of the intersecting tetrahedrons, also known as the star tetrahedron. Along with the geometrically sketched Mogen David, or Star of David, the combined figures of the three-dimensional star on top of the two-dimensional star were known as the Cube of Metatron. And among the ancient rabbis studying the mystical Qabalah, Metatron[2] was considered chief among the archangels. In some mystical circles he was known as the king of the angels.

As the sheets of paper took on more of an air of sacredness than weirdness, Nick was convinced that the angels not only were contacting him, but would continue to do so. The two references to the manuscript, of which Rick knew nothing, were a harbinger for Nick. He no longer felt alone, isolated with this information. Others around him were being brought into the circle of support that allowed him to feel more and more comfortable about the strange fact that angels were steadfast and certain in their effort to speak to the people of the Earth.

Nick expressed gratitude to Rick for his role as messenger, explaining to him the significance of 4:44 and how Abe had also been awakened. Matter-of-factly, Nick let Rick know he had been visited by angels. Nick conveyed to Rick how certain parts of his writings had been revealed earlier when Sara had conveyed those messages from Nick's angels. If any more material were to be presented,

---

1. Spellings vary, including Kabalism and Cabalism.

2. Also Metratton, Mittron, Metaraon, Merraton, etc.—the angel charged with the sustenance of mankind. In the Talmud and Targum, Metatron is the link between humanity and the divine.

Nick said, Rick was to feel completely comfortable in approaching him with it. As Rick left, he felt relieved, knowing full well this would be the end of it. *The absurdity of it all: angels working through me, Rick Eckard. What a joke.* This was a once-in-a-lifetime event, there would be no more material. Or so he thought.

❧

A week and a half later, on the 24th of January, Abe flew into Portland International from Geneva to meet with Nick. Substantial progress had been made regarding their business dealings. It was now time to sit down with Nick to iron out the details. While in Switzerland, Thomas had agreed with Abe that particular transactions could better take place through Nick's own business relationships. Nick received Abe with open arms. The two were becoming fast friends. Over the next week they worked closely together, meeting with local companies during the day while getting to know each other in the evenings.

Abe became a regular guest at Nick's home. The two of them also shared evening meals at some of the best Portland restaurants. Business was discussed and set aside to make room for a more important topic: angels. Both men exchanged many personal insights regarding information the angels had provided through Sara, as well as what Rick Eckard had gone through, parallel to Abe at 4:44 in the morning. Nick was developing a great respect for Abe. The two of them shared similar backgrounds. Like Nick, Abe had come from a very humble heritage. Both had been high-school star athletes, Abe in gymnastics and Nick in football. Both had made money the old-fashioned way: they earned it. And both had made their money with integrity and honesty. Neither of them found any pleasure in dealing with ruthless businessmen or unscrupulous businesses. To them, business should reflect a man's character, and not the other way around.

Abe's twinkling blue eyes and cherubic smile contrasted with his up-front approach to life, as well as with business. Along with Abe's forthrightness, it all proved to be a winning combination that Nick appreciated. It warmed him to be able to talk business transactions, the exchange of monies, and corporate strategies in one breath while switching the topic to angels in the next. At one point, Abe decided to ask Nick if he thought it inappropriate for him to call Sara, himself, and get information from his own angels. Nick only smiled, encouraging him to do so.

The next day an appointment was set up. It would be at 5:00 p.m. on Tuesday, February 2, the same day his business partner, Thomas Tsoi, was scheduled to arrive from Switzerland. Abe eagerly awaited the passing of the next week as Tuesday neared. He was not disappointed. The conversation with Sara was as sensational to Abe as Nick's had been. Not only were his business questions answered, but so were his personal questions, with extraordinary detail. When his angels began discussing Abe's son, he almost choked with emotion. They knew about his son's ailment and offered health remedies as well as other suggestions. She had also conveyed from his angels that Abe and Thomas would be forming a partnership with Nick. Though not surprised, he was delighted to hear the news. It was something he already had sensed in his heart.

After he hung up the phone, Abe was swimming in thoughts. However, Thomas was due to arrive within the hour. There was much to tell him about all he had heard concerning their business future, but there was so much Abe wanted to think about alone. He wanted to call his wife and discuss the family issues that had come up. He wanted to sit with Nick and relate the entire story. He felt pulled in different directions and was about to explode with the excitement of it all. There was not one iota of doubt within Abe that he had experienced a genuine communication from his angels. The details of information regarding his own private life as well as those of his immediate family were overwhelming evidence of truth. From that point on, Abe, like Nick, never questioned the authenticity of what was happening from the heavenly realm.

As Abe and Nick drove to the airport to pick up Thomas, they listened to the tape of Abe's phone conversation with Sara and his angels. After parking, they sat absorbed in conversation, as if they had arrived at a drive-through conference room. It wasn't until a jumbo jet flew overhead that one of them thought to check his watch.

"Wow! We're late. Thomas' flight has already arrived." The two of them took off at a trot, mimicking the athletes they used to be. A quick search found Thomas waiting for his luggage in the baggage area, looking as calm as a bag of rice. Nick beamed with anticipation as they walked up to the "Asian man with glasses." He was different than Nick had imagined from the many references made by the angels.

Abe and Thomas shook hands and exchanged pleasantries. Thomas noticed the fire in Abe's eyes. He knew something was up but said nothing. That was Thomas' way. Little needed to be said. Life spoke more loudly than words. Nick watched as the two partners swapped stories while waiting for the luggage. Thomas had the face of a man in his twenties, which belied the fact that he was actually in his early forties. He was a handsome man with an intellectual look, accented by his black-rimmed, wire frames. He stood just under six feet and was impeccably dressed. Nick could not help but notice the beautiful smile on his face. Thomas seemed cloaked in light. Nick would grow to realize that the smile was an almost permanent fixture that came from the heart. Thomas was truly a man filled with love and kindness, even during the tensest moments.

As the three men drove from the airport, Thomas was engrossed in the latest update in the angel chronicles. He listened as each man described not only the information but the person through whom all this information flowed. Listening intently, Thomas scarcely spoke. It was delightful to see his old buddy Abe so excited. He was still trying to size up Nick as they reached the hotel. Nick looked different than he sounded on the phone. His well-groomed, curly black hair obviated Nick's Eastern European ancestry. The fading gray eyebrows over his powerful, green eyes left Nick with a truly warm but capricious face. Thomas could understand how such a face had managed such impressive business deals with the movers and shakers of the corporate world. He would soon learn, as Nick would, that the two of them could not be judged, as books often are, wholly by their covers. Though the kindness reflected in their faces could be taken for granted, these two men also required, and deserved, respect. They were not only men of peace. They were also men of strength who knew the right and wrong ways to wield power.

After hours of conversation, Abe and Thomas bid Nick farewell as they headed into the hotel. It had been a long day, and Nick was looking forward to a good night's rest. For the next few days the three men worked their business wonders, engaging in a hectic business schedule, interviewing different companies while looking for a local institution in the Portland area that could facilitate their financial transactions. It required a company extremely well-versed in their field of expertise, a company with the talent to make things happen, and make them happen on time. The three of them knew what they were looking for and would not settle for less. Abe and Thomas marveled at how well Nick could articulate his thoughts and motivate people, while Nick was impressed with their financial savvy and experience. It was the beginning of an inevitable partnership, just as the angels had suggested.

Two nights after Thomas arrived, the angels decided it was time to perform once again. They wanted all three men to know beyond a doubt that divine forces were actively involved in their lives. Their first visit was to Nick's bed. Wakened out of a sound sleep, Nick's wife, Mary Jo, rolled over and began shaking Nick by the shoulder.

"Nick, Nick, something amazing has just happened. Something woke me up. I looked at the clock and it said 4:44 a.m." She could not explain the euphoric feelings that filled her.

"Uh, that's just the angels, dear," Nick mumbled, not to be cheated out of his night's sleep. "Welcome to the club," Nick muttered as he rolled back over. And that was that. Mary Jo lay there wondering what to make of it. All she knew was that she felt great. She was half-tempted to shake Nick once again. Had he become that used to having angels around?

Later in the morning, Nick drove over to pick up Abe and Thomas at their hotel. He found them sipping coffee in the lounge. A twinkle was dancing across Abe's blue eyes as Nick sat down. Nick could tell something was up. A broad grin erupted on Abe's face as he set his coffee cup down. "It happened again last night, Nick. The angels woke me up at 4:44 a.m."

Thomas looked a bit left out as Nick described Mary Jo's excitement at that exact time. The discussion was short; there wasn't much more to be said. Besides, there was business to get to.

But it did not end there. Arriving at his office, Nick found Rick Eckard waiting at his door again, with paper in hand. Sure enough, he, too, had been visited at 4:44 that morning. Rick wasn't wearing the blush of apprehension as before. As Nick approached, he handed him the paper. "It happened again last night, Nick. Let's go into your office. I want to show you what they wrote."

Nick peered at the paper while settling into his seat. He saw in large numbers in the middle of the page "4:44."

At the top of the page had been written, "Does the name 'Howard' or 'Walter' mean anything? Or 'Howard Walter,' 'Walter Howard'?" Nick looked up from the sheet of paper and shook his head.

"Never heard of him."

Then below, in quotes, it said, "Don't be afraid. Nick will teach you to pray."

Nick leaned back in his chair to absorb all that was happening around him. If the angels had wanted to make an impression on him, they had. The realization that all these heavenly hosts were in league in preparing not only Nick, but the earth itself, for events yet to come, enveloped Nick with a sense of profoundness. Why the manuscript seemed so important to the angels was no longer a matter for conjecture. It was now a matter of simply getting it published, regardless of the consequences.

With a turn in his chair, Nick faced Rick with the story of the other events of the previous night. The story about Abe and Mary Jo had a deeper impact on Rick than one might have expected. It was more than finding out others had been awakened, it was a realization that Rick was not alone, was no longer burdened with the self-made label of being the oddball. What might have seemed a divine comedy was now edging into celestial theater. Rick could no longer feign doubt or skepticism; he was somehow a part of a grand design. And that design was being created by heavenly beings. As he wandered out of Nick's office, he wondered what would be next on the heavenly agenda. The very thought caused him to chuckle quietly. *Me ... Rick Eckard ... contacted by angels. Right.*

That evening, Thomas, Abe, and Nick convened in the hotel's cocktail lounge. Business was set aside as all three mulled over the simultaneous awakenings at 4:44 that morning. After lighthearted comments were tossed back and forth between Abe and Nick, Thomas emerged from his stoic silence. In his Confucius-like style of talking, palms placed together with fingers pointing toward the ceiling, he interjected a comment.

"How come the angels wake you up, Abe, at 4:44 and do not wake me up?"

Abe couldn't miss this opportunity. "Maybe they're afraid you won't say anything." Abe angled back against the booth as he took a deliberate sip of his cocktail, his eyes laughing, knowing full well that Thomas wouldn't be able to reply. Though Thomas' silence could be unsettling at times, Abe had come to respect his friend's minimalist approach to language. Thomas spoke when he had something to say, and not before.

Nick joined in on the fun. "My guess is that they knew you needed your sleep too badly and didn't want to wake you up."

Thomas had already figured out how to read Nick, whose face could say one thing, but his eyes another. Nick's eyes were dancing. Thomas quietly grinned as Nick and Abe chortled. With a measure of light embarrassment, he ran his smooth fingers through his midnight of hair. His head nodded forward as he acted out the humor of the moment.

≈

A booming sound startled Abe from his sleep. *What the hell is going on?* he said to himself. *Sounds like someone breaking the door down.* He tried to look at the clock on the hotel nightstand, but his eyes weren't awake enough. It was early morning. *Has to be Thomas,* he thought. Abe swung the door open to see Thomas standing as if ready for inspection. A smile as big as the Columbia River was on his face, his short black hair neatly groomed. He was completely dressed and ready to begin the day.

"What?" was all Abe could croak out.

Thomas pointed to his Rolex. "Look, Abe, the angels did not wake me up. But look what they did."

Abe leaned forward to see all three hands of Thomas' watch stuck on the number four. The hour hand, the minute hand, and the second hand were all lined up. *It's not possible for a watch to do that,* thought Abe. *The gears inside won't allow the hands to line up like that.* And besides that, as the manufacturers of Rolex watches will tell you, *Rolex watches do not stop!*

The two men stared into each other's eyes and burst out laughing. Thomas had gotten his wish. Abe was amused but also moved by the incredible, loving joke the angels had played on his friend. Thomas was now a member of the 4:44 club.

Chapter 3

THE SOUND OF WINGS

*A*mong various religious traditions, the presence of angels has meant one thing: something is about to happen. These messengers of the heavens have manifested themselves in different ways for many different reasons. They have appeared as children, as agents of death, as deliverers of divine messages, as men completely dressed in black, as women healing the dying, as beings of light pouring out an ecstasy of love, as deliverers of plagues and saviors from plagues. Their scope and measure in the divine is beyond comprehension.

Not even the many weaves of religions throughout history agree on exactly who these beings are, why they are here, or how many different variations exist. In Christianity alone there are several schools of thought regarding these heavenly beings: some say there are ten choirs of angels, others say there are twelve orders, and still others say seven celestial halls of angels. And the names? The only consistency is to be found in their difficulty of pronunciation. Even Judaism, Islam, Buddhism, and Hinduism contain a plethora of angelic regions, hierarchies, realms, or orders.

The world of angels seems only limited by the human experience, the human condition. But on a planet pulsing with microchips and cable vision, where do these mysterious creatures fit in? And why are they now returning in a somewhat obvious fashion?

The members of the 4:44 club were no different than others throughout history who have been touched by angels: their lives were forever changed. When every clock encountered through the day is no longer looked at just for reading the time, one knows the world has been jarred from its mechanical foundation. These timepieces are no longer simple geared machines or digital signposts of the hours. No, they now are possible expressions of the miraculous. Just looking up and noticing that it's 10:44 or 4:44 or 7:44 brings a smile to your face. Having a meeting with a client whose office number is 444 no longer brings an empty thought. Now you wonder about the person, or about the meeting, or think of God and wonder if the divine is about to visit you once again. Angels can have that kind of effect on you. One thing was consistent with all the members of the 4:44 club—they all had felt that euphoric feeling when they were visited—that sense of well-being, calm, even divine love. And once felt, it is not easily forgotten. And so it was to be with Thomas.

Even though the week with Abe and Nick passed swiftly through the many business meetings and related accomplishments, Thomas still wondered about the angels and why they were here. What was it about Nick's manuscript that made these business sessions so extraordinary? Everything that Sara had predicted regarding business affairs was happening. He and Abe had tried before to make things happen in their business dealings, but doors would not open for them. Now they were opening widely. Was it the angels, or was it Nick's marvelous business savvy in these matters? It nagged at him. What was the real source of their growing success?

As the week progressed, the three men developed a stronger relationship with one another, and with a company president who appeared to be the candidate to accommodate their business transactions. Things were going well. Pieces of the business puzzle were falling into place. It looked as though Abe would be able to fly back to Canada on Friday to be with his family and take care of personal matters. Both Thomas and Nick were glad for Abe. Sara's conversation with his angels had given him plenty to think about, causing him to miss his family for more than the usual reasons. And Thomas was glad to have an opportunity to talk to Nick.

After seeing Abe off on a plane for home, Nick and Thomas took some time to talk at one of Nick's favorite restaurants. The conversation started with a review of recent business activities, as well as the role of the angels in business decisions. Thomas had an open-mindedness that respected his associates' experiences regarding the angelic happenings. But, true to his namesake, Thomas was also safely skeptical. He liked to deal in facts. That had been the secret of his business successes. What had happened to his Rolex was fact, but not altogether convincing in and of itself.

In an effort to better understand Nick's take on these events, Thomas gently moved the conversation toward more spiritual matters, even asking Nick questions about the manuscript. Abe had lent him his copy of the document, but Thomas had only glossed over it. What he was looking for were spiritual facts, spiritual certitudes—if such things even existed.

"Nick, I was wondering if you could tell me about the manuscript. Abe has told me something of what it contains. How did the manuscript come to be?"

Nick's thoughts went back to his first meeting with Abe, through a mutual business associate. He fondly remembered the many hours of business negotiations that had brought the two men close together as they worked with various companies and executives in pursuing Abe's original business needs. Nick had only heard of Thomas at the time, not knowing then how productive this marriage of talents would become.

There was one evening in particular when Abe and Nick sat deep in conversation for several hours in the cocktail lounge of Abe's hotel sharing their private and spiritual lives. Abe was the kind of fellow with whom you felt you could talk about anything. Not only was he affable, he was genuine. He spoke from the heart, and, in the process, had a knack for opening the hearts of others. Nick was no different. He had shared with Abe the contents of the manuscript and the story behind it. And now Thomas wanted to know that background also. Nick remembered how intrigued Abe had been, how he had asked for a copy of the manuscript to take with him to Europe. A half-grin snuck across Nick's lips as he remembered how he had assumed that the publishing of the manuscript was no longer an issue. Publishers had seen it, publishers had expressed an interest in it, and publishers had rejected it. It was over with.

Thomas' question still hung in the air. Where to begin. "It all started in the spring of 1977," Nick stated matter-of-factly. "I was forty years old, married, with four young children, and very involved in the business world. Although described by many as an overachiever, like most overachievers, I didn't think so. Business came easily to me, and I was constantly looking for new challenges."

Thomas settled into his seat. This sounded like it was going to be interesting, and long. He loved to listen. He was good at it. As the words poured from Nick's soul, Thomas watched the intimate details of each sentence animate Nick's face. This man was good, even compelling at speaking. Nick's green eyes were almost as expressive as the words he spoke describing this tale of wonder and mystery.

"I had just finished volunteering part-time in an unpaid position as special assistant to the governor. A number of prominent businessmen and political groups were asking me to run for Congress. While I was considering that decision, George Mack, a dear friend of mine, told me of a psychic he had visited. George was, and still is, one of the senior partners of a very successful CPA firm that handles many important clients in our region. He is a devoted Catholic and a man of tremendous integrity.

"George told me how impressed he was with this psychic, named Duane Berry whom he had visited in Portland. Duane predicted many events in George's life, some very positive and, unfortunately, some not. All except one became reality, according to George. He suggested I might want to see this gifted man. I had never seen a psychic before and decided why not give it a try.

"I made an appointment with Duane through a phone conversation with his wife. She did not ask my name or any information about me. She only stated their address, the time of our appointment, and that a contribution was strictly voluntary."

As the two men slowly progressed through their meal, Thomas couldn't help but notice how strongly Nick embraced life. Though fortune-tellers and I Ching diviners were common in Hong Kong, he himself tended to trust his own good sense and mental dexterity. It made for a predictable life—perhaps too predictable. But this Nick, he was a bit daring, dynamic, a risk-taker. In fact, he seemed so unpredictable, Thomas thought it would be almost impossible for a psychic to simply guess anything about him. Nick went on.

"When I arrived at their simple home, I was greeted by his wife in the living room. She offered me a seat on the couch and, while I waited, shared with me some of the poetry she had been writing. I found it extraordinary in that it kept changing styles. She told me she was getting her writing style directly from famous poets who had passed away."

A twinkle danced in Nick's eyes. "I had no idea what she was talking about. I didn't believe in that sort of thing. To be candid, I didn't believe in psychics. But I was looking forward to meeting her husband, after hearing what George had said about him.

"After about ten minutes of conversation, she told me to go into the kitchen, where Duane would be waiting for me. When I walked into the kitchen I saw a young man who was in a trance, with his eyes closed. There was incense burning in the background and spiritual music playing. He had a handsome face with a three- to four-day growth of beard."

As Thomas watched Nick eat, he was reminded of cultural settings of Hong Kong, in which meals were almost sacred, surrounded by custom and tradition. It half-amused Thomas to think of the strict protocol of some Chinese meals in comparison to the meal he was having with Nick. For Nick went through food the same way he went through life—with spirit. And he had no problem talking while eating. In some Chinese environments, this would have been considered rude. But Thomas felt oddly pleased by it all. There was no pretense about Nick, no pretense whatever. He might be impossible to predict, but he was also without guile. This was a man he could trust.

Nick took a quick peek at Thomas to see if he was following the story, then continued. "As soon as I sat down, Duane began talking. He disclosed information to me that I can only describe as incredible. How could he possibly know what he knew? How could he talk about my past as well as my current life, matters so private that, in some cases, only I knew of them? Yet he was reading me like an open book.

"What he told me set me off on the journey that ultimately led to the writing of the manuscript. He said some Portland businessmen were considering inviting me to run for an important political position. He told me I would accept that challenge and run for the position. He then said there would come a day when I would be speaking in front of audiences of thousands, and on television in front of millions. I thought to myself, *Surely I will be elected.* I thought maybe I would have to be in some kind of high-profile office in order to justify the audiences that I would be addressing.

"So I asked him, 'Then I do get elected to office?' And he answered, 'No, it has to do with the time when you walked with the Master.' I had no idea what he was talking about. So much information came out during the session that it never occurred to me to go back and ask him what he meant. My energies and thoughts were focused on the subjects I understood. Should I take them seriously? How should I deal with them? I can tell you unequivocally that, with the exception of the prophecy about my speaking in front of live audiences of thousands and TV audiences of millions, everything Duane Berry predicted in 1977 regarding my life has since come true."

Nick was still surprised at the strength of his emotions regarding an event that occurred so long ago. He stabbed another piece of steak as he decided how much more to tell Thomas. Thomas continued his meal in his usual stoic silence, forming no judgment about what Nick was telling him. Thomas was, himself, a man of truth who simply sought to know the truth about the manuscript. Ultimately, he might even want to read it. But for the moment, he was fascinated not only by the story but also by Nick's telling of it. Nick was as verbally convincing across a dinner table as he was across a conference table. Thomas wanted to hear more.

"Later that year, I declared my candidacy for Congress in the First District," Nick continued. "In 1978 I campaigned hard for the position but lost to the incumbent. It was one of the major congressional races in the country, one in which the political experts in Washington, D.C., felt that a challenger could beat the incumbent. But that did not happen. I lost, in the general election, to a very talented and experienced opponent." A mirthful grin matched the shine in Nick's eyes. "And, today, I am grateful for the outcome."

It was true. He was grateful for the turn his life had taken since then. Life had been not only exciting, but it had been his kind of life—not some bureaucratic drama in which all the people are players on a stage. "And I am also grateful for the experience of having run for the office," he added parenthetically.

There was a pause in the conversation as the waiter cleared some dishes. As was his custom, Nick struck up a friendly, teasing conversation with the fellow, asking him how his life was going. Thomas marveled at Nick's ease in carrying on such a warm conversation with an apparent stranger. Certainly, he might have been served by this waiter before. But even so, Nick spoke to him as if they were buddies. Somehow, he was able to treat almost anyone around him with such homespun welcome—unless they were seated on the opposite side of a negotiating table. You never knew what you were going to see from Nick when it came to business. He was almost legendary among his closest business associates.

One of Thomas' favorite stories was the one about Nick negotiating a settlement resulting from litigation. A very large corporation hadn't taken seriously Nick's determination to have them honor a contract. They considered themselves too big to lose a court case. But there they were, sitting across a table, ironing out a settlement after Nick had won the lawsuit. Nick and Anthony Brambilla, a junior partner of his, along with their attorney, stared eye-to-eye with the founder of one of the bigger corporations in North America and his entourage of four lawyers. Nick had instructed his attorney not to say one word, but to leave the entire negotiating process to him.

The first settlement offer from the corporation's attorneys was minimal, and Nick knew it. "Our best offer," they had insisted. But rather than argue the absurdity of their opening offer, Nick turned to his partner, sitting on his left, and began speaking in broken Italian. Those who knew Nick knew that his Italian was limited to a few insults he had learned on the streets where he grew up. But that didn't stop Nick on this occasion. What words he didn't know he made up. The English equivalent of what he was saying to his partner was something along the order of "Your mother wears army boots."

Anthony, who spoke four languages fluently, stoically retorted in sparkling Italian, "Nick, you are crazy. What are you doing? Get serious."

Nick smiled, turned back to his guests, and simply stated in English, "No!" That was it. There they all sat, staring at one another. The attorneys across the table huddled together with their client, then came back with another offer, twice as large as the first. Nick once again turned to Anthony and started reciting the Lord's Prayer in a variation of Latin and Spanish that almost caused his partner to burst into laughter.

Once again, this time in pristine Spanish, Anthony retorted, "Nick, you are the craziest man I ever met. But this seems to be working. Keep it going. At least my mother isn't wearing army shoes this time."

And, just as before, Nick sternly turned to his opponents across the table with a punctuated, "No!" And once again, there they sat wondering how to react. This time, the founder of the company motioned his team of attorneys away from the table for a huddle. When they returned to their seats, the lead attorney again doubled the offer. Nick went through his routine with Anthony one last time, and then offered a hand to finish the deal. Nick settled for slightly more than $1 million, rather than the $300,000 his own attorney had recommended.

Thomas had never met a man who loved oratory as

much as Nick. Yet here he was, this tiger of the business world, engaged in mellifluous chat with the waiter, who might as well have been the CEO of AT&T.

As the last remnants of the meal were carted away, Thomas returned to the thread of their conversation. "So how did the experience with Duane Berry lead to the eventual writing of the manuscript?"

"There were other unexplainable incidents," Nick offered. "A year after the elections, while I was doing a substantial amount of business out of state, I developed a friendship with a woman named Beth Jarman. Beth had a Ph.D., had been previously selected as the Woman of the Year in her state, was a former state legislator, and, at that time, was the first woman to hold a cabinet position there. She eventually became my business partner in one of my corporations.

"While visiting her, following a business meeting, she invited me to join her to meet a friend of hers after work. Her friend was a psychiatrist with a downtown practice. During our visit with the friend in her offices, somehow the conversation got around to age regression, under hypnosis, and past-life experiences. The psychiatrist asked me if I believed in past lives and if I had ever been hypnotized. I told her I wasn't sure whether I believed in past lives, and that I hadn't ever been hypnotized.

"I had gone through different spiritual phases in my life. As a youth I was extremely spiritual, then I became an agnostic, then, briefly, I claimed to be an atheist—although I wasn't, really. Also, I had studied reincarnation and understood the concept but had not accepted that metaphysical belief as an unequivocal possibility. Do you understand?"

Thomas nodded. He himself was going through various stages in his own spiritual life. His Baptist upbringing was yielding, more and more, to a sort of pantheistic holism of all religions. Like Nick, Thomas' spiritual values did not get checked at the door of Business like some hat or coat that could be worn at one's convenience. He took his spiritual values seriously. And, not unlike Abe, that seriousness had resulted from testing his beliefs and asking hard questions. Thomas could see the broadening picture of who Nick was as he listened more and more to his gracious host.

"I agreed to be hypnotized. She took me through an induction, which eventually led to my imagining that I was on a train going through a tunnel and that when I arrived on the other side of the tunnel, I would be in a past life. She gave me no suggestions as to what past life I would experience but left it up to my memory, or my imagination, to select one.

"After I passed through the tunnel, I was amazed to find myself standing approximately ten feet off the side of a road on a gentle slope. My fists were resting on my hips, and I had long black hair and a beard."

Thomas watched as Nick seemed to drift into a different place while describing the scene.

"I was dressed in clothing that came to midthigh. I wore leather shoes with straps around my ankles, and a short-sleeved upper garment, like a tunic. I didn't know who I was. I appeared to be a person of authority, as I watched the scene in my mind's eye. People were walking in front of me on a dusty road, wearing coarse clothes and tunics. Many wore head cloths, trying to protect themselves from the sun and dirt. I did not know who they were.

"I then experienced one other scene. I was now the same individual, but older and thinner. My beard and hair were longer and streaked with gray. I was wearing a loosely fitting, simple robe. Extended in front of me was a large map. There was an individual looking over my left shoulder, and two others on my right side. I still didn't know who I was as I described the scene to the psychiatrist and my friend, Beth. After it was all over, I didn't know what to make of it.

"A year later, Beth joined my Arizona organization. We formed a company and were doing business in the Phoenix area. At that time, there was a substantial amount of metaphysical activity in that part of the country. It was very easy to find a hypnotist or a psychic.

"One day, Beth and I decided to make an appointment with a local, well-known age-regression hypnotist in the Scottsdale area. His office was equipped with the latest gadgets, including a voice reverberator and other sound effects, as well as visual devices. I specifically asked him to take me back to a time that might have been biblical, if I had lived during that time in history."

Nick hesitated as he relived the scene in his memory. "He hypnotized me, providing suggestions to take me to biblical times, if such a lifetime actually existed for me, and if there was such a thing as reincarnation." Nick paused at this point. It was here, in the story, when he wondered what people would think. Many do not believe in reincarnation, just as he had not believed. He knew what he was about to say might be difficult for others to accept. However, his conversations with Abe led Nick to believe that he could tell Thomas about this event. He looked up at his business associate, eyes meeting eyes. Thomas sat almost breathless, waiting for the rest of the story. Thomas had never undergone hypnosis but had heard about the phenomenon. He hadn't made a judgment about it one way or the other—yet.

"The first scene I saw under the hypnotic regression took place in a house with floors made of wood. There was a round table. I was one of three young boys being tutored. I wore a white tunic, fur-trimmed on the hem and sleeves, which came down midthigh. I was about eight or nine years old, the youngest of the three children. The scene lasted less than a minute."

Again Nick hesitated, looking intently into his memory. "In the next scene, I was a young man in my twenties, sitting on the hillside of a valley, on a large slab of rock.

The valley slope was covered with vegetation and was fairly narrow. I could distinctly see the other side of the valley and the stream bed in the bottom of the valley. Seated to my right was Jesus. I felt great joy. There were only the two of us, me and Jesus, engaged in conversation."

The memory of the event took Nick back to another time, another place. Thomas could see moisture collecting at the corners of Nick's reddening eyes. Nick was not an outwardly emotional man, and Thomas knew that. Watching even this much response forced Thomas to sit back into his seat and wonder at the power of the event. He had to ask. "How did you know it was Jesus?"

"It's difficult to explain." It was a question Nick had asked himself many times. After all, he had been given no religious training while growing up. He knew nothing about Christianity but had always felt an inexplicable yet deeply personal fascination for Jesus. "Imagine you are regressed back to the age of sixteen, and you find yourself talking with your best friend, and someone asks, 'How do you know it was your best friend?' Your response would be, 'I know my best friend.' In the same way, I knew that was Jesus sitting next to me."

Thomas tried to remember what his best friend looked like thirty-odd years ago. Then he tried to imagine how someone could *know* Jesus when he saw him. Had Nick known Jesus that well? By now, Nick was accustomed to Thomas' paucity of words and resumed the story.

"The next scene was one filled with tremendous emotion. I was sitting in a tavernlike environment, such as an inn. My arms rested on a rough wood table that was almost circular. To my right was some individual, and to my left sat Jesus. In front of us were containers of wine. Jesus was telling us a story, and my other companion and I were roaring with laughter. When Jesus was finished with the story, the three of us were laughing so hard tears were flowing from our eyes. I reached out and placed my left hand on his right arm. I was overwhelmed with the love I felt for him. I also remembered feeling tremendous admiration for his sense of humor. But the love that I felt for him was greater than any love I have ever felt before in my present life."

Thomas could only wonder what it must have been like. He puzzled over how he himself would actually feel to see Jesus, to be sitting next to Jesus. But what he could imagine paled in comparison to what Nick had described. It wasn't how Nick had told the story, it was how the story shone on Nick's face as he told it. Thomas had never known Nick to be deceitful about anything. And his face was as convincing as the way he was telling the story.

"When the hypnotist began to take me out of my regression, I pleaded with him not to. I felt so much joy and love in my heart, I wanted to continue with those feelings, but it was too late.

"Beth Jarman still lives in the Phoenix area," Nick said. "She was with me during the entire session. She and I had many discussions after that experience. What did it all mean? I was now able to connect three experiences with what Duane Berry told me in 1977 about a previous life-time when I had 'walked with the Master': the two scenes I had experienced in the office of Beth's psychiatrist friend, and the vivid, emotional experience with the Scottsdale hypnotist.

"A series of events led me to the unfolding of information in the manuscript. I know this doesn't fully explain the manuscript, but it's getting late. Shall we continue tomorrow? Why don't you come over to my house tomorrow for the day? Are you any good at cribbage?"

"I could be," Thomas smiled back modestly. His statement was so understatedly Chinese. Thomas was good at cribbage, but not for the usual reasons. As with business, winning and losing were not important to him. But with someone like Nick, winning stood to be fun as well as a good forum for social interaction.

"How about staying for dinner?" Nick asked. "Maybe some backgammon along with the cribbage?" Thomas grinned at the thought.

As was the Chinese custom, Thomas refused the invitation, not wanting to impose. But Nick insisted, and Thomas then agreed—a very Chinese thing to do. He would come over on Saturday afternoon and take Nick on in some cribbage. As was his way, Thomas said nothing about the fact that he could be a merciless cribbage player. It would be better to surprise Nick, who thought himself almost unbeatable at the game. They had agreed to a tournament of backgammon, cribbage and gin rummy. Thomas had requested the gin rummy. If nothing else, he could provide Nick with unmatched competition in rummy.

On any other day, the snowcapped majesty of Mount Hood reflected sharply off the lake. But today the weather was in a changing mood. High clouds had already snuck in. The thick coat of evergreens surrounding this end of the lake made Thomas think he was in a national park instead of Nick's home. Never had he seen such beauty in a suburban setting. Portland's skyscrapers were hidden by the ripples of hills around Oswego Lake. Development across the lake had been minimal, leaving one with the sense of being out in nature. With a deep breath, Thomas took in all the beauty.

"Gorgeous, isn't it?" Nick interrupted, handing Thomas a cup of tea.

"We don't have this kind of beauty in Hong Kong. One should appreciate it while one can."

"Too bad you can't see Mount Hood today. It's quite spectacular, a tremendous view," Nick commented.

Thomas edged to the railing, extending one hand toward the mountain, the other hand open over his heart. "I can feel the mountain," Thomas volunteered.

"You can feel it?" Nick found himself increasingly surprised by Thomas. He could be so silent about most topics and so unexpectedly expressive about others. Nick watched as Thomas seemed to focus totally on the shrouded mountain. He wasn't kidding. He really was serious about this. Thomas was so spiritual in his own way, Nick felt.

"Yes. It has its own power, its own energy, its own *chi*," Thomas said.

Nick loved having guests who could savor this scenery before them. He had always felt that his home, hugging the bluff some thirty feet above Oswego Lake, was a kind of gift. And he liked sharing this gift with others. The architecture of the house, which he had designed, allowed a commanding view from any window, whether upstairs or down. Even after six years of occupancy, Nick had not tired of the house or its view. It truly was a dream house that still spoke of dreams that had come true.

After leaving Thomas at the window, Nick returned to the room with cards, cribbage board and backgammon board in hand. So, Saturday afternoon would be a battle of the fittest. The action would take place on the round, limestone table in the kitchen. Sleeves were rolled up and refreshments readied. Mary Jo would be gone the whole day. So it was man against man.

"You know, I'm world-ranked in cribbage. I never lose," Nick kidded. He prided himself on his wiliness at these board games, especially cribbage and backgammon. They were like mini business encounters: part smarts, part luck, part bluff. He relished a good contest and suspected Thomas would be up to the task.

Nick wasn't one to talk about it, but the truth was, he was a whiz—at most everything he did. He first became aware of this while a sophomore in high school after taking a series of tests. The principal had called him into his office, sat him down, and with a most serious face had stated, "Nick, I have great concern about your future." Nick's mind had grappled with the possibilities of what he could possibly have done. "It seems you have received an academic rating equivalent to a twenty-one-year-old at Harvard University." In the years that followed, he would be confronted with other tests telling him the same thing—he was a genius.

Frankly, this had always puzzled Nick. Why did people think he was a genius when he hadn't done all that well as a student? And why did he always find it difficult, if not unpleasant, to try and piece mechanical objects together, or take them apart? He could not play a musical instrument, as much as he would have loved to. If he was so smart, why didn't he show any interest in many of the things that one associates with higher intellect? It would only be later that he would find the answer to these questions from his angels.

Today, Nick was in his element. There was a contest to win, and Thomas was the opponent. It had been agreed upon: five games of backgammon, five games of gin rummy and five games of cribbage. Nick took the first game, but Thomas rebounded with some clever maneuvering in the second. He had done the unthinkable: Nick had been beaten. This was more than black tiles against white tiles; it was intellect against savvy, the silent Eastern strategist against the talkative Western tactician.

In the background, the Gregorian chant CD played against the backdrop of beautiful scenery and determined game-boarding. The monks' voices filled the cathedral ceilings of the house with a sacred fervor. The cards were shuffled and the hands played like generals negotiating surrender. Thomas had the edge in gin rummy. He was simply too good to be beaten by luck. And Nick was lucky. Thomas had never seen such luck. Or was it luck? It made him wonder if Nick had any unseen help.

It was time to replenish the munchies as the cribbage round was set to begin. Nick felt invigorated; Thomas found himself feeling more and more welcome in the company of a man who welcomed all but played backgammon as if his home were at stake. Nick didn't display emotion or feign battalion behavior. No, it was his intensity, silent as it was. His moves were not hesitant, nor were his tactics. He knew what he wanted, knew what he was doing. He took risks, and luck seemed to favor him. As clever as Thomas was, he could use such opposing strength to his favor. Whenever Nick overreached with his strategy, Thomas countered. He was swift with retribution when the opportunity presented itself.

Hours of tournament play seemed only to enliven each man. The cribbage board was now the new battleground, wooden pegs the new soldiers. Thomas was just about to move one of his soldiers when something caught his eye. Out the kitchen window the most extraordinary scene was unfolding. He had to look twice to make sure his eyes weren't playing tricks. "Look, Nick. Look at what is happening."

Nick turned to face the full openness of the high kitchen window. His eyes first scanned the deck to make sure everything was OK. Then, through the wrought-iron railing, he saw white objects floating to the lake like giant snowflakes. They were birds, beautiful white birds, hundreds of them. And hundreds more seemed to be floating from the sky from all directions, like some giant snowstorm. The sight was transfixing.

Oswego Lake was not a big lake, about seven miles long and roughly 400 yards wide from where Nick's property sloped into its waters. The birds appeared to be congregating in the vicinity between Nick's property and the opposite shore. Their sheer numbers slowly filled this end of the lake. From the north, south, east and west they came. Whole clouds of birds seemed to be descending from above. In Nick's six years of living on the lake, he had never seen such a sight, nor had he ever heard of one.

Thomas continued his move, keeping one eye on the cribbage board and the other on the lake. And still they came, by the hundreds. Nick would think about his next move, make it, and then turn around to catch the progress of the white throng settling on the water's surface. Cribbage was starting to take a back seat to the continuing cascade of white birds. Hundreds upon hundreds continued to float from the sky. The number of birds was now so great that there was more white than blue between Nick's property and the opposite shore. Finally, one of the men spoke. "Let's go see what's going on out there."

They abandoned the cribbage tournament and embraced the cool air on the deck. Dusk was settling in, the sun already hidden by the hills behind them. The birds continued their gathering, now numbering more than a thousand. The glow of sunset painted the cloud of birds in iridescence as they unceasingly poured onto the lake. The sight before them was no longer a matter of curiosity, it was now a vision of wonder. How much longer would this continue? What was bringing all these birds here? As the two men stood there on the deck, both now felt that something mystical was taking place before them. Finally, as if on cue, the white feathery clouds stopped. More than 2,000 white birds huddled on the surface before Nick and Thomas.

Then, as if some divine conductor had given the signal, several of the birds began calling, followed by the entire assemblage. The sound reverberated back and forth between the hills, filling the air with a kind of wild music. It was too much. The power of the moment permeated Nick to his soul, filling him with a sense of the profound. Both he and Thomas raised their arms heavenward and said a silent prayer. The throng of birds responded with immediate silence. It was as if they knew the two men were the purpose of their presence. Nick prayed in a strong but quiet voice, and Thomas echoed the prayer in Chinese. What was unfolding before them was tugging at Thomas' previous

58

skepticism. He didn't know what was responsible for this sight; all he knew was that it spoke to his soul. Without a word being said, Thomas and Nick knew some spiritual event was being orchestrated by the angels. There was no other explanation.

As the profundity enveloped them, more amazement swept before their eyes. Three huge bands of orange-gold light zoomed toward them from the opposite shore and stopped directly where the two men stood, hands still elevated in prayer. The phenomenon was as inexplicable as the descent of birds. The band of light in the middle was close to fifteen feet in diameter, while the other two bands, to the right and left, were each about ten feet wide. Was this a vision, they wondered? Nick looked across the lake to see what could be producing such a display of light. But there was nothing. The opposite shore was relatively undeveloped. There were no windows, no houses, no cars, no street lamps, nothing that could have created this sight.

Nick decided to open the French doors leading onto the deck to let the Gregorian chant music empty into the vision before them. He walked into the family room and turned the volume of the CD even louder. Sound merged with light. Nick returned to the deck and whispered something to Thomas. The two exchanged words quietly to each other. It was like being in church.

Without warning, a whooshing noise came from directly overhead. Both men looked up. It was as if some great bird with a giant wingspan hovered just above them, ready to land. Each could distinctly hear the sound of wings. But nothing was there—or at least nothing they could see. The wing sound whooshed rapidly, staying stationary, constant. It hung above the two men for five or six seconds. Each kept searching for the source of the wing beats. Not finding it, both looked at one another, smiling broadly. "Angels!" each announced simultaneously.

Momentarily the sound left. Ten minutes later the

sound of giant, beating wings returned again. And again both tried to find the source in the dimming light. The whooshing ceased, then returned, a third time. After the fourth occurrence, the sound of wings left for good. Nick and Thomas were filled with amazement over all that was happening.

Night descended, leaving the lake pitch-black except for the three bands of light, which appeared to grow larger as they remained suspended between the far shoreline and two men keeping watch on the deck. The patter of rain gave the impression of tiny applause as the white birds nestled quietly on the waters below. Nick went inside to fetch a flashlight, returned, and aimed the spotlight on the swarm of white. They were all there, still, silent as snow.

Two hours passed before the mysterious bands of light disappeared in the showers of rain. Mary Jo arrived with dinner for all. As food was served, Thomas and Nick retreated into the kitchen to disclose the marvelous events that had unfolded. She couldn't help but concern herself with how this must be affecting her husband. Her heart went out to him, knowing the responsibility that must inevitably come when the contents of the manuscript would be published. But for now, Heaven had to wait. It was time to feed these menfolk, angels or not.

Thomas was speechless with joy. The magnitude of what was happening made him wonder what role he played. Originally, he had complained to Abe about being left out by the angels. But now, he wondered what the consequences were of being a part of such moving events as he had witnessed. Surely these blessings had purpose. The question now was, what was his purpose in all this?

Nick invited his guest to stay the night. True to his tradition, Thomas politely declined, and returned to his hotel. The following morning, the birds were gone, replaced by six inches of freshly fallen snow. It was as if the white blanket of birds had been magically changed to a blanketing snowscape. All was pure, quiet, and rich with beauty.

Days later, Abe, Thomas, and Nick proceeded with the formation of a new company, making them all partners. Once again, what the angels had foretold came to pass. Both Abe and Thomas joined with Nick to make sure the manuscript would see the light of day. Their new company would also be committed to making preparations requested by the angels to ready the world for a new way of living. The three men did not see themselves as anything special. Quite to the contrary, they were being made increasingly aware that they were simply part of a greater whole being addressed by these forces of Heaven.

As in the days of Bethlehem, heavenly messengers once again seemed to be bending near the earth with their harps of gold. Abe, Thomas, and Nick felt their touch, and in the most uncomplicated of ways, their collective souls whispered back, "Yes."

Chapter 4

VISITS AND VISITORS

*O*n Sunday morning, March 26, at exactly 4:44 a.m., Rick Eckard experienced his third angelic encounter. It had been more than seven weeks since the last "visit." Unlike before, Rick had a growing awareness of what was happening around him. He no longer felt singled out, and it gave him a feeling of deep reverence to be visited once again. Nick had shared with him the experiences of Abe and Thomas, as well as other incidents involving neighbors and friends. The angels seemed to be touching a growing number of lives, and Rick felt grateful for being included, even though he remained perplexed over the events unfolding before him. What he was being told to write down still seemed mysterious and unrecognizable to him. Perhaps it was meant to be that way. But what if it wasn't? What if he was supposed to be doing more? Yet, he didn't know what more he could do, except play his part. It was obvious the angels were up to something. But was it simply the publishing of a manuscript, and nothing more? He wanted to know.

Nick felt an ever-growing respect for Rick. Of all the people involved in the angelic encounters, Rick had the least to gain. All he was being told to write down was meant for others, most specifically, Nick. Surely there must be some reason that Rick was the conduit of this information. But then, Rick pretty much already lived a life dedicated to helping others.

His generosity and dedication were never more evident than in the work he performed in providing college scholarship opportunities to boys and girls in the Pacific Northwest. Many of these student-athletes simply would not receive aid for higher education if not for this forty-year-old man with three children. He always had time for those who needed help. His entire life centered around making life better for those who had the good fortune of meeting him. Yes, perhaps it was understandable that the angels had awakened Rick once again.

"Nick," Rick announced, "another message from you-know-who." This time the writing was scribbled on a single sheet of letter-sized yellow paper. On the right-hand side was written 4:44 a.m. Underneath it:

Awoke—looked at digital clock on the dresser—4:44.

Printed beneath that was

2-3 weeks forward, matters for Nick will make an aggressive turn, positive. Eighteen months from now Nick will (should, must?) retire—Kevin, his son, or someone else will take over management of Nick's offices.

Nick reread the lines. So now the angels were telling him he might have to hand over the business to his son. Kevin had an office in Nick's suite of offices. Kevin was a handsome man, prone to wearing conservative business suits, yet easygoing in his own way. He even seemed to take the news of a younger brother "in the oven," twenty-seven years his junior, with good humor. After all, Nick was his father, and there was nothing typical about Nick.

Rather than try to figure out what the angels might be up to, Nick simply trusted in what must be coming. He read on. Most of what followed was of a personal nature, echoing what the angels had already said in his first phone call to Sara. He assumed the angels just wanted him to understand that they were, indeed, speaking also through Rick.

Three days later, Rick handed Nick another message. It was short, scribbled on a telephone pad of paper:

> *4:44—to show us the way ... can communicate any time ... we will get better at receiving. Someone in government ... will be chosen ... also very high—secretary/state? Same message ... they will cooperate. They will somehow aid in education ... bring very high government clearance. May surface after this book is published.*

Each man stared at the other and shrugged. Someone high in government? And what could the angels possibly mean about a government clearance? Whatever the meaning, apparently it would have to wait until the manuscript was published. Nick stepped into his office and filed this paper away with the other messages, knowing he would simply have to wait to discover what the angels had in mind. He assumed they were preparing him with news about the future, as they had done so many times already.

As Nick came back out of his office, Rick was still standing there. "Nick, do you think you ought to give your angel lady a call again? Maybe she could provide some insight into this, maybe she could tell me what my role is in all this. You know, why is all this happening?"

Was this the same Rick who only a few months earlier had pooh-poohed all this? Nick once again felt compassion for the man. It did look as if the angels were having him operate in a vacuum. It spoke well of Rick that he could change this much in such a short time, that he could be this accepting, this helpful.

"You may be right. Perhaps it is time to give Sara another call."

In truth, Nick was now in touch with Sara on a regular basis. He had not asked for a second session with his angels but had simply gotten to know this gifted lady better as a person. They had become good friends since the first phone call. But Rick was right. Why not see if Sara could throw a little more light on this subject? It had been a while since there had been any action in the publishing arena. And the angels had made another reference to the manuscript through Rick.

Nick's agent, Jennifer, already had checked out the name the angels provided during his first call to Sara. She discovered that a woman by that name had, indeed, been recently hired by a major publishing house, one of the publishers they had previously contacted. At Nick's request, Jennifer reconnected with the publisher, specifically aiming at the offices of the new editor.

After receiving the query letter, the new editor called Jennifer and asked for an air-expressed copy of the manuscript. She stated that she was impressed with the information Jennifer had sent and was looking forward to getting the document. It looked as if the angels were still on a roll. But thirty days passed with no word.

Jennifer tried to reach her by phone several times, but her calls were taken by an assistant. Most recently, Jennifer had been told that she had gone on vacation and wouldn't return until the end of March. She would get back to Jennifer the first week in April. It was now April 1, and Nick was interested in what knowledge his angels could tell about the status of the manuscript. Consequently, Rick's request for more information was timely. Perhaps it was time to set up an appointment with Sara.

Sara began the second session the same way as the first. As her prayer of protection came to a close, the angelic realm opened. "The first thing I want to say to you is that Thomas is going to have to do some business in Switzerland," Sara commenced. "There is going to be a lot of activity around you. And you may have to take a trip, between one and four months." There was a brief pause, as if she were listening to someone, then she continued.

"Thomas is very much a humanitarian. How can we say it? What is the word? They are telling me he is very slow to let you know this because, you see, if people find out he is a humanitarian, everyone will come toward him and ask him for favors. So, since there seems to be honor building, they are showing me bridges, large bridges between the two of you. As time goes by, you will see this, you will see this unfold before you.

"There is another man with brown hair involved in this trip. There will be talk about appropriation and distribution of funding, something having to do with Switzerland, so watch for this opening."

Sara's bubbly voice went on, "There will be an opportunity within an eighteen-month period, discussion around you, about money going toward different types of satellite equipment. Something having to do with satellite receiving and sending communications. Something on the forefront of technology having to do with equipment like this."

Nick was pleasantly surprised to hear this. He was having discussions with the chief executive officer of HTW Inc., a California company in which he had recently invested. Their talks centered around technology that would facilitate transmission of medical data between doctors and hospitals. Nick was pleased to hear from the angels that this was going to become a reality in the near future. It would benefit not only him personally, but the company he had set up with Abe and Thomas.

The next twenty minutes of the session dealt with his son, Nicholas, and other members of his family. Nick listened carefully, recording the conversation on cassette tape. He then asked if it was OK if they move on to a different subject. It was. Would the angels talk about his new company, partnered by Abe and Thomas, and the business activities associated with it?

Sara responded, "Yes, they are telling me there is a conflict ... yes, there is a conflict there. The receptor on the London end is being stubborn—somehow being stubborn. And I don't know what that means. My sense is that the actual person Thomas is dealing with ..."

"But is it going to be successful?" Nick interrupted, "Or is that end of it not going to happen?"

"Oh, it's going to happen. The angels tell me, oh yes, it is going to happen. There are many appointed, so this *is* going to happen."

Nick was puzzled. "Many appointed? Do you mean many people working on it, or many angels?"

"Many angels, not people."

Nick apologized for interrupting, hoping he had not offended his heavenly companions with his query. Sara continued, "Yes, many angels have been assigned to this event. It is going to happen, and they are showing me on the calendar ... May 5 is when the window is wide open. In particular, May 10 and 12 are highlighted on the calendar as well. The 10th and 12th seem important dates, but the window opens up on the 5th."

"So I shouldn't be anxious for things to happen in April?" Nick wanted to know.

"No, this is one of the few ways your own soul is being tested. You have to understand, you don't give your angels much to work with. You wait, for your patience is being tested."

Sara could not see Nick's grin as he mused, "What is that? They want to test me? Could it be they want me to develop patience?" The tone of his voice gave it away, and Sara chuckled at his mock indignity. Nick joined in the laughter. He had been told more than once by friends and family what a dynamo he was. He tended to see possibilities more clearly than most, and he wasted little time in making them happen. He liked to seize the moment and didn't like to see time frittered away. Patience often cost money.

Sara continued, "Yes. The way your life is before you, they tell me, what else do they have to work with? This is a test of faith for you, Nick. This is one of the few ways, with your life structured as it is, for you to learn and grow. For them to, how can we say, get your attention, to administer certain lessons to you.

"Take a step back, Nick, a step back to receive. This is not a time to push your energy out. No. Let it come to you. Take a step back and let it come to you. The angels say you are very good at pushing. This is your prior mode of operation. It is your forte. This is one time it will not work. Right now it is time for stepping back, for everything is energy. Try to pacify your ego by just thinking of it as willful thought and by taking a little step back, just a little step back, from your forceful energy—thinking that you have to do something. The ego is running you ragged, always making you feel and think you have to do something. This is not the right time to do that. Does that make sense to you?"

As self-reliant as he was, Nick was not *so* self-reliant as to ignore good advice. He responded humbly to the angels' suggestion. It *did* make sense to him. The message continued.

"It's more about the London energy. It's more about the person at that end, and the liaison between them." Though it wasn't clear, Nick assumed this had something to do with Thomas, since he was in London, and another Asian man, whoever that might be. Perhaps Thomas was negotiating with an Asian man. Nick took note of this part of the session, thinking he might say something to Thomas the next day.

"The two in London, the Asian man—how can we put this?—are a reflection of the butting of heads. This is when power meets power. That happens." Nick wondered if Thomas was having a tough time with the negotiations. It wasn't anything that concerned Nick because he knew Thomas could hold his own. Unlike Nick, Thomas was the epitome of patience. He did not push a business deal, he simply laid it out like a sumptuous banquet and invited you to eat. If you wanted to partake of the feast, that was great with Thomas. If you didn't find the feast appealing and wanted to pass, that was also fine with Thomas—your loss. Thomas was so adept at his craft that he believed one man's loss would simply be another man's gain. If one client did not want to do business with him, well, there would be another who would. It was the heart of his business success. Quite different from Nick.

"This is not a delightful scene to talk about. When someone is not one to cooperate, there is a bashing of heads, with power. So they are working right now, the two men, on separate issues. You are involved, but his is a separate issue, also."

Again, it was not totally clear to Nick exactly what Sara was conveying from his angels. It sounded as though Thomas and the other Asian gentleman were locked in negotiations, that they were hammering things out from different perspectives, probably different business philosophies. But it also sounded like the angels just might have to take a hand in these matters, since it was apparent the "butting of heads" was part of each man's personal issue. The impasse might be a reflection of each man's personal philosophy, personal hang-up, personal problem. Nick would have to wait to find out.

Sara continued, "This will all unfold around the first of next month, which is May. Is that right? They tell me that somehow it has attached itself to London? That the transaction has indirectly attached itself to London? Are there a lot of papers, securities in this issue? That's right, OK. So that's right." It amused Nick to listen to Sara carry on these sidebar conversations with his angels. But she was right. Critical negotiations were taking place in London with some heavy hitters. Other references had been made about negotiations in Switzerland. Why, he didn't quite understand. But that would probably make itself known later. Nick hadn't heard any updates from Thomas, so the angels were most likely accurate that there was some head-butting going on.

"You have to wait just a little bit longer. There is nothing to do right now, for the next week at least, OK? This is how your ego deals with things. Tell your ego that you have honestly agreed to do nothing for one week."

Nothing? For one week? His voice echoed back in surprise, "One whole week?"

Sara answered, "Yes, one whole week. Agree with the ego, you will do nothing. It is not yours to do. In other words, put it at bay, calm the ego. Calm the pushiness, the ego energy. For one week you will relax and stop putting out that energy that is actually blocking, a little bit, the London transaction, and Thomas. Let him do his thing. Pull that energy back. Relax, just for one week. So now my sense is that Thomas is dealing with the man in London who has glasses. He is a very powerful man—big lessons that will affect the world and the man Thomas is dealing with. The angels tell me he is nervous, believe it or not."

Just hearing that made Nick want to pick up the phone and get involved. But he focused on what Sara was trying to say to him. "Is that good or bad?"

"It is good. The angels tell me that the London connection knows about Thomas, has checked up on him. He knows what Thomas needs. But he also knows from Thomas' history that Thomas will find another way of getting what he needs if the London connection does not come through. And because the other Asian man knows this, he knows he has to interact with Thomas. It is just a matter of time. These are the dynamics of what is going on. It's going to be fine. It's going to unfold before you."

Nick almost laughed, feeling sorry for the Asian man who was the London connection. If Thomas dealt with this man the way he dealt cards for gin rummy, it was all over for the other guy. Thomas could be a force to be reckoned with. Not like a bomb blast, more like the tide that inevitably takes over the shoreline. Nick realized now that he had to leave Thomas to his own skills and not try to intervene.

"Is it OK to move on to another subject?" Nick asked.

"Yes, the angels have nothing more to say on this topic."

"Regarding the book—by the way, I sent you the transcript—the question to my angels is, will they publish it? And if so, when? If not, how will I get it published?"

"OK," Sara began, "they are showing me they have a hand on it. If they put a hand on it, they want it. I don't see them letting that go. So everything must be going fine. There seems to be a deterrent."

"Regarding the book?" Nick was uncertain what she meant.

"Regarding the book, yes. The angels are telling me that it is going to take a little more time for them to process the book, to get clarity on it. So, it may be toward the end of the month before there is a need for you to go to New York."

Then the angels began to get into information already revealed in the first session, telling Nick that major events would take place in the world between now and the year 2000. Once more they reminded him how important it was for the manuscript to be published before these events occur. The events would be preceded by a band of lights, like a continuous rainbow, although of different colors, which would encircle the globe.

Nick weighed this information in his heart. He had come a long way since the manuscript had first been created. Nick's concern for his personal and financial well-being, which had sabotaged the first efforts to get the manuscript published, had faded. Now he knew that the welfare of humanity may well rest in the revelations embedded in the manuscript.

"Ask my angels if they want me to share with other people what the event is going to be."

"They say that even though the event is going to be a very positive one, they do not want you to reveal it yet. Rather than telling people what is to happen, they prefer that you do it in code. Part of your function has already been fulfilled in code, and you will address this issue in a coded way. In other words, you will not come out with this information in an aggressive, male way. You will not be direct with it."

Nick asked Sara if she had heard of this information in other angel readings. Her response was "Absolutely not." She had never before been told of these events. With a sense of knowing responsibility, Nick assured his angels he would honor their request and would not share the information until such time in the future when they would direct him to do so. He understood how some people might fear the coming changes instead of embracing them. People need time to prepare, to hear of the returning Age of Miracles. Then they could understand the coming events as they were meant to be understood—in terms of love.

Once more Nick asked the question, just to be sure. "Should I be subtle about this information, should I be subtle in how I speak about it?"

Sara answered, "Yes, yes. Because the man, Jesus Christ, is coming to you in person, in a very intimate, personal way. It is a very intimate, deep, emotional, spiritual experience for you. And so, by approaching the sharing of this information with the same kind of energy that you feel with Jesus' closeness to you, that kind of intimacy, that kind of love will be reflected in all you share, say and do. So to answer your question, yes, you will, in a very sensitive way, very coded way, very intimate and loving way, at some time in the future, reveal what is going to happen to everyone at an intimate, personal level."

Nick was a bit unsure about what exactly was being communicated. But in his heart, he knew what he was to do. He must not be explicit about what is to happen. He understood the angels' concern about misinterpretation, and that some people would want to proclaim that the end of the world is coming. An apocalyptic end was not what this was about. He knew the events to come would be positive. How he could communicate this in a coded fashion was not clear. He wasn't sure what that meant. But he felt certain that when the time was right, he would reveal all.

Setting aside the weight of this knowledge, Nick decided to ask about the birds on the lake. "Thomas and I had an experience with white birds on the lake while we were standing on my deck. Would you ask my angels if they had anything to do with that? If that was a sign from them, or whether it was just a coincidence?"

Sara interrupted, "They tell me that in nature there are no coincidences. None of nature knows a coincidence. It is something that they ..."

Nick returned the interruption. "Were they there? We heard whooshing noises overhead while thousands of these birds landed. Were they with us?"

"Yes, they told me yes. Also they tell me that you bring others good fortune. I get a big yes from this. Regarding Thomas, it was assigned to him that you are together. That you bring each other good fortune. That you have a lot to do here. He comes to you from a different religious background than yours, but it doesn't matter. They tell me that they were with you. Also, I see them tapping. So that was their way of letting you know their presence. And then, also, you may have noticed being touched. You may have felt something was brushing up against you."

Nick acknowledged that he had felt something touching him. Knowing that the event at the lake was neither imagination nor coincidence, Nick felt a warm peace surround him. It was now time to ask about Rick Eckard and his being awakened several times at 4:44 in the morning. He reiterated the tale to Sara, telling her about the notes, and asked if the angels could tell him what that was all about.

Sara responded, "It's true, yes. Regarding the three actually being four, they told Rick of the Father, Son, Spirit and angels. It is confusing enough for people to try and understand three beings in one, let alone four. But there truly are four. The notion of the oneness of God is a stretch for people. People can't begin to comprehend that abstract concept.

"But they are saying that Rick is a messenger for you. They tell me that Rick doesn't know what he has to offer you, because he doesn't feel—we are talking about his ego—his ego doesn't feel that he is of a mental stature, for lack of a better word, to offer you advice. He is a very good person. He has a good heart, and so this is the way that his Higher Self can ask his angels to communicate with you. It's more a meeting of the minds then."

"That's fine," Nick said, "that's good. I appreciate the angels doing that because they have now brought under the umbrella five people who have had the 444 experience. And every time it happens, it gives me a greater confidence and greater understanding that the angels are with me."

As they began to wind down the session, Nick had one last thought to share with Sara, regarding his difficulty in meditating. It genuinely bothered Nick that he could not meditate, only adding fuel to the personal doubt that smoldered within him. It was still awkward to consider, if not hard to believe, how a businessman could be involved in all this spiritual unfolding. He confessed to Sara that he had tried normal meditating techniques without success. "Ask them what I should do to be able to communicate with them."

"Well, they tell me that's what you do. Your ego doesn't have to know, Nick. 'Why do you feel you need to know?' the angels ask."

"Well, because it's not a question of ego," Nick answered. "It's just that I don't know if I am communicating. For example, I don't know if what I am saying is just me saying it or writing it, as opposed to whether I am getting information from some other source."

"They tell me that you are accessing another dimension. So, it is you. You and the angels have direct access to each other. It is a partnership you have with them. When you think in your mind, you are getting answers in your mind, because they are sharing information directly with you. You are thinking in a higher dimension, Nick. This is a tremendous gift."

Sara continued, "You are in a partnership, Nick. You have not been clear on that. Now you are clear. Just acknowledge them. The angels are saying that you should rely on your intelligence, that you know this is a gift. That you are given intelligence, knowledge, and wisdom. You should rely on these and know that you can depend on them.

"And secondly, you must understand that you asked for this intelligence. You asked for this power. You asked for it and agreed to it, in a prior agreement. On some level you're able to be responsible for it. They hope you understand."

With a knowing nod, Nick replied, "Yes, Sara, I understand. I want to say good-bye to the angels for now. No, I don't mean good-bye. I know they are always with me."

"Oh yes, they understand Nick, they understand."

With that, the session ended. Nick stopped the tape recorder attached to the telephone and stared out his office window. There was so much to think about, so much to consider, so much to do.

Nick was scheduled for a trip a few days later to Southern California to help out with one of his corporations. It was not uncommon for Nick to make such trips, for he sat on the board of directors of several visionary, high-tech companies. Since he was going to be in the area, Nick made an appointment with Sara and with a man named Michael Wiese.

A friend of Nick's had sent a copy of the manuscript to Wiese, who lived in the Los Angeles area. Wiese was actively involved in creating videos and documentaries. He had played an active role in the Shirley MacLaine video-tapes. Normally, Nick did not permit the manuscript to be sent to strangers. In this case he had made an exception because of the integrity of his friend, who thought Michael Wiese could be helpful. Nick didn't know anything about the man until Wiese called him soon after receiving a copy of the transcript.

"I thoroughly enjoyed your story," Wiese had said on the phone. "I'm quite excited to see your book get published. What kind of progress are you making in that vein?"

At the time, Nick was reluctant to give any details to a man he had not met but did let him know some extraordinary circumstances had surrounded the manuscript up to that point. Michael countered Nick's reluctance with an affirmation of the manuscript's content, trying to convince Nick how completely he believed in it. Nick warmed to the man's sincerity.

Wiese encouraged Nick to feel comfortable sharing

any information with him, regardless of how much spiritual understanding one might need to appreciate it. Wiese suspected that the two men probably had a lot in common in their spiritual belief systems.

After having given it some thought, Nick decided to let Michael Wiese in on some of the latest occurrences regarding the angels and the manuscript. When he mentioned that the angels had participated in placing the new editor in a position of responsibility with a major publishing company in New York, Michael cut in.

"I know who you mean." He seemed almost excited. "I know her well. We've worked together. What an amazing coincidence. So, she is in possession of the book?"

Nick had remembered Sara's comments from a few days earlier: "In nature, there are no coincidences." Apparently other forces had been at work. From that point on, the conversation between the two men became more relaxed. Michael had been astonished by the synchronicity of events that had apparently brought him and Nick together. To top things off, Michael volunteered to contact the editor and encourage her to publish the manuscript. He also asked Nick to contact him should Nick ever visit the Los Angeles area in the near future. Thus, tomorrow would be their first meeting.

Michael joined Nick for dinner at Nick's hotel. The two men spent three and a half hours rapt in each other's stories, Nick telling the background that had led to the writing of the manuscript, Michael going into how he found his own personal calling in spreading the stories about people like Nick. Because Michael was good at asking questions and Nick in the mood to answer them, the two men got into a level of detail that Thomas and Nick had not.

Nick recounted the events that followed the initial revelations from Duane Berry—what had happened at Scottsdale, and beyond. The food, the company and the ambiance of newfound friendship proved to be nourishment for a growing story waiting to be told. Nick carefully laid out the sequence of unsolicited events that kept occurring, as if directed by an invisible hand, where the same scene was being played out time after time. He was being told that he had walked with the Master. And each time more information would come out. He not only was with Jesus during his time on earth, but he was also being told who he had been and what he had done after Jesus' death. The manuscript told it all, but in the most careful way. For Nick was troubled by all he had been told. There were many times when he would spend hours lying awake at night, trying to understand, looking for direction. What was he supposed to do with this information? Ultimately, he came back to the same conclusion time after time: He had other priorities. Children were growing up. Business responsibilities were growing greater by the year. Life was to be enjoyed. He had worked hard to establish his financial holdings. It was time to enjoy life. Step back a bit and breathe it all in.

But the knowledge continued to torment him as the years rolled by, as would unexpected occasions when a psychic or a friend of a psychic would announce all over again that which he tried to ignore. Nick had moved into a beautiful home overlooking a private lake. He was dating a beautiful woman whom he loved who eventually became his present wife. It was time to think of retiring. Yet he had too much energy and too much knowledge. Life would not let him fade away into anonymity and leisure.

Nick confessed to Michael that his greatest concern had been that people simply would not believe him even if he had tried to make this information public. What if his financial structure came tumbling down when this information got out? Wasn't there a conflict between his business life and his spiritual life? Even if he had wanted to move forward with these revelations, how could he accomplish anything meaningful with what little information he had available to him? Yet, Nick also felt a tugging concern that he would find himself on his deathbed, years in the future, filled with remorse because he had done nothing. He imagined himself regretting not having chosen the spiritual road, for not having traveled its path sharing what he knew with the world. He thought about what it would be like to feel such terrible failure for not having pursued his purpose in this lifetime. It gnawed at his soul. It was a conundrum that, for the longest time, had no solution.

Michael urged Nick to consider making a documentary about all that had happened to him. He wanted to begin immediately. Nick declined. He wasn't comfortable with the proposal. There were already too many things to take care of. He didn't need any distractions now. However, he left open the possibility of a documentary in the future. The two agreed to stay in touch, shook hands, and called it a night.

The following morning, Nick drove down to Orange County to attend his corporate meeting. He was aware of tremendous mental and physical energy running through him, far beyond what he knew as normal. It could mean only one thing: his angels were present. Why? He did not know, but he was thankful, nonetheless. The three scheduled appointments went off without a hitch. He was glad for having made the trip.

At midafternoon Nick was back on the freeway headed for his appointment with Sara. So much had happened since that first phone call. The two friends were anxious to meet, finally. Nick was aware that telephone friendships didn't necessarily translate into the same kind of friendship in person. As he arrived at her apartment complex, he realized how close he was to the ocean. The entire scene of palm trees, stucco architecture, and tanned bodies was so Southern California. The weather was perfect. The whole day seemed to have been perfect. He could even smell salt in the air as he walked up to Sara's front door.

The knock produced an immediate response. There she stood, this gifted woman who spoke to angels. Each looked startled to the other, as if their human bodies contrasted inappropriately with their many spiritual conversations. Both smiled and embraced in friendship.

Sara welcomed Nick in. She was an attractive woman in her late thirties, with deep blue eyes and high cheekbones that gave her a look of elegance. She dressed very casually, in contrast to Nick's business suit. Her apartment could only be described as "California funky." The bubbling voice he had heard so often on the phone, filled with a wonderful enthusiasm for life, started right in where their last conversation left off: spiritual matters. There were no pretenses or affectations about Sara; she wore her heart on her sleeve. What you saw was what you got.

After the two friends caught up on the latest angel "info," dinner was in order. A local restaurant two blocks away seemed the perfect place to continue their dialogue. Even though the place was crowded and the table small, both Nick and Sara delved so deep into conversation that the restaurant seemed to fade into the California background. It was as if they were in another world.

Sara told how she had grown up in the Midwest, and as early as she could remember—maybe as young as two or three—she had seen angels in her life. She had assumed that having angels in her room, and talking to them, was a normal experience for every child. When she shared her stories with her parents, they initially thought it was her childish imagination. As she got older, and her parents realized she was serious, they told her to stop talking about angels. Apparently they either didn't believe her or had thought it was unhealthy. Either way, Sara stopped discussing her angelic friends for a while—until she came to her own conclusions that they were an important part of her life. And she could not deny them. They were more than playmates, they were her best friends. From that time on, her angels were her constant companions.

When she became a young adult, Sara moved to California, living there ever since. She eventually served as intermediary for hundreds of people over the years. Listening to this made Nick wonder how she ever acquired such a gift from God. He made sure to tell her how thrilled and honored he felt to have met her, to have been able to share in her giftedness. He, indeed, felt blessed in her presence.

After dinner, a walk along the beach served as the perfect dessert. Both felt the presence of divine company as they continued to convey to one another their spiritual discoveries, their knowledge of the unknown, the other world. It is rare to be able to speak of the unspeakable, to share what seems unsharable with another. This was the parting gift they gave to one another, and each was sorry to see it come to an end. They bid each other a fond farewell, and Nick was on his way back to his hotel, a good night's sleep, and the return trip to Portland.

A few days after their meeting, Nick received a beautiful card in the mail. Attached to the card was an angel bookmark. Written in Sara's unique handwriting was the following inscription:

The bookmark that comes with this card is for your book, which is already published. We are just catching up to our future as we know it has been ordained—the publishing of your book. The birth of your son brings with it so many blessings and new beginnings. Congratulations on everything that is now coming to fruition. God has prepared you carefully. I am in awe of how, together with God and your angels, you have blended your energies with the One source.

Nick did not feel worthy of the accolades Sara had showered upon him. Nonetheless, he felt honored by her respect. Joy and harmony fused him with the One source Sara spoke of, as well as with the angels who watched over him. Life swells us with such euphoria when all is in harmony. However, there are some things that even angels cannot control. And Nick was about to find that out.

Chapter 5

A CLASH OF WILLS

*O*f all that is held sacred about humanity, nothing is held more so than free will. In all of human history, there has never been an incident, a story, or a legend in which the will of man has been usurped by Heaven. In fact, legends intimate that the fallen angels rebelled against the divine plan that put human souls, bestowed with free will, in oneness with the Christ. It is said that the angelic realms constantly gaze toward the face of God, dedicated totally to the Divine Will in all its manifestations. But humanity? Humanity can stand before God with an arrogant "No!" and leave the Creator with no choice but to allow us the consequences of our own decisions.

How many times have humans wailed in their own darkness over the horror of wars, over the inhumanity of humanity, over the fate of nations? How many times have we heard "How can God allow this to happen?" when the real question ought to be "How can we *not* recognize our own role, our own responsibility?" We are inheritors of the divine. That is how sacred our own free will stands before the cosmos. That is how powerfully we shine before Creation. And if we choose to destroy ourselves and the

Earth in the process, then so be it. The divine experiment of free will shall simply fade into oblivion, forgotten like a bad dream.

One can only imagine with amusement Nick's angels watching the match they described as "the butting of heads" between Thomas and "the Asian man"—one man's will battling another's. How typical it was of these sacred messengers to have warned Nick to stay out of it, to let the process take its own course. It is in the nature of angels never to override human will. Nick possessed a will of such force that it had already thwarted the plans of Heaven on one occasion. He could make things happen simply by willing them to take place. If the adage weren't so old, some would suspect it had been Nick Bunick who had coined the phrase, "Where there's a will, there's a way."

But Thomas Tsoi lived by a different philosophy. He moved with the flow of life. If a person decided not to go along with what he perceived to be the best path, Thomas either chose someone else with whom to do business, or he selected a different path. With Thomas there were no obstacles to overcome, just different options from which to choose. He trusted in life, a life deep with spiritual richness. What the angels had seen as "the butting of heads," Thomas saw as an engagement of continual communication. He saw no adversary, only another man living life as he knew it, as he believed it to be. True, he was engaged in critical negotiations with "the Asian man" and his assistant, just as Nick's angels had accurately relayed through Sara. However, from Thomas' perspective, whatever happened was merely a ripple in the river of life. There were other ripples, eddies and currents, but the river would inevitably reach its ultimate destination.

Before leaving for his Los Angeles trip, Nick couldn't help but think about Thomas and the importance of his efforts. The message from his angels about the head-butting made Nick want to join Thomas on the battlefield. But he had given his word to let Thomas work this out singularly. The business wizard was to take a week off, letting his counterpart work his own magic.

Nick thought it over and decided it would be appropriate to send a fax to Thomas, letting him know what the angels had said. He wanted to encourage Thomas, tell him that he was in the company of a "light-being," as described by Sara. After all, Thomas had been in London for several weeks, negotiating with several individuals, trying to conclude business deals on behalf of their company, their new partnership. A fax would let Thomas know he had the support of a friend as well as the blessing of higher forces.

The day before he took his flight to Los Angeles, Nick faxed Thomas a letter to his hotel room. It read:

Dear Thomas,

Yesterday I spent two hours on the phone with Sara and the angels. And though I had written down many questions I wanted to ask, they immediately began talking about your efforts in London. They shared with me the difficulties you were having, in particular with an individual with whom you are "butting heads." They told me you would be successful in your efforts and that it would also involve your going to Switzerland.

They also told me they were with us on my back deck the day the thousands of birds came, that it was not a coincidence, and that it was definitely a sign from them. They said that you understand and know that. They shared other things with me that were very positive, as well as telling me what our relationship is to each other. I support your efforts.

They told me something else at the same time they were talking about you. There is a "light-being" who is now

85

*with you, as well as with me, providing you with a
tremendous amount of help. This entity is an extremely
high-level being and has never been in the flesh. This
being's participation is in addition to many angels that
are helping you accomplish your objectives. Again,
they said that our efforts would have tremendous, positive, worldwide implications and that you are a humanitarian in the deepest sense.*

Take care of yourself.

Sincerely,
Nick Bunick

When the fax arrived, Thomas held it in his hands for
the longest time. He was having the same reaction to the
fax message as he had with the shrouded Mount Hood. The
chi was quite strong, much stronger than he had experienced with the mountain. The paper itself actually felt
warm to his touch. It was as if it contained an energy apart
from his own. The more he thought about it, the more
Thomas figured it must have something to do with this
light-being Nick had described. He had not felt this strength
of *chi* before. After rereading the fax, and smiling once
again when he came to the part about the butting heads, he
slipped it into the inside breast pocket of his suit. Whenever
he felt the need, the paper would be retrieved, and each
time the warmth was there, the energy was there, the *chi*
filled him. Never had Thomas, the man of facts, had to deal
with such bizarre phenomena. It was not something the
mind could understand, but neither was it something the
mind could dismiss. Facts were facts. And what he felt each
time he took this message into his hands was a fact.

The negotiations continued, and, unexpectedly, as
Nick's angels had predicted, Thomas found himself now

staying at the Zurich Hilton Hotel, in Switzerland, still negotiating with the Asian gentleman. Thomas made it a practice never to mix business with his spiritual life. His spirituality was not a topic for debate. It was too personal for that. He lived his whole life in harmony with his spiritual beliefs.

It was the Asian man who had drifted into the topic of things spiritual during one of the evening get-togethers. Thomas did not try to understand why, he just listened. It was not uncommon for others to feel comfortable sharing their private lives with him. Thomas nudged the topic a little further along. The Asian man pined for a happiness he once had possessed, a life full of spiritual value and rich with a kind of peace he no longer possessed. As a young man, he had practiced an extremely holy way of life, studying to become a priest in a religious institution. Because of his devout spirituality, he was destined to have a great religious future. But certain choices he had made changed all that. Unfortunately, he had gone astray, had become involved in several vices. As a result, he had dropped his religious studies and lost his spiritual well-being. He now carried with him a great amount of sorrow for having lost what he felt had been the most important part of himself.

Thomas was touched by this executive's story, made all the more poignant by the knowledge that this man was quite powerful within financial circles. He was one of the heavy-hitters in Asia, and commanded great respect from those in business. Yet here he was, confessing to Thomas intimate details regarding his past spiritual life. And why? Thomas had made no personal remarks that could have been construed as spiritual. But words had not been necessary. To those who did not choose "blindness," Thomas was the proverbial good tree with good fruit—fully aware that "a good tree does not bear bad fruit, nor a bad tree good fruit. By their fruits you shall know them." And apparently this former student of the spiritual life knew Thomas for what he was—a good man of pure heart. How had Thomas gotten this far in business without compromising that spiritual purity, as he had done?

Setting aside his usual tendency not to speak of such things, Thomas decided to disclose to the Asian man and his assistant some of the events he had encountered recently. The conversation grew even more open. Not certain he was doing the right thing, Thomas decided to tell the gentleman about the fax he had received, how their own efforts would have tremendously positive worldwide implications.

"Would you like to read the fax, hold it in your hands?" Thomas politely asked.

"Very much so," responded the Asian man, his assistant looking on pie-eyed.

With near-reverence, Thomas crossed the suite to retrieve the fax from his coat. The fax was placed in the Asian man's hands. He unfolded it as if it were made of gold instead of paper, and began to read. A few sentences into the message, he looked straight up at Thomas.

"It feels like heat is coming from it. A vibration. What is it?" Thomas only smiled. The assistant took a step back. He knew his boss well and had never heard him talk this way before. The assistant felt privileged to have heard stories never before revealed in his boss' presence. But what was this powerful man doing talking about paper seeming as if it were on fire? To the assistant, it looked like ordinary paper with printing on it. The startled expression left no doubt that the paper was making a convincing impression on his boss.

The gentleman continued reading the fax, finished it and looked over at Thomas. Like his assistant, his eyes were as big as bowls. "Oh my God," he gasped, staring in Thomas' direction. "There are angels in this room with us." His arms became animated with excitement trying to describe what it was he saw. His assistant took one more step back. Angels?

"There is one angel surrounded with a great light; he is very elderly, wise looking. He is standing behind you, Thomas, almost holding you, embracing you. Do you see him? Can you feel him?"

Thomas had expected a reaction to the fax, but this was too much. Caught off-guard, he was searching for the right response. He didn't know whether to take this man seriously or not. Like his namesake, Thomas tended not to believe what he could not see. Yet, he did not want to insult his guest, nor, for that matter, the angels.

"No, I don't see him. I can feel a strong presence around me, but I have been feeling that for a while."

It was true. Thomas had felt a presence around him since receiving the fax. He considered the fax phenomenon, the heat, the energy, to be a manifestation of this light-being. Rather than totally dismiss what the Asian gentleman was seeing, Thomas tried to remember how he had felt at Nick's house when he himself had concluded he was in the company of angels. How different was that from what this man was experiencing? The look on the Asian man's face revealed everything. He was, indeed, seeing something.

The amazing scenario did not end there. The gentleman now swung to his right, entranced with what was before him. "Do you see that?"

"See what?"

"Through the door. This beautiful woman has walked through the door. She has a very large blossom in her hands, like a lotus."

The assistant froze. His boss, his mentor, was now frightening him. The tremendous respect he accorded the older man forced him to conclude that something extraordinary was happening. The door had not opened. And no one had walked through, from what he could tell. Yet, he could smell the flower. There was definitely the aroma of a flower filling the room.

"She wants to hand me the flower," the executive stage-whispered. "Thomas, will you join me in receiving it?" Thomas moved toward the gentleman. With a twist of the head, the executive signaled his assistant to join them. As if on legs strapped to stilts, he edged into the circle.

The three men stacked their hands, one on the top of the other, to accept the gift of the blossom from the beautiful being. The three sat in a circle, hands together in that fashion. With long-forgotten humility, the executive began to pray, Thomas joining him. After finding his tongue, the assistant choked out his own prayer, along with the other two.

The flower was placed into the collective hands of the three with a gracious solemnity. Its perfume filled the nostrils of the assistant. His emotions rose to his throat. As with his mentor, his eyes filled and tears began to trickle from their corners. Thomas could feel surges of blissful energy coming through his hands. And as unexpectedly as she had arrived, the angelic lady left the room the same way she had entered—ghostlike, right through the large wooden door.

The executive stared at the flower for the longest time. It began to shrink in size, becoming smaller and smaller, until only a single petal remained. Then the petal flashed into a beam of light that permeated the three men. All saw the flash, all shuddered from the laserlike wave of light that surged into them. Thomas' entire body felt the force of the energy; it was like being shocked with electricity. The doubter could not doubt this. Like the sound of wings he had heard with Nick, this, too, convinced him he was once again in the company of angels. As his guests continued to weep in their emotion, Thomas was moved by a peace that passed understanding.

The three men joined hands in their intimate circle, each man's right into the other's left. The assistant appeared nearly panic-stricken, overwhelmed by forces he simply could not understand. The older man continued his prayers of thanks in sync with Thomas. The assistant was beyond speaking. He could not understand why he was weeping. He only knew he reeled with bliss.

⮞❧

Later that night, Thomas called Nick to thank him for the fax and to try to describe the indescribable. The soft emotion in Thomas' voice moved Nick. He had not heard his friend talk this way before, as if he were filled with awe. Joy swept through Nick as he heard how the angels had made their presence known at such a critical time—a time when butting heads had turned to praying hands. All these events played deeply within Nick's soul.

Thomas ended his evening the way he ended every evening and started every morning—he gave thanks. He prayed with reverence for the beauty of this particular day. To Thomas, every day possessed beauty for which he was thankful. But this day would be among the most beautiful of his entire life.

Shortly thereafter, the Asian executive contacted his business colleagues to inform them of his decision. He would do business with Thomas Tsoi, on terms agreeable to both. He then notified Thomas, requesting they all fly to London to conclude their dealings and put an agreement together. And it was done.

⮞❧

Spring began to fill the Willamette River with snow-melt from the Coast Range and the Cascades. The Oregon crocuses had bloomed, leaving center stage to the tulips and daffodils. The winter rains had yielded to sunny days and showery evenings. Nick's world was alive with the optimism of spring. He waited with great anticipation, expecting to hear from the New York publisher. Certainly it was only a matter of time before they would send the good news about deciding to publish the manuscript.

Nick's agent, Jennifer, continued calling the editor's office for updates, hoping to learn what progress had been made in reading the manuscript, but the editor's assistant told Jennifer that her boss was too busy to talk to her. And, no, she had not yet read the manuscript. Assurances were given that the manuscript would be reviewed, as soon as the editor could clear her desk.

As agents are prone to do, Jennifer created a schedule of "tickler" phone dates, checking back on a regular basis. The next call yielded a different excuse. The editor was going on vacation soon and would not be able to read the manuscript until she returned. Two weeks after the editor's scheduled return, Jennifer called the woman again. Still, she had not read the manuscript.

In the meantime, Michael Wiese, good to his word, had sent a fax to the editor, reminding her of the work they had done together in Los Angeles. The fax referred to Nick's manuscript:

> *I wanted you to know that I have read the draft of Nick Bunick's manuscript. It is my understanding that it has been submitted to you. This is a phenomenal, real-life story that is still unfolding. While it is still in rough form, the prospects of this material are staggering. I suggest that you take a look as soon as you are able.*

Michael was hoping the publisher would move on the story soon. It would enable him to negotiate film rights, thus providing the publisher with an additional motive to publish the book. His fax conveyed to her the news of his meeting with Nick, describing Nick as "an individual whose spiritual life had entered extraordinary dimensions."

He suggested that she, too, ought to meet with Nick personally.

Three days later, Michael received a response from the editor. Her return fax read:

> *Dear Mike:*
>
> *Of course I remember you. Thanks for being so understanding about my being buried. I'll look forward to reading Nick Bunick's manuscript and will call you as soon as I do.*

Adding additional punch, Jennifer followed with a fax of her own. Nick would be coming to New York in a few weeks. His schedule would be flexible should she wish to meet with him. If she could give some indication as to which day would be better for her, Jennifer could make flight arrangements from the West Coast to New York. She never responded.

A few weeks later Nick received a phone call from Sara. Her usually effervescent voice was solemn as she greeted him.

"Nick, I have important information to relay to you. The angels have told me that your book has been rejected by the publishing company in New York. However, they want you to proceed with a different book first, one that deals with the angelic experiences you are having. They said they will help write the new book."

The news took Nick by surprise. He had gotten used to the accuracy of the angels' predictions. It was not clear in his mind how to proceed. He had not yet received a formal reply from the publisher. He let Sara know that he would have to think things over, that he would have to wait to hear from the editor's office.

A few days later, the bad news arrived. A letter from the editor's assistant read, "Thank you for sending your proposal for Nick Bunick's manuscript, which I did enjoy reading." Her letter continued, explaining that the format did not meet their needs at this time, the proposed book would be hard to market, and "We wish you good luck" in placing the book elsewhere. It was a stock rejection letter.

As it turned out, the editor never even read the manuscript. Unfortunately, she didn't connect with that part of her being that could have heard the urging of angels.

Nick's disappointment was lessened only by his recollection of the role he himself had played in sabotaging the first round of publishing negotiations a year earlier. How dynamic, this free will, how powerful. Even when the forces of Heaven are aligned to produce a particular outcome, a single person can change that outcome. Like Nick, the editor had exercised her free will. The manuscript would not be published. Not yet, anyway.

The question that lay before Nick was what to do about the manuscript. According to the angels, time was running out. There was only one option left: to work with the angels in publishing the manuscript independently. Such a decision had greater implications than simply starting a new publishing house. It was small comfort to Nick that he would take the lead in deciding his own fate. Publishing the manuscript meant embracing unavoidable changes, perhaps alone. He had hoped others would help him face those personal challenges. It now seemed that it was up to him and his angels to release the message embedded within the manuscript. He was free to choose whether to do this or not. But in his heart, the choice had already been made.

Chapter 6

THE CONFESSION

O n a Wednesday in April, Rick was again wrenched from a sound sleep. This time he did not feel the usual need for pencil and paper. Instead, there was a driving compulsion to turn on the television. He found himself staring at the religious channel, and a Christian preacher was quoting from St. Paul. "All credit must go to God," exhorted the televangelist. Somehow, Rick knew this was what he must convey to Nick. It was intended to let Nick know that everything happening in his life was God's will, God's doing. He was not alone.

It was no secret that Nick had an ego. Not so much the kind of ego that makes you feel you are in the same room with an arrogant know-it-all, but the kind that feels compassion for others but at the same time knows what the problem is and how it needs to be addressed. It was the kind of ego that says, "Let's not waste time here. Let's get this taken care of." Nick's will was a power to behold. But there are times when other measures are needed. Those measures require one to be still, to watch, to listen.

The publishing company episode was a testimonial to

the power of free will. The reason behind the decision was immaterial. What mattered now was getting the message out to the world. That was going to take harmonious cooperation, and Nick had to know he was not alone in his efforts. He also needed to keep in mind that his heavenly companions still required room to operate. What they had said to him before remained true even now: They required space, opportunity and openness to allow things to happen.

Such was the case in the "butting-heads" incident. The executive had given these divine messengers opportunity, perhaps an invitation, to come into his life. All that he had hoped for in his spiritual quest flooded in on him at that moment in a way few shall ever know. Because his heart was open and his ego set aside in the presence of Thomas and his divine companions, wonders prevailed.

Nick began to review all that had happened to him since Rick's first message and that first phone call to Sara. He remembered certain phrases in the original message, which referred to an aspect of himself few knew about. Rick had written "Pauline Le Master" more than once in the message and had no idea what it meant. Nick knew, but had said nothing. Buried on the fifth page, Rick had scrawled an obscure phrase: "Letters of Paul ... St. Paul ... New Testament."

❧

Since the initial predictions by Duane Berry fifteen years ago, a series of recurring revelations had haunted Nick. Those disclosures had caused him to search for more answers, more information. Ten years had passed since the Berry revelations when Nick was jolted by an encounter he would never forget. The last decade had seen his children grow up. Two were in college, a third had graduated, and his youngest was in high school. Nick's business had flourished, allowing him financial independence. He had led a very active social life, physically and intellectually. Religion still played no significant role in his life, though he considered himself a spiritual person in continual pursuit of insight concerning the revelations that had come before him.

Nick had been told of a prominent psychic in the Portland area, Laurie McQuary, and decided to call her. The yearning to understand more about himself had tugged at him over the years. Perhaps someone with her talent might be able to help. An appointment had been made for a half-hour reading. Little did he know how that half-hour would change his life forever.

A ten-minute drive from downtown Portland took Nick to Laurie McQuary's office. He had been warned she was all business, that when the reading began, Laurie would press a button on a tape recorder to start a thirty-minute tape. When the time was up, the button would pop up, and you were out the door.

As Nick walked into Laurie's office suite, he found himself impressed with its professional atmosphere. It could have been a doctor's office. An attractive, thirty-something woman introduced herself with businesslike mannerisms. "I'm Laurie McQuary. Welcome. Would you like to come into my office and make yourself comfortable?"

The two of them settled in, she pressed the red button on the recorder, and they were off and running. "Is your right knee still bothering you?" she asked.

Here we go again, Nick thought. His daily seven-mile runs had taken their toll in recent months, and he, in fact, had been experiencing pain in his right knee. She went on to tell him he was involved in a new relationship (Mary Jo) of which her parents did not approve, not only because he was not of her faith but also was divorced. She told him both parents would become very ill the next year and would be hospitalized. One of them would pass away. She would be proven right: Mary Jo's parents both suffered heart attacks the following year and were hospitalized—her mother passed away.

Laurie continued with the reading, and about halfway through, her face become very animated and her voice excited. With great enthusiasm, she burst out with, "Oh my God! You knew Jesus! YOU KNEW JESUS!"

Nick sat silently, not surprised by the now common announcement. What followed was not so common. "When are you going to start doing what you are supposed to do?" Laurie interrogated. "You know exactly what I mean. When are you going to move ahead and do what you are meant to do in this life? You are supposed to be a teacher. I don't mean a schoolteacher. Well, you know what I mean. When are you going to move ahead and do what you are supposed to do?" Nick stared stone-faced without answers, choosing to sit in silence.

"You were Paul the Apostle. You have returned. And you possess the power to heal. This is a carryover from the lifetime of Paul." She then proceeded to tell Nick he had refused to fulfill his purpose in other lifetimes, following the one with Jesus, and that he must deal with it this time. She was adamant that it was his responsibility in this lifetime to teach the truth regarding the beliefs, philosophies and life of Jesus.

Other psychics had already told him that he possessed the spirit-mind and soul of Paul of Tarsus, but this was something altogether new. At thirty minutes on the dot, the record button popped up, bringing the tape, and the session, to a halt. Laurie rose from her chair stiffly, marched over to the tape deck, and snapped shut the cassette cover in a single motion as she handed the tape over to Nick.

A year passed before Ms. McQuary bumped into Nick again. For him, it had been a year of more questions with no answers. "Could you meet with me? I have to talk to you," she insisted. Nick agreed to meet over lunch.

Less than a week later he arrived at the restaurant, spotted Laurie, and walked over to her table. Without a greeting, a "Hi, how are you," or a "Nice to see you again," she confronted Nick immediately as he tried to sit down.

"When are you going to move ahead and do what you are supposed to do?" Laurie was exasperated.

"What do you want me to do?" Nick responded as he sat down. "Should I call a radio talk show and tell the audience that I lived a past lifetime with Jesus? That I was Paul of Tarsus in a past lifetime? Or should I put an ad in the newspaper?" Previous psychics had expressed excitement about discovering this return of the apostle Paul, but none had ever given Nick a reason for his return. Certainly, none had confronted him in this way. The previous two years had found Nick wrestling repeatedly with the dilemma about his role in this life. He had spent many hours searching his mind and his soul, but he could come to no conclusions that would have led to action.

"Just open up. It will come to you. It will happen," she exhorted. *Easier said than done,* Nick thought. He had tried to come up with answers.

"A series of events will happen around you," she offered. "First, you will write a book. Then you will be involved in traveling and speaking engagements nationally and internationally. Of this I am certain."

"But how do I start? How do I 'open up'?"

The rest of lunch was taken up with Laurie's continued efforts to convince Nick that the answer dwelt within him. He knew what he had to do—he just needed to let himself do it. Nick sat back and watched with admiration as Laurie tried to help. She had given him even more to ponder.

Another year would pass before Laurie and Nick stumbled into each other again. She found him at the neighborhood grocery store. Without hesitating, she came up from behind and tapped him on the shoulder.

"Nick, would you call my office and make an appointment with me?" He had obliged her, making an appointment for three days later. It would be three years before he would make his phone call to Sara, in January of 1995.

Nick arrived expecting another reading, but none was offered. Instead, Laurie began with the familiar admonishments about his failure to move forward with his task in life. But this time she didn't leave it at that. She said a friend of hers, Julia Ingram, was a respected psychotherapist who used past-life regression as a means of helping her clients. Would Nick be willing to meet with her?

Two weeks later, Nick and Laurie met with Julia over coffee. Julia's lanky, confident form was accentuated by her short auburn hair and no-nonsense glasses. Her dress covered her as if she were a piece of sculptured art. She looked strong as a frontier woman, yet her voice was as peaceful as a lullaby. No explanation had been given for the gathering. Julia sat patiently listening to Nick explain the purpose of the meeting, with Laurie adding necessary detail. Nick did not try to persuade Julia, only inform her. Would she consider taking him as a client? Would Julia try to learn about Nick's past life with Jesus?

It was Julia's decision whether to accept Nick as a client. She was pleased with what she had heard and seen in him. His credentials were strong. He spoke assuredly, acting neither excited nor doubtful about the story he presented. She was willing to work with Nick to determine the validity of his story. The first session was scheduled for the following week in her office.

Nick was a good judge of people, and Julia left him with a sense that he would be working with a credible person. Julia's professionalism was important to him. If it were true that he would be going public with this information, Nick did not want to become aligned with someone who appeared irrational, impressionable or radical. Julia was intelligent, scholarly, nonjudgmental, as well as open-minded. He looked forward to that first session.

Julia's office looked over one of the more bohemian neighborhoods of Portland, above one of the better known vegetarian restaurants. The streets were flanked by beautifully restored Victorian houses and renovated brick apartment complexes. In one section of the neighborhood were odd shops where craftspeople sold handmade items. A bakery across the street filled the avenue with the old-fashioned smells of hot-cross buns, warm muffins and breads accompanied by the competing aroma of espresso. Parking was always at a premium, for not only did people desire to live in the area, they also loved to window-shop or people-watch as well as mingle. Julia had chosen her location carefully. Even though her thriving practice would have allowed her the luxury of moving to finer quarters in one of the new high-rises, she chose to keep her cozy office above the busy street where life flowed with a pleasant verve.

Will Vinton's claymation studios snuggled in amongst the northeast section of Northwest Portland, while the hilly Forest Park, one of the largest urban parks in the country, guarded the southeast section of the neighborhood. Joggers could be seen at all hours of the day. Men in business suits walked side-by-side with aging hippies and Generation X street kids. Those with dreadlocks or nose rings were as welcome as those with crew cuts or High Sierra fashionware. Men with earrings—right ear, left ear, both ears, it didn't matter—chatted easily with those wearing ties, or Rip City basketball caps. Nick's Jaguar wasn't even noticed by the blend of passersby, its wheels hugging the curb in front of the nearby health-food store. Yes, part of what Julia observed out of her upstairs window was a community of rich diversity that celebrated all that was harmonious about life and good about humanity.

Nick had no idea what would transpire in the session, but he felt a sense of arrival, a chance finally to meet a part of himself that had eluded him for years. Little did either of them suspect what would unfold. They would not, could not stop at just one session. Both Nick's and Julia's lives would be forever changed by these sessions. And both would come to know that the world would be waiting to hear, once again, the Messages they both had uncovered.

It would be a year after these sessions that Nick would reveal to Julia the contents of his first phone conversation with his angels. He had made a transcript of that conversation and delivered it to her. She read with knowing eyes what the angels had conveyed. Emotions that had stirred within her during the regression sessions touched her once again as she read Sara's reaction to what the angels were saying:

> *Nick, oh my Lord, Nick, the angels are telling me that you lived at the same time as Jesus and were very close to him. Nick, they are saying that you were a very important person during that past lifetime, that you lived at the time of Jesus, and that your ego is struggling with it.*

> *Yes, they are telling me that you are a higher being, and that you were Paul! My God, Nick! You are a brilliant soul. I am honored to be able to talk to you, as well as with your angels. They are incredibly evolved. The energy is just extraordinary in my apartment, now. Candles are flickering, and it is just going crazy here. Nick, I am honored to know you. You are a very special soul.*

As Nick worked with the various principals involved in making the publishing of the manuscript possible, his angels continued to lend support. The stories and events that surrounded Nick sometimes made him laugh. At other times they kept him awake until the early morning hours as he attempted to glean their meaning, their underlying message.

On one occasion, Nick was meeting with the president and founder of the Portland company that handled the financial activities for the new partnership. The conversation drifted into matters spiritual, and Nick's growing boldness enabled him to tell much of the story about the angels and what was in the manuscript. The man was deeply moved by the story. If the story were true, he had stated, all involved were indeed blessed. The implications of what was transpiring caused the financial executive to examine his own role. What if the story were not true? The question made him think of one of his favorite business axioms: Money talks. And businessmen understand that credo. It was one thing to talk about angels and past associations with Jesus but quite another matter to have the whisperings of angels turn into unquestionable business success.

Not long after his conversation with Nick, the Portland businessman took his wife and children to Disney World in Orlando, Florida, for a vacation. They returned a week later, on a Sunday night. After preparing the children for bed, the man and his wife entered the kitchen together and found their large digital clock flashing 4:44. It couldn't have been due to an electrical outage because the clock blinked 12:00 when that happened. He phoned Nick the next day and told him the story. Nick's only response was, "Welcome to the club."

Another episode involved Mark Wagner, Nick's attorney. One evening, Mark and his wife were guests of the Bunicks' for dinner, and Nick revealed to them his continuing experiences with angels. Mark was a lawyer outside the office as well as inside. He listened attentively but with polite skepticism. The next time Nick heard from Mark, he was recuperating from an accident. Mark had decided to cut down a tree in his yard, an old forty-foot maple that had been there far too long. He had not notched the tree correctly, and it fell unexpectedly toward him. The last thing he remembered thinking was how the tree was going to crush his head. He had turned his back to what he thought was his certain death. Then, inexplicably, he found himself conscious in the ambulance wondering how he had escaped. The tree had miraculously missed his head, injuring only his back and shoulder.

"Nick, guess what time they admitted me into the hospital."

"I don't know. What time?"

"At 4:44 p.m. And guess what room they admitted me to."

"Room 44?" Nick guessed.

"No, room 444." There was a pause on the phone.

Mark was now feeling fine and would be back to work soon. Nick was listening to a different Mark, different from the skeptical lawyer he had known for years. This Mark was trying to convince Nick that he was certain that angels had spared his life. He insisted there was no way the huge tree could have glanced away from him. The 444s were the angels' way of letting him know why he was still alive. Mark was indeed a different man after that incident.

Sleep was becoming difficult for Nick. He found himself possessed of so much energy it seemed as though he did not need sleep at all. However, the realities of a new morning proved otherwise. He began to pray for more guidance, more help, more affirmation.

Sometimes Nick would lie awake until dawn reflecting on all that was occurring. On one late-night occasion, around 1 a.m., he asked the angels for a sign. And they delivered, waking up Mary Jo in the process. The telephones were always taken off the hook before bed every night, but that didn't stop the angels. Both lines began blaring through the handsets shortly after Nick asked for a sign.

Thereafter he was more careful about asking for verifications.

Nick kept an "angel journal" in which he wrote letters to his angels every few nights. It seemed to give him connectedness, a sense of calm about all that was happening. The number of 444 occurrences were getting too numerous to remember. Or a certain business decision might cause him to wonder whether he had acted in the best interest of his purpose, prompting him to write to his angels.

On a night like that, he asked his angels for a sign that they were with him on a decision. He lay in bed waiting for an answer, dozed off, only to be awakened by little Nicholas fussing in his crib. There was a radio monitor in the master bedroom connected with Nicholas' nursery. The baby's fussing increased. Mary Jo awoke. They decided the little one would go back to sleep if left alone. But Nicholas was adamant, and his crying grew louder. Nick rolled out of bed and glanced at the clock. It was 4:44 a.m. He smiled as he went in to tend to his infant son. "Even you are a part of this, aren't you Nicholas?" he cooed. There was no crying or fussing after that. All these things Nick recorded in his journal and kept in his heart.

These continuing 4:44 incidents with Nick, Abe, and Thomas served as constant reminders of the importance of their efforts. No longer was Nick agonizing over whether to make the manuscript public; it was now a matter of how to do so. Whenever he felt the need for reassurance, he simply asked for it. And without fail, he would find some kind of sign or event that would remind him of his constant companions.

Chapter 7

CHRISTMAS

December in the Portland area is whimsical at best. Some years bring early ice storms that topple trees for miles around. Streets and freeways are transformed into skating rinks. Icicles dangle from every twig, phone wire and car bumper, creating a weird crystalline panorama. And Portlanders can be as weird as the weather. Newscasts show video clips of bus patrons at 39th and Burnside holding up makeshift scorecards. Hastily scribbled-on sheets of paper are raised high above their heads, giving ratings as cars skid down the sloping crossroads through red lights and bash into other cars. Applause is heard from the "judges." It's the Portland Winter Fender-Bender Olympics.

"Great donut!" is heard as one car executes a 360-degree spin. The bundled-up, self-designated judges display 9.6, 9.5, 9.5, and 9.3, as if some Olympic skating event were being staged solely for their enjoyment. Another cluster of folks dances across the glazed streets to help dazed motorists turn their vehicles, sending them on their slippery way. Only the real fender-benders bring the flashing blue lights of Portland's finest. A few judges flash 2.5 and 1.5 as the bus finally arrives.

December can also bring what is called "false spring." Flowering cherry trees display hints of blossoming as El Niño effects bring balmy weather. True to form, some Portlanders can be seen running through the Salmon Street Springs fountain, fully clothed, acting as if summer were on its way. Bystanders laugh nervously at kids playing tag with the fountain spouts. One kid guesses wrong, touching one of the silent spouts just as it sends out a whoosh of water, soaking him to his skin. Portland weather is as unpredictable as Portlanders.

Nick was rather like the Portland weather. When he and Abe got together on one of their many trips, it was impossible to predict what would happen. In New York, both men would be on their way to dinner after a long day of business arrangements. The streets would be crammed and the cabbie conversational. He would ask what the two men did for a living. "I'm a businessman," Nick would volunteer. "Abe here is a world-famous dancer." Abe would turn his head to the side window, trying not to betray his stifled grin. By this time he had grown accustomed to Nick's flights of fancy.

"A dancer, eh?" the cabbie would question, stretching his neck toward the rearview mirror trying to capture some evidence of dancerlike traits. No telling what direction the conversation might go after that. Abe had grown familiar enough with his made-up occupations that he could go along with the charade no matter what angle Nick might take with it—famous flamenco dancer, or noted ballroom dancer here for a competition, or even you-should-have-seen-him-in-West-Side-Story dancer. Wherever these gifted men went, they carried the fun of life with them. Perhaps it was some kind of Portlander "thing" with Nick, or perhaps these two men simply loved to laugh, and hear others laugh with them.

In more serious moments, Nick could have a silent, delving side. Lately, that part of him questioned his role in the unfolding events looming large before him. Sometimes Nick wondered about his own spiritual fortitude. It was a recurring topic during sleepless nights. Was he worthy enough? Was he spiritual enough? He discussed this one day with Sara over the phone.

"You know, Sara, I don't feel I am enough of a spiritual person. I don't go to church. I have a hard time praying, and I find it almost impossible to meditate." She seemed amused at his concern.

"Nick, the angels don't go to church," she explained. "They don't have a religion—they aren't Catholic or Protestant or Jewish or Muslim or Buddhist. They're just part of God."

Nick thought about that. It made sense. "The reason meditation doesn't work for you, the reason you can't stay focused, comes from the fact that you are operating on another level. You have constant contact with the heavenly. Conversations with the spiritual realms are constantly going on in your thoughts and your heart."

Nick was not aware of this phenomenon. Perhaps he had been taking it for granted, or hadn't really noticed. There did seem to be a part of him that felt in constant contact with Jesus. This was especially true during his childhood, even though he had never been taught anything about Christianity. It was as if he had a silent obsession with Jesus. As he grew older, these feelings faded. But he never forgot the inexplicable affection for a religious figure he knew very little about. Had this not always been a matter of the heart for him?

He felt much better after talking this issue over with Sara. But the nagging thoughts still lingered. He had eyes that saw how society conditions us from the time we are children to express spiritual values in certain acceptable ways. We are not always taught that there are other realities and other ways to communicate with the divine.

Nick was becoming aware of how cultures centuries older than ours used many different avenues to commune with the sacred. Going to church seemed to fulfill the lives of many, while others were quite content with meditation techniques as varied as the people practicing them. Yet Nick possessed a quiet admiration for those who were content with the simple, effective ways in which they had learned to speak to God. He respected those who led such simply good lives.

How was it that a man of Nick's vision could not see his own spiritual veracity? He questioned the choices he had made years before that took him deep into the business world and, as it seemed to him, away from his past spiritual centeredness. To those close to him it seemed strange how Nick could not appreciate the importance of what business had taught him in preparation for what was to come. Was he not learned in strategy, organization, human interactions, negotiations, power used and abused, finance and politics? All these skills would be valuable in facing a harsh environment of skeptics, idolizers, or iconoclasts. It prepared him for the best humanity was capable of—as well as the worst.

Sometimes Nick called Sara because he questioned his own judgment; other times it was to hear her affirm what he already knew. On this occasion he wanted to check in with his angels regarding certain choices he had to make before one of his business trips. Tickets had been purchased for a late December flight to London, and Sara knew nothing of the trip. She started off the session by telling Nick of a man the angels said he was going to meet in Switzerland, describing him in vivid detail: stocky build, well-dressed, with black hair, about six feet tall. His last name would begin with an "L." Nick knew he wasn't going to Switzerland but said nothing to her.

After three nights in London, Abe and Nick received a communication requiring them to make a trip to Switzerland to meet some people. The first night in Geneva, Nick met the man Sara had described. His name was Boris Lopatin. He would eventually become the fourth partner the angels had hinted at months earlier. At that time, the angels seemed to waffle between three and "maybe" four partners. The reason for the uncertainty would become apparent later.

Thomas Tsoi had played his part in bringing the partnership to its present place. It was time for another to take the partnership to the next level. Later, the angels would indicate that Thomas would play a future role with the partnership. Nick was very fond of Thomas, but he understood the need for each man to play his part, and, if necessary, move on. Their primary concern was to enable what had been foretold: to prepare the way for a better world.

Boris brought considerable talent to the partnership. In addition to his knowledge of several languages, he was a man with a world view. Though Boris was born in Kiev, Ukraine, Nick called him a man of many countries. His worldwide connections were remarkable, especially in various parts of Asia, and Japan was by far his favorite place to travel. Japanese food was one of his staples; he even had a Japanese assistant, Toshi-san, to help him. If Boris could have arranged it, he would have been born Japanese.

Without question, Boris was a man of high spiritual integrity. His determined search through life had taken him into various spiritual traditions to where he was now—a man of universal beliefs who honored all religions and welcomed broad spiritual thought. He confirmed that universality in his everyday business and personal life. Abe loved to watch Boris during business deals sitting there so silent, even serene. He could hardly wait until afterward when Boris' scalpel-like intellect would reveal any disguised problems or hidden agendas. He missed nothing. If there was a flaw, Boris would expose and excise it during their post-meeting discussions. Anything to do with contracts gave him an edge. His understanding of international finance constantly provided the partnership with added advantage. Pitfalls were often missed because of Boris' skills. He served as the perfect complement to Abe and Nick.

Nick and Boris became close friends in short order. Not only did Boris feel that Nick was his intellectual equal, he also recognized Nick as his spiritual equal. It would take several conversations over sushi before Boris would understand the full measure of Nick's giftedness. Their spiritual lives, as well as their business lives, were a great match.

Boris was soon to discover he had become the subject of Nick's humorous shenanigans. Abe loved having company to balance out his many made-up occupations. The three had become regulars at an Italian restaurant in London, where dinner conversation and business strategy mixed well with the superb food. The owners and waiters alike loved hearing Nick toss around his street-Italian. Laughter could be heard the length of the streets when the three were together. And Abe was no silent participant. He could give as well as he got. Nick had the Italian waiters convinced he was Abe and Boris' father. Anytime Nick was in Portland while Abe and Boris were taking care of affairs in London, the Italian waiters would surely ask, "Where is your crazy father? When are you going to bring your father?" Inevitably, it would get Boris laughing. *That wild man Nick,* he would muse, *What a joy!*

In a way, Boris and Abe were much like the brothers Nick had made them out to be. Along with Nick, they were dedicated to fostering a better world. Boris had no difficulty at all accepting the notion that angels were behind the partnership. And when asked to join, he did not hesitate. These were special people for a special time. For Boris, the unusual had been the norm throughout his life. In all his years he had always depended on "outside" help to guide him through life. The angels who worked with Nick, Abe and Thomas were simply one more instance of "outside" help.

The 4:44 events occurred more regularly now. Each case would be noted in Nick's angel journal. One night, while staying in London with Abe and Boris, Nick asked his angels for help, writing the request out in his journal. He also asked that they would show him a sign to let him know they were there. The suite Nick occupied at the hotel had two rooms, one a bedroom and the other a parlor. Nick never used his parlor because the three men usually met in Abe's suite. Abe was a smoker, and neither Nick nor Boris wanted the stale smell of smoked cigarettes in their own suites.

The morning after Nick requested a sign from the angels, Abe knocked on his door to announce it was time for the meeting. He invited Abe to wait in the parlor while he finished dressing. As soon as Abe entered the parlor, he called back, "Nick, you've got to come in here immediately." Nick rushed over to see what had happened. Abe was pointing to a large clock on top of an armoire. All three hands had stopped dead on the four. They immediately called Boris, who had not yet witnessed this phenomenon; he had only been told about it. The only one among them with an engineering degree and knowledge of gears, Boris examined the clock carefully and noted, as Thomas had, that it was not possible for the hands on a working clock to stop directly over the four. If the hour hand and minute hand are together at 4:20, both hands are one-third the way past the four. But the hour, minute, and second hands were all pointing right on top of the four. Boris smiled one of his big Russian smiles.

Seeing the clock left Boris with a sense of the angelic presence that his colleagues had felt. It not only pulled him closer to them, it provided a pathway for further discussion of ideals and common spirituality. Boris believed our planet was in need of healing at several levels. He believed humanity was capable of returning to the Age of Miracles, and had already put in place the concepts for creating learning centers and healing centers. Some five years earlier he had participated in bringing Chinese *Qi Gong* masters to the United States. Sponsored by the World Research Foundation, these masters began showing others how they use their powers for healing. It had created quite a stir. When Boris discovered Nick embodied the return of Paul the Apostle, he only grinned that big grin of his. It told him how timely his own personal convictions were. It was, indeed, the time for the return to the Age of Miracles. He felt blessed to be instrumental in fostering it.

The three would dedicate their efforts toward the creation of centers for healing, learning, and leadership training where the finest young minds on the planet could gather, learn, grow, and develop into the leaders of tomorrow, blessing the planet with their dynamic lives and the force of their creative imaginations. Others were working with them in these efforts. Infrastructures were being readied in coordination with the coming heavenly event which the angels had spoken of.

Boris believed that, basically, people are good. Humanity needed to be reminded of its own potential, the magnificence of our collective good will. The more love we give, Boris insisted, the more love permeates the world. Nick's vision was similar. He saw a world ruled by universal compassion, truth, and love. This vision portended a new paradigm in which all people live in harmony. There would be no need for war or the weapons of war. There would be no crime. For justice would follow from the precepts of compassion and love. Leaders who did not exemplify compassion, truth, and love would simply be voted out of office. Businesses or businessmen who operated out of greed or self-interest would be boycotted. Those who could not add to the harmony of life would be marginalized by their own ignorance and lack of caring.

Nick, Abe, Thomas, and Boris would attract other like-minded, like-hearted business executives, financiers, and spiritual adepts around the Earth. This project would not be an isolated one. Before all was said and done, Boris believed a consortium of international concerns would join this common cause. He felt in his heart of hearts, that, indeed, the Age of Miracles was returning.

§

Christmas was near, and Mary Jo decided to put on a party for close to 140 friends and associates. It seemed a marvelous time to bring people of good will together. As a sidelight, she enlisted the services of a local respected psychic named Patty Reed. Like Sara, Patty also spoke with angels. She was a truly sweet lady who reminded one of the Mona Lisa, only slimmer. Her ivory face displayed the most infectious smile. She was the hit of the Christmas party.

As she sat giving readings to people from their angels, she would look far off as if she were watching these divine beings while listening to them. Patty was not a commercial person; she gave readings at parties because she was devoted to helping people. And if it took a party or home gathering to help people, well, then that is where she would go. It didn't have to be a private or professional setting for her. Her gift had not come to her easily, and, consequently, she was rather generous with it.

As a child, Patty had been constantly sick with recurring blackouts and seizures. During one of those episodes she experienced a vision in which she was visited by angels. They asked her to participate in a ceremony where she would dedicate her life to helping others. At first she refused, but their constant urging caused her finally to agree. Her seizures and blackouts stopped from that day forward. From then on, she was able to see and communicate with angels, to the benefit of others.

This was a grand night for Patty, for never had she seen so many spiritual people under one roof. The light she now saw around the guests told her these were not the typical people she had helped in the past. These people had beautiful light around them. One man in particular had a bright, white light around him that seemed to fill the entire room. He had just arrived thirty minutes earlier—from London, someone had said. She stared, wondering who this man could be as he made his way over to her and introduced himself.

"Hello, I'm Nick Bunick. I'm your host this evening." Nick was not aware she was the psychic that Mary Jo had invited. Instead, he thought her to be one of the many guests.

After the party, Nick received a request to go downstairs. Would he mind if the lady doing angel readings did one for him? It didn't take long before the two were deep into discussion, especially after Patty's announcement that "You were with Jesus." Patty reminded Nick of Sara in some ways. However, she was able to carry on a casual conversation while gleaning information from the angels. In contrast, Sara would enter an intense prayerful state.

During one point in the conversation Nick said, "I don't pray very often. I feel very guilty that I don't pray, that I don't meditate. But Sara told me that I think in another realm, at another level."

"That's absolutely right, Nick," Patty confirmed. "Do you know who you communicate with?"

"I assume with my angels."

She smiled as she pointed toward the ceiling. "You're getting yours from the Boss."

"What do you mean?"

"What is happening with you is so powerful, so powerful that you don't need to be concerned about not being able to pray the way most of us have been taught. Because of who you are and the state of your consciousness, you are constantly in spiritual communication—but not in the way we normally think of prayer."

"You know, I don't feel like a spiritual person. I really don't."

"Nick, I see a color around everyone. Some would call this an aura. To me, it's just light. I don't see this light intentionally, it just happens. It happened to me after I got healed. I started seeing this light around people. When I first saw you, I saw how you filled the room with this light. You have this huge white circle around you. No one else tonight had a white circle like that around them. Only you, Nick. Believe me, you are spiritual, so don't worry about it."

Nick eased a bit. "OK, I'll accept that. Thank you." It was the last time Nick would express anxiety about his spiritual worthiness. Both Sara and Patty had come to the same conclusion. Hearing it from independent sources allowed Nick's delving mind finally to accept the possibility that he truly was a spiritual person, whether he thought so or not.

Like December weather in Portland, Nick sometimes could not be figured out. At times even he had trouble understanding the various facets of his character. In one moment he could tell you, "I have ice in my veins." Two minutes later one might see the telltale watering in his eyes.

Something had stirred that big heart of his once again. Boris and Abe often commented to one another about these different aspects of Nick. Sure, they loved his gregarious side that kept the Italian waiters doubled over in laughter. But they also honored and respected the ardent business-man he reverted to when it was necessary. If Nick had ice in his veins, then he also had a furnace for a heart. And both men loved and admired him for it.

Julia Ingram had developed similar feelings while working with Nick during the regression sessions. Not only had she come to respect Nick as a friend, she had also come to love and respect Paul of Tarsus, a man she had previously disliked. During the thirteen sessions, she had acquired a level of knowledge that enabled her to see that Paul was more than epistles and interpretations. She saw that history had fashioned a legacy of the man that in cer-tain ways was inaccurate. She recognized that Nick even-tually might have to deal with these misunderstandings and preconceived notions, some of them centuries old. Paul of the New Testament was as multifaceted as Nick of today.

Julia and Nick had many conversations after the ses-sions were transcribed. What Julia had heard in the sessions had broadened her spiritual knowledge. She was certain this material should be made public. And with that conviction she stood behind the manuscript, with her professional expertise and credentials as back-up when they traveled to New York to meet with publishers.

As a psychotherapist, she had recognized in Nick what Sara had heard through his angels: "They are telling me that your energies are holding the book back from being published because you are concerned for your family and your financial structure." Months later, Julia had smiled on hearing about Sara's warning because it verified what she already surmised. Nick's angels had been right, and Nick now realized it. How ironic that Nick's renewed decision to pursue publication of the book had met with the editor's decision *not* to publish it. Sometimes Julia wondered if the manuscript would ever see the light of day.

❧

Considering the manuscript's rejection, all Nick had been told weighed heavily on his mind. It became obvious that if the manuscript was to be published, he would have to publish it himself. But how would he communicate coming events in the coded fashion the angels had suggested? And how could he ensure that those who needed to hear the message, who wanted to hear, would hear?

Nick remembered how he had felt the previous time the manuscript almost reached publication. He smiled to himself as he recounted his feelings of living a dichotomy. Half of him had felt compelled to move ahead with the book. The other half truly did not want to give up the life he sincerely enjoyed.

There was no question about it. Making this manuscript public would change his life. He recalled how he had selfishly wondered if publication would interfere with his enjoyment of NBA games. He had been a longtime fan of the Trail Blazers and held season tickets. Would he be too embarrassed to attend a game and sit in the arena with 20,000 other people, wondering if they were staring, thinking he was a fraud or out of his mind?

All that was behind him now. The angels had seen to that. Nick was aware of the importance of the material and how it stood to positively influence many lives all over the world. Yet, he still needed time to assimilate all he had been told by the angels, all he had been exposed to in the hypnotic regression sessions. Certain conversations with Sara continued to echo in his memory, especially parts that were difficult for him to understand.

"The angels are telling me that you have the same personality and intellect in this lifetime that you had in the lifetime 2,000 years ago. They are telling me, Nick, that you are the same person you were at that time."

He didn't know what to make of such talk. He had tried to visualize himself walking among the populace 2,000 years ago, had tried to put Nick Bunick in the body of Paul. Part of him found it impossible, yet another part of him felt as if he were wearing an old familiar coat. The contrasting sensations made him shiver. Was he Nick Bunick, or was he Paul? Were they one and the same, or were they different? The truth seemed to lie somewhere in between. This was the 20th century. Different values, different cultures, different worlds made Nick Bunick who he is. Yet he was also aware of certain timeless values, truths, and traits that were the same now as they had been then.

"They are saying that before the year 2000, a major event is going to happen to the world. They are saying that there will be a band of light that will go around the entire world, almost like a continuous rainbow, although different colors. They say that you were exposed to this energy before, during your lifetime as Paul."

Nick understood a new world would result from this influx of energy, and to prepare for it, humanity needed to put its spiritual house in order. This event would usher in the thousand years of peace. After publishing the book, he would speak more directly about how people might change their lives by returning to the original Messages Jesus brought to the world.

Late one night Nick wrote in his journal a message to himself. After reflecting on it, he was sure the angels were the author.

You must believe in yourself at all times. You must never lose faith that you are capable of doing anything in life you choose to do. And you must always choose the highest. It is not enough for you to choose that you must achieve excellence. For you must believe in your-

self enough to accomplish that which others cannot accomplish.

To believe in yourself, you must have courage that exceeds the need for the consideration of courage. It must be a natural part of your life that avoids any need for decision-making based on whether you have courage to do that which you must. This must be a belief beyond personal questioning, beyond personal doubt, to a point when it can no longer be considered courage but rather a way of life. This shall be so, for you will believe in yourself.

You must have character that is beyond criticism and is a permanent part of yourself. It is not imagined or pretended. Every moment of your life must be naturally conducted with pride and dignity that cannot be confused with arrogance but recognized with respect. Your character must always contain compassion and concern for others. This concern will be genuine, for you will never lose sight of your background in trying to understand those you have difficulty in identifying with, for they are the majority of the world and the ones that need help the most. You must believe in yourself so that your character never bends, never compromises and is consistent.

You must believe in your intellect that no task is beyond your ability to succeed. Your intellect is a gift that you shall not waste and you shall use to its greatest capacity. You must have the patience and tolerance to realize that others will not always agree with or understand you. But rather than find fault, you shall try harder to reach them, for it shall become your responsibility to serve them. This is your calling. You cannot question it. You must accept it.

Nick would read and reread this message many times during the coming months. It became his manifesto. For he did feel called, with Abe and Boris at his side in that calling. These men were actively dedicated to creating the infrastructure for the arrival of a better world.

Book II

HE WALKED WITH THE MASTER: THE MANUSCRIPT

PROLOGUE

As Julia sat across the table from Laurie McQuary and her client, Nick Bunick, she glanced back and forth between the two. In the past, Laurie had recommended other clients, but rarely had she gone to the trouble of arranging a meeting, let alone arrive with a client in tow. As Laurie opened the conversation with a minimum of information, attention turned to Nick as he began to describe his fifteen-year adventure with past hypnotists and paranormals. Julia's trained eye watched his mannerisms. She listened to the way he told his tale, noting carefully what kinds of details he left out. Nick's concern that others treat his revealing history with respect and discretion was compelling. Something significant was happening to this man. She spotted immediately that he was choosing his confidants carefully. He probably was an executive, she surmised, someone who knew not only how to deal with other people but knew how to carry himself. He was confident, eloquent, and affable.

When Nick finished describing his past life with Jesus, Laurie turned to Julia, and with the subtlety of a midwife delivering another's baby, popped the question, "What would you think if we told you that Nick is the reincarnation of Paul the Apostle?"

Julia cradled the question for a moment and replied in her typically honest way, "I don't know." Her eyes met Nick's. "I would like to know more. I believe in reincarnation; I have regressed hundreds of people to past lives, some of whom have been able to find physical evidence to substantiate their reports." She noted how rare it is to meet someone who was a past historical figure. Contrary to popular myth, rarely do regression therapists run into clients who claim past lives as known historical figures. Most of their clients are ordinary people living ordinary lives. "But what about extraordinary figures?" she asked, half-rhetorically. "They reincarnate, too. Just look at the Dalai Lama. So I believe it is possible."

Nick was now observing Julia as closely as Julia had observed him. He understood why Laurie recommended Julia. She had experience, and she knew how to address difficult issues professionally. Not only did she observe him like an investigator, she also handled him delicately with her open-mindedness. Perhaps Laurie was right. Maybe it was time to see someone like Julia Ingram.

Julia found Nick's story most intriguing. If it were true, then she faced a rare opportunity as a regression therapist. And if it weren't, there still existed significant research potential in discovering why he thought the story was true. The human psyche is both a minefield and a star field, completely unpredictable at times. Modern-day psychology is only beginning to tap into the evidently endless resources of human consciousness.

Nick asked Julia, "Would you be willing to guide me in a past-life regression?" Julia was pleased with his directness, as well as the other qualities she had observed in him. His credentials were strong. He spoke assuredly, acting neither excited nor doubtful about the story he presented. She was willing to work with Nick to determine the validity of his story. The first session was scheduled for the following week in her office.

That night Julia stared out her living-room window while sipping her favorite tea. She didn't know who Nick Bunick was. Had she subscribed to the *Oregon Business Journal,* a weekly newspaper, she would have recognized his name. Later she would learn that his name appeared there frequently. Between the tea and the nudging of her dog, who could easily be mistaken for a horse, her thoughts returned to wondering what Nick was hoping for. If he were Paul, what were the ramifications of his return? Perhaps Nick just wanted to find out why people had said these rather unbelievable things about his being Paul. Or perhaps a detailed journey via past-life regression would provide Nick with the luxury of having his own experience, his own knowledge of who he actually was, and what that meant.

Laurie had confessed to prodding him for several years to explore this information and why he had returned to our times. Something was obviously bothering Nick about this phenomenon. What it was would have to reveal itself later. But what was it about this man that she found so interesting, so impelling? He hadn't tried to convince or impress Julia at their meeting. His presence had been strong, his intelligence evident. She remembered how her surroundings had faded away when his clear eyes had brimmed with tears when he had mentioned Jesus' name.

She lifted the cup to her lips only to find it empty, for the second time. *What an adventure this is going to be,* she thought. Nick was a mystery better than any novel she had read. He struck her as a man of truth. His eye contact with her had not been from good sales technique but from a surety of the soul. From a therapist's point of view, the only thing Nick needed was the opportunity to face his own doubts or his own convictions. And it seemed the only way *that* was going to happen was to see if he had, indeed, lived during the time of Jesus. What truth there was to be found, Julia would help uncover it.

What Julia was about to undertake certainly had implications as research. The field of psychology has yet to fully understand the therapeutic "how" or "why" in employing past-life regression. Theories abound—but the fact remains that they are still theories. While the science of therapy struggles with the unknown, the art of therapy—healing—must progress. Julia was a clinical member of the American Association for Past Life Research and Therapy (APRT). Her active membership reflected her dedication to her work. She had seen extraordinary results with some of her clients, one who had been considered psychotic, another hopelessly obese. What standard psychology had not been able to address, past-life-regression work had.

Julia's office wall was not papered with her certificates. Though she possessed an M.A. and was certified as a Licensed Marriage and Family Therapist as well as a Licensed Professional Counselor, her solid reputation was at the heart of her successful practice. Her open-mindedness served her profession as well as it served her clients, allowing colleagues such as Laurie McQuary to refer clients her way.

Julia's becoming a regression therapist was not the result of scientific pursuit. Quite to the contrary, it evolved from her personal efforts to stretch her spiritual understanding. After years of clinical experience, Julia opened a private practice in 1978. The Far East beckoned her in 1981 as she endeavored to broaden her personal life. Her exposure to other cultures and other ideas fomented her initial fascination with the concept of reincarnation.

In 1986 Julia heard about a hypnotist who claimed to "regress" people to past lives. She believed one could remember all life events using hypnosis, but she still did not know if she had lived before. So she scheduled an appointment. The power of the encounter opened up a place inside her that convinced her she was indeed a soul inhabiting a body, that she had lived before, and, best of all, that she had all the time she needed to become the person she desired to be.

Still, the psychotherapist in her struggled to understand how this other world of consciousness functioned. How did the human psyche operate in allowing such worlds to be unveiled? Had she really remembered a past life? She couldn't prove it, but her feelings during the regression were genuine—that was undeniable. Was the past life an actual living occurrence, or was it a psychological metaphor? Was it a spiritual inheritance or an envisioned reflection of Carl Jung's notion of cosmic consciousness? Her joining APRT meant engaging in the ongoing professional debates about what this ability of humans really is: Are we tapping into soul memory, ancestral memory, collective unconscious, archetypes, dreams, imagination, or what? These were questions that stayed with her for years. It is only now, as Julia begins to appreciate more fully the incredible complexity of the human mind and spirit, that she has formulated her own theories and understanding about how people are able to have access to previous lifetimes.

On the appointed day of her first meeting with Nick, Julia's mind and heart played a game of volleyball, bouncing back and forth between the mind of the therapist and the heart of the adventurer. As Nick walked up the stairs to her office, the volleyball game ended. She welcomed him with the handshake of Julia Ingram, licensed professional therapist.

But let's not cloud this event with secondhand commentary. Let us have Julia tell the story from her own perspective. What she encountered few will ever encounter, whether in this life or another.

When I first meet clients, I get a feeling for the way they access memory (seeing, hearing, feeling, sensing, intuiting) and their level of willingness to collaborate with me. This requires a certain level of trust. While clearly a powerful man, accustomed to being in control, Nick was a cooperative hypnosis client.

In his first session, as he relaxed in my recliner, I gently guided him deeper into a trance state. I suggested he imagine himself standing at the entrance to a tunnel, suggested that this tunnel would take him back in time, back to an earlier lifetime. I suggested that if he had indeed lived on this planet 2,000 years ago, that he return to that lifetime as he mentally passed through this inner tunnel.

Normally in past-life regressions, clients visit a single lifetime in one session, hitting the highlights, identifying the beliefs and lessons, and reconciling the material with their present lives. Sometimes in one session a client will recall several different lifetimes but with a single theme that ties them to the present life and, usually, to the problem for which they sought therapy.

During this first session, Nick stuck to the details of his life as a young man. When I attempted to move him into the future to see if he had met Jesus, he wouldn't move forward and stated that he hadn't KNOWN Jesus. I concluded that (1) there was an intention to recall this lifetime chronologically and in great detail, and (2) that this was not Nick's imagination. Otherwise, he would have confirmed his acquaintance with Jesus. After all, that was the reason he had come to see me.

Nothing was assumed during these sessions. I did not plan ahead nor ask leading questions. While I was familiar with the biblical version of Paul's life, I did not consult the Bible during these sessions. I felt any preconceived notions on my part would tend to bias the

*sessions. In the same way, Nick wanted his recall free
from expectation, and during the period the sessions
were conducted he scrupulously avoided reading mate-
rials that might give him any knowledge of Paul's history. He had never read the New Testament and had no
training in Christianity. He had not studied any of the
languages of that time while in college. I did, in an
attempt to keep track of the geography, obtain a book
with first-century maps of the area when he began
speaking of his missionary journeys.*

*Because spontaneity was essential in these inter-
views, certain details and events may have been over-
looked. A person under hypnosis rarely offers information, only answers to questions. Therefore, there are
many things Nick undoubtedly knows about Jesus,
Jerusalem, and that time period that he didn't report,
simply because I didn't ask the questions.*

*At the conclusion of our first session, Nick ex-
pressed satisfaction that he had indeed recalled a lifetime 2,000 years ago. He was pleased at the level of
detail and enthusiastic about continuing. We scheduled
another of what eventually led to thirteen sessions. As
Nick walked out the door after that first session, I
leaned back against my chair.* Here it is, *I thought to
myself,* What will we learn from here? *I was very curious about how this was going to unfold.*

(Editor's note: To preserve the integrity of what occurred in the sessions,
every attempt was made to preserve the exact wording used during the
interviews. Any time grammar or confusing verbiage is corrected or
changed, such changes are enclosed in brackets.)

Chapter 8

YOUNG SAUL

Regressing people in time can be accomplished using different techniques. It can be done by key events, or dates, or whatever seems appropriate for the client. In the case of Nick Bunick, what seemed best was to trust the circumstances that had brought him to this moment. That meant not cueing him but simply letting events and memories unfold as we began.

My office is upstairs in a renovated building on a street where houses once stood as family dwellings. Almost all these houses are now offices or shops. This is a part of Portland that has what one might call "personality."

I closed the blinds and made sure Nick was comfortable while I explained my method for inducing my clients. Nick seemed at ease, and so we began a journey, the likes of which I may never witness again.

As the information began coming through, I was being told of a young man whose name is Saul. Saul is nine years old and is playing in the fields where his father's sheep often graze. Saul describes his home, his parents and his formal relationship with his father. His father is a landowner of considerable wealth. During a later session, as a young man, he identifies his home as having been on the outskirts of Tarsus, in the region of Cilicia, which today would be in the country of Turkey. At that time it was part of the Roman Empire.

Saul is most enthusiastic when he describes his education. He speaks of his tutors, one of whom is Greek, and his favorite subjects—languages, mathematics, and philosophy. He identifies his favorite philosopher as Demosthenes, a famous Greek orator who lived approximately 300 years before Saul's time.

He is extremely bright, well-educated, speaks three languages, is enthusiastic and confident. We are now hearing the words of a young man who is still in his teens. Saul discusses with his parents his desire to leave home. They do not try to dissuade him but instead encourage their precocious son to experience life. Because they are wealthy, Saul is given funds to help him in his pursuits and to take care of any costs incurred in his upcoming adventure to Judea. He leaves home at the age of eighteen.

Julia (J):   Tell me about your travels here.
Saul (S):   Well, I went by foot and rode a donkey some of the way. I stopped along [the way in] different villages until I came to the sea.
J: You came to the sea?
S: Yes. (In a later session Saul identifies it as the Great Sea. Today it is known as the Mediterranean Sea.)
S: And I went on a ship, a merchant ship. I would talk and meet with the people on deck. They're very interested in hearing what I have to say. I can tell that I command their respect, and they respond to me very much, in terms of interest and my opinions of things.
J: What are you talking about to them? A variety of things, I imagine?
S: Oh, the state of affairs, what is happening, the Roman

occupation. They're not as educated as I am, so I have to be careful what I talk about. I wouldn't talk about philosophies with them because I recognize that they don't have the same background I have. So I try to talk about things that they're interested in and to learn their viewpoints of things that they have experienced.

J: Sounds like you're wise as well as intelligent, even at eighteen. Does "wise" feel like the right word?

S: Well, I don't think of myself as eighteen, and they don't either. But that's fine.

J: You feel older?

S: I don't feel the fact that I'm eighteen has any relationship to how they are responding to me because some of them are much older than I am. They realize I'm more educated than they are. So it's not a factor.

As the ship completes its sea journey from Cilicia, there is a growing excitement in the young man, not unlike a present-day small-town lad who has come to the big city. Saul stands on the wharf soaking in the sights in the early morning air.

S: All the people are exciting. All the activity going on. A lot of these people are from different places in the world. Selling, trading—very crowded—a lot of activity.

J: How are the goods moved from the port? When they are on the dock, how are the goods moved? Can you see?

S: There are people you can hire, [who] stay around the docks, who will transfer your goods from the docks to where you want. They have carts with long [wooden] handles attached to the platform where the goods sit, and there are wheels, two wheels. And they push it. They can't have animals there because it's too noisy and too crowded, and the animals would be spirited and distracted. You know, would react—frightened.

Saul informs me that he eventually finds a family to provide him room and board in this seaport community. The city is called Caesarea, and it affords Saul his first exposure to the many groups and philosophies in the area. I decide to see if this is where Saul first hears about Jesus.

J: I'm curious if you have heard of a teacher, some call him Jesus, some call him the Christ. He is a teacher.

S: No.

J: You haven't heard of him? Move forward in this lifetime to the point when you first hear about a new kind of teaching, a different way of thinking about God, or when you begin to learn about a man called Jesus.

S: Well, there are all different kinds of teachings about God. We have different people who have different interpretations of religious beliefs in terms of their relationship with God.

J: Is this of interest to you?

S: Yes. I seek out groups of people I think are more educated or more interesting, to be able to discuss these matters. It's easy to do because there are people of many different nationalities. They are more interested in the Judaic philosophies.

I did not pursue the question regarding Jesus further at this time. It was obvious he had not heard of him.

J: Thank you. It would be interesting for you to remember a group. I would enjoy hearing about one of the groups you enjoyed meeting with to talk about philosophy and religion.

S: They meet almost on a daily basis, and we are about

six or seven people. They change sometimes, one or two more, one or two less. Some of them are very interesting, and some of them are argumentative and opinionated. But that's OK. I enjoy listening to what they have to say. I'm a newcomer to them right now, so I listen more than share my own thoughts.[1]

J: How old are you now?

S: Almost nineteen.

J: What are some of the concepts you find interesting as you listen?

S: Well, where I came from, I was basically exposed just to one concept, a very strict interpretation. My father was a Pharisee. And his friend was a rabbi's brother. But here I get exposed to the Essenes and the Sadducees, a real cross-section of the Judaic philosophies, and how they should be interpreted. Some of the people are fanatics. Some are very liberal, and there's a great deal of humor and cynicism. It's all good-natured, though. They argue good-naturedly.

J: And do they argue from passages?

S: No. Not passages, just what is happening of a more contemporary nature.

J: And what is happening? What are you hearing?

S: In this particular area there's a lot of activity. There are many foreigners living here because it's a very active seaport. I'm only going to be here a while, and then I'm going to go on to Jerusalem where it's more of a holy land. Here there is such a melding of other influences, which makes it very interesting. Many activities happening that I'm enjoying. It's novel. But it's not where I want to be. I'm just visiting here for a while.

---

1. Saul usually speaks in idiomatic American English, since this is Nick's native language. However, during the course of regression sessions, Saul also used certain words and phrases in Greek, Aramaic and Latin, languages of which Nick has no knowledge.

J: You have something in mind in going to Jerusalem?

S: I want to settle there indefinitely and establish some roots. I want to see the holy places. I want to walk through the temples. I will have fewer distractions, even though I'm enjoying the distractions right now.

Saul remains in Caesarea for another three or four months before he boards a ship once again, heading for Jerusalem. Though he has enjoyed his stay in Caesarea and has made a few friends, Saul meets no one special enough to keep him from heading south for the next port city of Joppa, west of Jerusalem.

J: Let's then move to your journey to Jerusalem. How did you get there?

S: Went south on a boat. Wasn't very long. Wasn't like coming from Tarsus. It was a short journey.

As in Caesarea, Saul informs me that he finds a family that provides him with room and board in Jerusalem. The head of the household is a rotund, accommodating gentleman named Jaceem. His round face, bald head and light beard add to his friendly, fatherly appearance. His wife, Salema, is a quiet woman of medium build who takes care of the rather large house, doting over her kind husband and grown son. Saul is a welcome addition. She provides him with a space in the house that allows him his privacy. There is an attitude of respect between Saul and the family. Saul's desire not to be an imposition keeps his relationship with Salema and Jaceem merely polite.

J: I'm assuming that you've come to Jerusalem to see and learn things, and to meet people.

S: Yes. This is my destination, really. I want to establish roots here. I have some money that I'll want to use to start making an income. I'm going to look for something. Maybe I can own a shop and rent out the space. Then I can have a monthly income from doing that. It's money my father gave me.

J: Move forward now to the next interesting thing that happens here in Jerusalem.

S: Well, I like Jerusalem. So much to see. A real cross-section of life here. Where I was before, the streets were very crowded and here we have both. We have some sections of the city which are crowded and other sections which are quiet. Some sections have nicer homes, and some of the streets are larger.

J: What's your favorite part of Jerusalem?

S: There's a meeting place that's a big open area. I don't mean big, really, but almost circular, where you can sit and talk and watch people. But it's not a market area where there are hundreds and hundreds of people. It's a nice place to go and sit in the sun and talk to people.

J: Do females come here as well as males?

S: There are females there, but not participating in our discussions.

J: So are discussions generally with males?

S: Almost exclusively. Yes. Just males. If the females talk about those kind of things, I am unaware of it. They maybe talk about it among themselves, but they are more inclined to take a quiet position and not be involved in arguing or confronting those kinds of things. They're more involved with taking care of their households—running the household.

J: So talking about philosophy, religion, and intellectual things is something that men do? As far as you know?

S: Yes. Almost all men do. And if the women do it too, they maybe do it on a much quieter basis. I don't think they have the time as much as the men do—busy running the households.

J: All right, thank you. You said one of the things you

were interested in doing when you came to Jerusalem was seeing the holy sites. What was the first holy site you visited? Tell me about that. Not necessarily the first, but one of the interesting ones.

S: There are the gates.

J: The gates?

S: To the outer temple. You go through those and there are gates to the inner temple. The temple is magnificent. So much larger than anything I've ever seen before.

J: Describe the gates, please.

S: There's an archway. And the gates are tall, maybe three times higher than a person. The gates don't open all the way because it's the archway between the gates that opens. But they call it "the gates." It takes you into the inner wall before you get to the next set [of gates] that's almost a duplicate of that. That takes you into the temple grounds. Then you go through the second gates, and then these wide, wide steps go up, before you get to the temple itself. [The temple is] very clean and light colored. White, a whitish gray. Very, very large. Activities. Large crowds. Large building. It's very impressive. It's cleaner than any I've seen before. I did not expect that. Obviously there is a lot of care taken to it.

J: Lots of people here to help take care of it?

S: Well, it's a big city. It's the most important temple in the city.

J: How do you feel as you stand in this temple?

S: I don't feel religious. I feel more impressed with the structure. It makes me feel as if I am in a big city. I don't feel in awe of it, or anything of that nature.

J: OK. Thank you. Are there other holy sites you visited that you would like to talk about now?

S: (Long pause.) I'm not a very religious person in [the] traditional sense. I'm just enjoying seeing the city, meeting people and deciding what I want to become.

J: So you're making it clear this is not a religious quest, but an intellectual ...

S: That's right. Learning. [The city has different sections.] You have your old section where the streets are very narrow; houses are very close together where people with less affluence live. You have [one] part of the city where all the markets are, and you have the other part of the city where things are built more spacious. Then you have the outside of the city, where the soldiers live.

J: Tell me about the soldiers.

S: They're Romans, and they don't bother us too much. They're more inclined to go into the part of the city where there are ... oh, what's the word? Where they'll buy wine, drink wine and ... and find women for entertainment. They're just there.

J: How do you feel about having Roman soldiers here?

S: Indifferent. There's no conflict. They are there just to make a presence so they can collect the taxes. They get part of the tax money that's sent back to Rome.

Saul explains to me how he is becoming financially independent. He has the instincts of a shrewd but honest businessman. His newly chosen profession is that of subletting. He starts by purchasing the leasing rights to two shop spaces. This allows him to charge his own rental rates and keep the rent money. Saul expands his leasing business as he becomes more established in Jerusalem. Between his business investments and the money from his father, Saul continues the life he has been accustomed to. His days are comfortable.

In a typical day, Saul walks into the city in the mornings and later meets someone for a meal. In the afternoons he involves himself in discussions. In the evenings he meets with other people. He goes by the shops once or twice a day to say hello and see how his tenants are doing. Even though the shops are managed by the renters, Saul's friendly character causes him to keep in touch with his tenants. "There's a lot to do. It's easy to make friends here," he says, feeling rather at home in Jerusalem, for a twenty-year-old.

J: In your meetings and sharing of information, study and curiosity, do you have a goal in mind? Do you have something you are trying to solve, or is there a question you are trying to answer?

S: No, I'm just learning and establishing roots. Making friends. Establishing a flow of income.

J: All right. Move to age twenty-one.

S: Yes.

J: All right. What happens during your twenty-first year? Move to that which is most significant for you, most interesting.

S: I think that people recognize that I am a person of character, and [they] are more inclined to look up to me now. [I am] established and [it is] being recognized that my education and my intellectual bearing [are] of a higher degree than the others. You know those [who] care about their own self-esteem? They recognize that I am a person of capacity and I don't abuse it. I have their respect. I'm no longer an outsider.

Chapter 9

SAUL MEETS JESHUA
FOR THE FIRST TIME

With raised eyebrows I thought about this last regression session. I muttered to myself, "That was interesting and, frankly, somewhat unexpected." What I had expected was a regressing right into the thick of things. I thought I would have met the adult Paul experiencing some dramatic event from his lifetime. Instead I was introduced to the young Saul, and with great detail.

Normally, hypno-regression clients come in for one or two sessions to work on some specific issue. The mechanism that operates to open the memory (I call it the Inner Healer) usually takes us right to the core, allowing us to get into the issues and work through the lesson for our healing.

This session with Nick had a very different flavor. It felt "contained," as if there were an intention to be more deliberate, to present great detail in chronological order. In the previous session, when I had asked if he had heard of Jesus, he clearly responded that he had not, in spite of Nick's previous exposure to information from psychics regarding this topic. I had every reason to expect that we would be accessing the memory that knew of Jesus or had met Jesus. Normally the Inner Healer would have taken us there, out of sequence, just to satisfy my question, and get to the core. But not so here.

Nick is an excellent hypnosis subject and recalls detail with clear pictures in his mind's eye. Sitting across from him, watching his face, hearing his voice, I had no doubt this was authentic.

I looked forward with great anticipation to the next session, wondering what else we should learn about young Saul, and if he really had met Jesus, contrary to what the Bible says. Since we had now reached the point where Saul was twenty-one, I decided to ask again whether he had met Jesus.

J: I'd like you now to move to that point in time when you first meet Jesus.

S: (Long pause.) Yes.

J: All right. Where are you and what's going on?

S: Outdoors. About seven of us—Jesus and three other people, myself and two other people. We meet. What do you want to know?

J: Is this one of your usual meetings, and are they guests? Or did you hear about him? How did this come about?

S: No, we heard he was coming through. We wanted to meet him. We heard he was a very unusual person, what he has to say, his personality.

J: So you were curious? (Saul frowns.) Not the right word?

S: I was looking forward to meeting him. It wasn't curiosity. It was a sincere interest.

J: Thank you. So this is the first meeting. Please describe it in as much detail as you can remember— what it was like, your impressions, what was said.

S: We exchanged introductions among us all. He'd just arrived. Well, he actually had stayed here the night before. He had slept over. So it's midmorning now. Now we are just exchanging pleasantries.

J: And then?

S: We visited maybe for an hour or so, and we invited him to meet with us that afternoon where we usually meet to sit and talk and have conversations.

J: And does he come to your afternoon meeting?

S: Towards the end of it, yes.

J: Please describe what he looks like, what he's wearing.

S: (Long pause.) Almost my height. He's thin, gentle looks, kind of brown—lightish brown hair, not a dark brown. Has a medium-size beard, and his eyes are light colored, kind of a blue-gray. He's wearing a robe, a light gray-colored robe, and sandals on his feet.

J: Thank you. You say he arrives at the end of your afternoon meeting?

S: About halfway through, yes.

J: Tell me what you can remember about the conversation—what he's saying, what you're asking.

S: We're asking him, oh, how he feels, what is happiness. How does one define joy and happiness in life? That's what we all were discussing.

J: And what does he answer?

S: He says that happiness begins within. It has nothing to do with material things. He [says] that one can be a slave and another a master, and it doesn't necessitate that the master is happy and the slave unhappy. The slave can be happy and the master unhappy because it has nothing to do with their positions. Happiness is something we can control from within to make it part of our life. Many of the things people seek, which they think will bring them happiness instead bring them unhappiness. He is very gentle in what he is saying. He isn't preaching to us, but what he [says makes] a lot of sense, in that we have complete con-

144

trol of our own happiness regardless of our status in life.

J: So Saul, as you sit here speaking with this man and getting to know him, you are forming some impressions. What are those impressions?

S: I thought he was very enlightening. There were about eight or nine of us there, and he was also listening to us. He wasn't trying to impose himself on us. I thought what he had to say was very, very enlightening.

J: So he's just joining in the conversation?

S: Yes.

J: Other people are speaking as well?

S: Yes, but they're not speaking like they usually do. They're not argumentative, or being as cynical or as confrontive. His presence has toned it down [so] people are speaking more gently rather than interrupting each other (Saul laughs) and shouting at each other as they usually do.

J: So his manner of speaking is having an impact on people.

S: Yes.

J: It seems to be touching you. (Saul had a huge grin on his face.)

S: Oh, I think it's funny that he was having that [effect]. Well, I don't think he was trying to—I don't know—but the conversations took on a different personality than they usually do.

Wanting to hear more from Jesus, the nine listeners invite him to meet with them the next day, when they would like to bring even more friends. Jesus agrees. So early the next afternoon, after the meal, Jesus returns to the same location. Several have gathered.

J: Tell me some questions and answers as you remember them.

S: We invited him to talk to us about how he felt about certain things, sort of just giving him a free rein to talk. So it was less of a conversation and almost more like a teacher talking to his pupils. He started talking about religion, about our relationship with God. He said that God is within every one of us, but some of us do not know it. Some of us don't acknowledge it, and some of us have a better understanding of that than others—that God was within each of us.

J: And is that something you also believed, or is this a new idea for you?

S: It was a new idea. I always thought of God as a separate deity. He said that we are all part of God, and that as we go through life we become, hopefully, closer and closer to God. He believed that if we do wrong we have to deal [with it] either now or sometime in the future—we have to rectify that wrong. It can either be done through atonement during this lifetime or dealing with it in a future lifetime. And the same is true of the good. If we genuinely and unselfishly do good, then we will be rewarded. We will receive the same, if not in this lifetime, then in some future lifetime.

J: And do you know how old Jesus is? Has he said?

S: I think he's three years older than I am, so about twenty-four. I think twenty-four or maybe twenty-five. About three-and-a-half years' difference in our ages.

J: All right. You speak several languages yourself.

S: Yes.

J: Are you aware if he does?

S: Well, he occasionally will use some expression that is a Roman word or a Greek word. But that's not unusual. Most people do that.

J: Most people use Greek words?

S: I speak Greek fluently. But most people, the others,

146

don't. Occasionally they use a Roman or Greek expression or word.

J: That would make sense with the occupation. All right, how did the afternoon conclude then?

S: We started early in the afternoon. He left while we stayed. He left with the two people he was with this time. We stayed and talked some more about what an interesting person he was, and about his philosophy, what he shared with us, until it was time to go eat.

J: As you were talking among yourselves, what was the concept that seemed most interesting to people?

S: He seemed to bring a gentleness into the group (Saul laughs) that stayed there after he left. And it was refreshing. Even those who usually argue didn't argue or challenge what he was saying—because it made sense. He wasn't asking anybody to give up anything. He was just offering them more than any of us could have if we follow that lifestyle or that belief system.

It is obvious by what Saul is telling me that he is quite taken with Jesus, his gentle manner, and his simple makes-sense teachings. The impact of all this on Saul's usually animated companions is striking. Again, their usual shouting to make a point is absent. Saul decides he must talk to Jesus privately. Jesus tells Saul he would like that, and the two agree to meet together two days later. They meet in the morning because the gentle man with the blue-gray eyes is scheduled to continue on his journey that afternoon. They eat together, spending three hours in conversation.

J: What did you talk about? I know that's a lot to ask of three hours. What stands out for you?

S: He wanted to know my background, and I told him about myself. So I shared with him who I was and some of my thoughts. Then I asked him more details about himself and what his belief system was. I wanted more information.

J: What did he share about himself? What did he say about his background?

S: He said he was very disturbed over—no he didn't use the word "disturbed." Concerned. He was very concerned over what the religious leaders were doing in trying to control the people, and that it was actually pushing them further away from God rather than closer to God. He was very upset at the rituals, and he felt the real spirit of God and love for God wasn't there. But [the religious leaders] were more interested in the rituals, and they were misleading the people because of that. He felt the people would be better off if they didn't go to the temples and the churches. They could find God in the fields. In their homes. In their hearts. And they couldn't find God in the temples because He wasn't there.

J: Oh. That's quite a thing to be saying. Is that what you were also thinking?

S: He had thought it out more than I had. He was more concerned than I was because I wasn't concerned about how it was affecting other people. He's concerned about how it's affecting the lives of other people. I wasn't concerned about that because I felt that was their [own] business.

J: Did he speak of his mother and father?

S: Well, his father repaired broken furniture. They had a shop in their little house, and it was on a street level where his father fixed things that were broken. That's how he made his living. Or he would buy things. I mean he would buy things that needed to be fixed, then to be sold. But they weren't new things, but like a chair or a table that were old. He would fix them and sell them. He said he'd been traveling for quite a while, so he didn't see them very often. He doesn't spend very much time with them, even though he spoke of them with respect.

In a future session Saul comments that Joseph had been about twenty years older than Jesus' mother, and that he had died while Jesus was a teenager studying in another country. It was apparent to me during this session that the two men were just becoming acquainted, so Saul was not able to answer in detail some of the questions I asked. Saul's respect for Jesus was very obvious. In addition, I sensed a sincere curiosity in Saul in that he was trying to determine what kind of man this newfound friend was.

J: What age was he when he left home? Did he say?

S: He left home more than once. I think he left when he was young. Maybe around thirteen or fourteen the first time, and went away and studied [in] different places with a group of people.

J: Did he say where?

S: I'm sure he did. I don't remember. But they were Essenes.

J: All right. Then he returned home?

S: For a short while. A couple of years. Then he left again and hasn't been back since, other than just to visit once in a while.

J: So do you talk about the next time you will be able to see each other?

S: Yes.

J: When will that be?

S: He's guessing. We don't know for sure, but probably a couple of months.

J: He'll be coming through again?

S: Yes.

J: All right. So we'll come back to that point again. This is a good time to stop.

S: OK.

J: And then we'll re-enter when his next visit to Jerusalem comes up. So now, begin to move back and away from this memory.

Chapter 10

A HISTORICAL PERSPECTIVE OF JESHUA, THE ESSENES, AND THE EARLY APOSTLES

Our next session took place on May 5, 1991. This session begins several months later in Saul's life after the point at which the last session ended. He is still twenty-one. Jesus has returned to Jerusalem and is to meet Saul and his group of acquaintances once again for a group discussion. The group now has grown to some 30 people. Saul informs me that different numbers of people show up at different times depending on the topic, their previous commitments and the weather. This particular gathering will be in the big courtyard of Solomon's Temple.

J: Look around, describe the setting.
S: We're in the big courtyard—of Solomon's Temple. One side's in the sunshine, and one side's in the shade. And depending on the weather, the time of the year, how hot it will be, we sit in the shade or the sunshine. We're sitting in the sunshine, the left-hand side of the courtyard as you go through the gates.

It is a sunny spring day, not too hot. Everyone has had their afternoon meal. The typical discussions, talks and arguments ensue. Saul then tells me that Jesus finally arrives with two men accompanying him. The two men are brothers.

S: He has some people traveling with him, and two of them are brothers.

J: Oh. They are blood brothers?

S: Not of Jesus, but themselves. Yes. They're from his area, from Galilee.

J: What are their names?

S: The older one he calls Cephas. The younger one is ... I can't say it ... Ara ... Arrisons. I don't know.

J: All right. Take your time and relax; hear it spoken. Just repeat it the way you hear it.

S: Arandon. Something like that.

J: Thank you. And he's the younger?

S: Yes. Cephas is the older one.

J: Arandon. He's the younger brother. They travel with Jesus?

At a later session, Saul explains that the brother he calls Cephas is also called Peter. According to the Gospels, this would indicate that the other brother is the disciple Andrew. Saul refers to Peter as Cephas quite frequently, although he does call him Peter later in life. Again, it is common for individuals undergoing age regression to have difficulty translating names from one language to another.

S: They used to fish in the Sea of Galilee with Jesus. His Hebrew name is Jeshua ... Jeshua. In Greek, it [would be] "Jesus."

J: What does he prefer to be called?

S: We call him Jeshua. He introduced himself as Jeshua.

J: Please feel free to refer to him by the name that's

most comfortable for you. Can you recall some of the things he says this afternoon?

S: He's talking about happiness and the joy that comes from within when feeling at one with God. It doesn't make a difference what your position or status is in life. Too many people place happiness as a condition of wealth. He speaks about people who have wealth and who are unhappy, as an example in showing that the two aren't related. That we have to become one with God inside of us, and allow that part of God that we have inside of us to become part of our conscious living so that we are one with Him.

J: Thank you. When he's teaching, or discussing a concept, does he use examples? For instance, you said he uses examples of those who have wealth but are not happy.

S: Well, he mentioned names that we recognized, yes.

J: Give me an example of a name he mentioned that you recognized.

S: He was mentioning the problems that royal families have had for years. They have been unhappy and fighting among themselves over leadership of different regions. He talks about some simple people that he knows where he's from, the region of Galilee, that are very happy people even though they're poor.

Saul relates to me that he just listens on this day, asking no questions. He decides to invite Jeshua to supper as his guest so they can talk privately once again. They meet at an inn on the road to Bethany, a short distance from Jerusalem. Jesus arrives first, with a friend, who then leaves. Saul also arrives with a friend who chats for a bit and departs as Jeshua and Saul begin their meal. Saul wants to know more about this curious and wonderful man. He decides to ask about Jeshua's family, and what his life was like before he started traveling.

J: What did he say?

S: He left home when he was sixteen, or somewhere around then. He went to Alexandria to study, and other places. His father was fairly old and died while he was away. [He] was much older than Jeshua's mother. So [Jeshua] had to return to visit with his mother and brothers.

J: So he went home to support his mother, or help her?

S: Yes. When he got the word, he went back to pay respects to the family, and then went away again after a while. Traveled.

J: Did he report his impressions or talk about what that was like?

S: He talked about Alexandria. Said that they had wonderful schools there, and libraries. He learned many things there. And he went to Mount Carmel [where] he studied with the Essenes. His mother was very much involved with the Essenes. His father wasn't very involved. His mother was involved with the Essenes since she was a little girl.

J: And did he say who taught him to read and write, and how this is ...

S: A woman who was part of the family taught him how to read and write when he was growing up. She wasn't related, but she was part of the family. But the Essenes took him in and took care of him while he was with them, at the temple and schools in Carmel.

J: How long did he spend at Mount Carmel? Did he say?

S: Most of the rest of his time until he started traveling. He started traveling first in his own region of Galilee, around Capernaum, Bethsaida, Tiberias, around the Sea of Galilee. That's where some of his friends who traveled with him were from—the brothers.

J: And where did he go as he traveled more widely?

S: He's been traveling just for a while—a couple of

years. He went through Samaria, on his way to Judea—to visit. Well, he's in Jerusalem right now. But [in] Samaria, they're not very religious there. They're Jews, but they're mixed bloods. They're not as pious as the Jerusalem Jews are, the ones in Judea. A lot of them intermarried when the Persians were occupying that area. There are mostly desert towns there.

J: And then he went to Mount Carmel in later years?

S: Yes.

J: And was Mount Carmel the base from where he traveled?

S: The Essenes had two colonies: one in Mount Carmel, one near the Dead Sea. And he stayed at the one in Mount Carmel, although there were Essene people scattered around Jerusalem, Bethany, Cana, and Canaan—places like that. Most of them lived, though, in the two colonies.

J: Are you also an Essene?

S: No. My parents were Pharisees. But I believe in a lot of the things the Essenes believe in. Some of the things they believe in, I don't. They believe, and I believe, in rebirth. The Pharisees believe in that, too, as well as the Essenes. But Essenes believe in the stars, too, and that you can tell what's going to happen in the future from reading the stars. I don't believe in that. I don't know anything about that.

J: Is he teaching on his own, or is he teaching as part of the Essene order. Or is that the right way to ask the question?

S: No. He's teaching on his own. He doesn't ... I mean, we're all Jews, and we all go to the same temples regardless of whether [we] believe in the Essene [or Pharisee] philosophy. We all have the same places of worship. It's just a matter of how you want to interpret the word of God.

J: OK. You were asking Jeshua questions about his travels and his studies. You've studied as well, so you must have ...

S: He was asking me about me too. We were talking. We were getting to know each other rather than just his philosophies ... wanting to know about each other's lives. He said he is a little disappointed with his teachings in the Galilee area because the people know him to be from that area, and most of the prominent people and teachers come from Judea rather than from the Galilee area. So he was having difficulty in getting the people to listen to him. He feels he will have [a better] reception in Judea than in Galilee.

J: Jeshua's not taken as seriously in his own home area?

S: Yes. Also, they're not as religious there, and a lot of the information he's sharing has to do with our relationship with God.

J: What did he find interesting about your story and the things that you've been doing?

S: Well, he respects me. He recognizes that I have—how do I say this? Besides my education, he recognizes that I understand more than the others. He's interested in knowing more about me as well as my opinions. He wanted to know what my goals were. I wanted to know what his goals were, too. I told him that I wanted to learn as much as I could. That I wanted to be self-sufficient, which I basically am now, and that I was probably going to stay here in Jerusalem and live here indefinitely. Probably some day I would have a family. Also, my interests are in learning, wanting to learn more about life ... philosophy. I'm very interested in the things Jeshua is teaching.

J: And Jeshua's goals?

S: He wants to be able to have as many people as he can reach, hear the truth, understand the truth and have it become part of their lives. He wants to touch as many people as he can, for he feels they will be better people and have better lives as a result of his sharing with them his beliefs.

J: Any other goals? Does Jeshua have a goal of having a family?

S: No. I don't believe so. He didn't indicate so. Judging by his relationship with his own family, I don't think family is very important to him. His brothers aren't very supportive of what he is doing. But his mother is.

J: Did he talk about his mother anymore during supper?

S: He said that she was a young girl when he was born. His father was much older. He didn't think they had a very ... Well, because of their age difference they were quite different. She was more active in things than he was. She was active with the Essenes, and his father was more quiet. He was an old man when Jeshua was traveling.

Saul goes on to tell me that after supper, Jeshua continues on his journey to Bethany, which isn't far away. Two days later Jeshua shows up again in the courtyard of Solomon's Temple, where Saul and his group of friends have gathered. Saul is glad to see Jeshua, and they embrace each other warmly in greeting. It is apparent to the others that Saul and Jeshua have been meeting. They are impressed and not resentful. Saul is not one to discuss his private life with others. In some Jewish traditions it is considered inappropriate to talk about others or oneself. The group is ready for another discussion.

J: All right. Talk about the conversations this afternoon. What's the topic today?

S: They're asking him questions like, how can God allow a child [to die] at an early age? If we attribute good things to God, then should we also attribute the bad things to God? Which would make sense if God is responsible. And he said no. That's not the way it works. God doesn't interfere with our lives. We're responsible for our lives. Our relationship with God brings us happiness and love, and love towards others. But God's not responsible for what happens in our lives. And the little child will be born again.

J: So a lot of people pray to God for help, for favors?

S: Yes. They're constantly asking God (Saul sounds amused) to do bad things to other people they don't like, as well as good things for themselves. As if God were their servant. And Jeshua is telling them it doesn't work that way.

J: It's their impression that God doles out both the favors and the punishment?

S: Yes.

J: Jeshua is saying it doesn't work that way?

S: Yes. He's saying that our relationship with God brings us happiness. But we're responsible for the good things and bad things that happen in our lives. That God is within every one of us. Some of us know it and some of us do not. But as we allow that part of us to become part of our everyday lives, we are rewarded afterward. We could be rewarded now, too. But we are responsible for the things we do that are wrong, and we will have to atone for them and pay for them until we have counterbalanced the wrong we do. We also will be rewarded for the things we do that are good. Everything that we do, whether it's good or bad towards others, will someday, either in this lifetime or a future lifetime, be repaid.

J: Thank you. That's clear. Is that a different concept than is commonly held?

S: Yes.

J: What is commonly held?

S: It varies among the different people. But the Pharisees

believe in being reborn again. They've never expressed it like Jeshua has. And the Sadducees don't believe. They don't know. They don't talk about being born again. They don't know about afterlife. They say they don't know, and that only God knows what happens after you die. They say you have to give things to the Church, the priesthood. That they'll pray for you, and that you're going to be rewarded by giving gifts to them. Then they'll take care of your relationship with God. Of course that's what Jeshua is saying is not true. He's saying that each of us is responsible for our own relationship with God.

J: And therefore the gifts to the intermediaries aren't necessary? Gifts of money and ...

S: Not only unnecessary. He's saying it's wrong.

J: That could be an unpopular concept. (Saul laughs, displaying a sense of humor and wit that begins to emerge more and more.)

S: Yes. I would imagine so. Particularly if you are the one that's receiving those gifts.

J: Would you explain the difference in the beliefs between the Pharisees and the Sadducees?

S: We all pray in the same temples. There are several differences. The Pharisees, of which I am, believe that our spirit and soul are immortal. We experience rebirth continually until we reach that level [where rebirth is no longer needed]. The Sadducees do not believe so. They believe that when you die, your spirit does not come back. They also say they do not know what happens to the spirit. But they do not believe in rebirth. This can make a difference also in one's attitude—how one lives one's life, particularly when we come to the High Holy Days regarding judgment.

J: Would you like to say more about that?

S: They both have great respect for the testaments that

have been written. But the Pharisees are more inclined to intellectualize and want to understand the meanings behind them, and less inclined to take the material literally, where the Sadducees do take it literally.

J: Can you think of one particular belief that they take literally that you as a Pharisee might not?

S: Some of the stories such as the miracle of Passover, or David and the slaying of the giant. Where we Pharisees would be inclined to discuss these stories to determine whether they are meant to be taken literally or whether there's a message in them, the Sadducees are more inclined to accept them and not question them as to whether they were actual events that happened or not. David grew up as a boy not very far away. He grew up as a boy in the Bethlehem area, which is not very far from Bethany. So there is much conversation about his life and stories. The Sadducees are inclined to accept all the stories as literally accurate without concern about possibly challenging them or questioning them.

J: Are these equally old sects? Do they date back to about the same time, or is one more modern than the other?

S: I don't know which one's older. There are many more Pharisees than there are Sadducees. The younger people, as they become knowledgeable in our religion, are more inclined to become Pharisees than Sadducees.

J: And the Essenes, how do they contrast with these other two?

S: They're thought of as radicals by the rest of us. Even though they also pray in our same temples, they have two particular colonies where they're very strong. One is by the Great Sea in the Mount Carmel area, where Jeshua spent a lot of time also when he was younger. The other is by the Dead Sea. But there are some Essenes who live scattered throughout the towns and cities. They believe in a lot of the philosophies of other countries such as India, Persia, and Mesopotamia. They believe in astrology, which I do not, and the Pharisees do not. Sadducees do not. And they also believe in rebirth as I do. They bring in other beliefs from other parts of the world into their system.

J: What other questions were asked?

S: We spent a lot of time on those questions. We're asking [Jeshua] to explain why sometimes things that appear to be hurtful happen to people who don't appear to deserve them. And Jeshua's trying to explain that we should know how to accept those things, for they're only temporary pain, temporary losses. And that these people could be experiencing something because of what they've done in the past. Or it could just be an act of nature, and that it's OK. It's not something that has to be interpreted as punishment from God because God doesn't punish. God is a loving God. We all have inside of us His love. We must learn how to use it.

J: God doesn't punish?

S: No. There are a lot of old stories in the old books that talk about God punishing, and Jeshua says it's not true. Those are just stories.

J: They're just stories? Then he's saying that God is a loving God?

S: Yes, and that we're all part of God, that He would not hurt us.

J: Did you ask questions?

S: No. I'd rather ask him when he and I are alone. I just listen when we're talking as a group. I'd rather ask him other things that I'm interested in when we're alone, like we did the other night. I think, also, he would prefer that, too.

J: The nature of your discussions is different than in these group meetings?

S: Yes. But, I just think in general, too, when we're talking to one person, we might give a different answer than when we're talking to a group of people who have many different thoughts and different backgrounds. So it was my own decision to be a good listener and enjoy what I was hearing, and learn from it. But if I have other things I want to ask him about, then I wait.

J: OK. One of the concepts that sounds as though it interests you a lot is that of life after death.

S: That's right. I think, for me, that what I believe in will have a very important influence as to how I lead my life.

J: Say more about that.

S: I think that if one were to believe—not just me, anybody—that when [one dies], that's the end of life, then one might not care as much about how to live life—other than for [one's] own pleasures. It's important to know we are held accountable for things we do that hurt others, as well as rewarded for things we did that are good. So I think it's very important to come to an understanding of life after death as opposed to thinking we can pay the priests and have them take care of it for us.

J: So, you are developing a philosophy that you are accountable, and you are deciding to live your life in that manner?

S: It [all] makes sense to me. I think it would make us all better people. And if we're better people, then we have more influence on each other's lives in terms of finding happiness for the right reasons, rather than [finding] just temporary enjoyment of something that doesn't give us happiness later on.

J: All right. When do you two get together again? During this visit?

S: Later. Much later.

J: Where is he going now? He's leaving Jerusalem shortly? Is that right?

S: Yes. He was staying in Bethany, which is just a little distance, and then he was going to travel some more to other places. He's going to go down to Salem and Anin, around there. I don't know what his schedule is, but I know that he was going to go for a long time.

J: To reach his goal of just trying to reach as many people as possible and teach to as many people as possible?

S: Yes. But I think also he was trying to find places that he can stay as he continues his traveling, so when he comes back again he'll have places to stay and know people. So he's not a stranger every time he comes in to visit these little towns and places. I think he's trying to make relationships in each one of them. He needs places to stay. He needs food and warm things. [He also needs] to develop a center, and learn who the people are in each one of those places, who can become helpful in his being able to talk to other people.

J: You said the word "center." You mean a center for these teachings in each place?

S: Yes. But I don't mean it has to be. Some places he'll preach at are a temple or outside of a temple. And other places may be near the marketplace. Mostly places where people would meet in the smaller towns would be near the marketplaces and near the wells, unless they have a temple, a big temple, which smaller towns do not have.

J: All right. So, he's gone for a while?

S: Yes.

J: So this has been an important new relationship for you?

S: Yes.

Saul tells me how Jeshua has provided Saul and his friends with new ideas to discuss. While Jeshua is gone, the group grows in size, due mainly to the lively topics now exchanged among the participants. What eventually will influence a nation, even the world, begins in the Temple of Solomon—minds are being changed, enlightened.

J: Now, let's see ... you're about twenty-one or twenty-two years old now?

S: I'm still twenty-one.

J: Still twenty-one. All right. And so we're looking at Jeshua, who is going to be away for a while. Then talk about what you're doing with your time these next few months, or however long he's gone.

S: I'm taking great interest in the conversations that we have. They have more meaning now. And I'm enjoying myself. Things are going well. I'm accumulating more currency so I am able to get some more stalls to rent which someday will allow me not to have to do that anymore. I'll have enough money coming in from these that I won't have to worry about it anymore. But I do that in the mornings—take care of those things, make some nice friends.

Saul reveals to me that he again is toying with the thought of having a family but decides he's not ready for that, in spite of his interest in a few women friends.

Jerusalem is a lively city, and Saul takes delight in listening to music, frequenting eateries with foreign foods. Warm spiced drinks from different countries are sampled during his long morning walks inside and outside of the city walls. This is a man who enjoys watching the multinational diversity afforded him within the gates of Jerusalem.

J: I know that you enjoy your conversations, your meetings and being with people. Is there anything that you do for recreation?

S: I listen to music. There are lots of things to do in

Jerusalem. There are places that have people playing music, and there are different foods from different countries. And each of those places have different atmospheres.

J: Move forward to twenty-two. Anything significant you'd like to report about your twenty-second year?

S: I don't think in terms of years. I don't think in terms of the fact that I'm one year older is what makes the difference. I'm growing my beard a little longer. I'm getting a little stronger. I've gotten a little bigger. I'm not as thin as I was.

J: Let's move forward to the next visit of Jeshua. Do you get word of his coming?

S: Yes. I heard he was coming. He went first, before he came here, to the river. He spent just a little time there before he came to here.

J: To the river?

S: So I heard—Jordan. So I knew he was in the area before he came.

J: And do you spend time together alone?

S: Yes.

J: Let's go to that. So it's nice to see each other again?

S: Yes. A lot of time has gone by, maybe a little more than a half a year. It takes a long time to travel the way he's doing it. He has to go through Samaria to get to Galilee. And it's a long [and tiring] trip. We're not old, but we're getting older. Of course it's harder on him than it is on me because of all the traveling he's doing. He's been spending most of the time just going [around] the region of Galilee, Canaan, Tiberias—along the Sea of Galilee. And he has some other people.

J: Other people traveling with him?

S: Yes. I don't feel as if we're strangers now. [Jeshua] sought me out that morning he came into Jerusalem, and I felt good about that. We only visited a short time, and Jeshua told me that he would join us the day after tomorrow at the outside of the temple.

J: All right. Go to that.

S: I've told others that he would be there. So there are more people—quite a few people this time.

J: When you say people, do women attend these as well as men?

S: Yes, but they stand on the outskirts. They don't get involved in the discussions. In the past, when our group was smaller, there weren't any women. Now that the group has gotten larger, there are women. But they stand on the outskirts of the group, and they don't—maybe they talk a little bit among themselves and whisper—but they don't talk in the group or ask questions.

J: I see. So remember for me what the topic was for today or the nature of the questions.

S: Well, it seems as if he's talking a little stronger, now, in that he's being more emphatic in what he's saying—so a slight change of style, but his same philosophy. I sense a little bit of anger towards subjects like the priests—what the priests are doing—less conversational in tone and a little more emphatic.

J: So he's angry about the way the priests are?

S: I sense some anger, yes.

J: Do any priests attend your meeting?

S: No, but there's a couple of people who are not part of our group that I think are, could be, messengers, could be listening [and reporting back to the priests].

J: Like spies or informants or ...

S: I don't know about spies. Individuals who I think are close to the priests, who would be inclined to go back and tell them what people are talking about, which is fine. There is no problem, nothing wrong. I mean, there are no laws against what he is saying or what we're talking about.

J: There are no laws against speaking against the priests?

S: Well, no. The Romans don't have any laws against what we believe in or don't believe in, and as long as [we] don't commit crimes, they don't care what we say. And the priests can't arrest you for what you're saying. That's not an issue. They might not like it, but I don't think it's an issue.

J: OK. So you say you have a perfect right to have these discussions?

S: Yes. They might not like it. I'm sure they won't like it when they find out what he is saying. But that's their problem.

J: OK. Anything else you'd like to recall for me today? What's different about this particular afternoon?

S: Just as I said, a different tone. Actually, what he's saying is even more compelling because he's saying it stronger, rather than before [when] he was speaking so softly and gently. [It's] as if he was giving you the option of wanting to accept what he's saying or not. But he's speaking more in a tone that is telling you to accept what he is saying as being truth.

J: Let's go to your next meeting with Jeshua.

S: [It's] nighttime, and he and I are walking and talking together. I can see he's getting frustrated because a lot of the places he's been to aren't accepting what he's saying. You see, they're not as educated in the Galilee area, and even though they're Jews, they're not as pious. They've had influences from other cultures that have occupied their areas at different times, and he's not getting the response that he had hoped for. But he's had some good things happen in the Judea area. There is a person on the Jordan, who lives around the Jordan River, who's getting people to come around that area and listen to him talk. I guess he's related somehow. But he's a mountain person. He said I should come and meet him. I would think that he was different. I guess you'd say he's a character. I told him I'd like to.

J: So we expect that will take place. We're getting close to a stopping place today. So we'll mark here.

Chapter 11

THE EMERGING MESSIAH

*A*s the next session begins, Saul is describing to me his traveling toward the Jordan River. The journey will take a couple of hours. Before reaching the river, Saul joins Jeshua and "one of the brothers," as he tends to call him. It is Jeshua's intention that Saul meet John, the one known as the Baptist. The three move through the nearby town and then to the river's edge. John is there.

J: What's your impression of John?
S: He's outspoken. He has an aggressive personality. He's a big person. Jeshua seems amused by him. He is kind of odd. He's like a preacher, an outspoken preacher. Rather than being in a temple, he's preaching outdoors, and lives outdoors. He obviously is educated, even though he doesn't try to give that impression. He tries to overpower you with his personality and his voice. He's not intimidating us, but I can see that's how he's accustomed to influencing people. I'm not quite sure of the relationship between [him] and Jeshua. They have two completely different styles.

J: Two different styles of relating to people?

S: Yes. Where Jeshua will study you and your feelings as a person, John is more inclined to just try to overpower you and not be particularly concerned about what your personality is.

J: Do you know how long they've known each other?

S: Well, they know each other. Their mothers are sisters. So they knew each other when they were younger. Then there was a period of years, as they were growing up, that they didn't see each other.

J: I see. So they're cousins?

S: But they don't act like they're related.

J: That is not what's bringing them together?

S: No. [John] and his mother moved. They were originally from the same area as Jeshua's parents, and then they moved from the Galilee region down to the Judea region. So they aren't that close as far as family, but they're both adults now.

J: Are they close to the same age?

S: I think John is just a little older.

J: OK. Thank you. So what is the gathering today? Or is it a gathering?

S: No. There are some people that come by, out of curiosity, to listen to him speak. He's at an area in the river where there is sort of a beach where a lot of people come to either just relax or bathe in the river. So there are people that come there, and then they go. Other people come, and I guess what he does is lecture and preach to them. Not that they are coming for that purpose, but he's taking advantage of their being there. There are people who do that, you know, that are thought of as zealots, who are always preaching the word of God.

J: So he's not the only one who does this?

S: No. And most of the time these people aren't taken seriously because they're not members of the priesthood. They're just individuals. But he has a strong personality.

J: Do you have an impression of how long he's been preaching here?

S: Well. I think he travels between here and some other place near Anin. He's an Essene also. The population [of] Judea think of the Essenes as being radical in their thoughts anyway.

J: What kinds of things are they teaching that are thought of as radical?

S: Oh, they believe in astrology. And rather than confining themselves just with Judaic philosophies, they study Indian, Persian, and Egyptian philosophies. They're not traditionalists.

J: Do you listen to him teach today?

S: Well, he's preaching more than teaching. We listen to him for a while. It's amusing. He's a lot into damnation and punishment and things like that, which neither Jeshua nor I are inclined. I mean, neither of us believe in that philosophy—that you have to do certain things or God is going to punish you. So, like I say, he's trying to intimidate. He preaches by intimidating the people. (Saul is smiling as he describes this.)

After a couple of hours watching, listening and musing over Jeshua's cousin, John, the two return to Jerusalem. Though Jeshua spends long periods traveling, he always visits Saul when he's in the area. Capernaum is Jeshua's home base, on the Sea of Galilee, where his family lives. He continues his travels, revisiting Canaan, Bethsaida and Tiberias—sometimes stopping in Jerusalem when holidays and festivals are celebrated.

J: If you would, recall one of your meetings when Jeshua's talking about his travels and how far he goes.

S: Well, I went with him one time.

J: Let's hear about that trip. Remember that trip.

S: He had with him, oh, five or six of his followers, and we were going north on the road through Samaria. I went, too. I hadn't been there before. It's mostly just desert, little towns along the roads. Small little towns located where there is water, where there are wells. And we talked a lot. We talked about his philosophy and his goals, his frustrations, his attitudes. And he asked me a lot of questions about how I felt about things. But I was more interested about how he felt.

J: Anything you'd like to detail specifically about his attitudes or his frustrations?

S: He didn't like the way people related to God, and didn't like the way those who were in power were teaching the words of God—that they were trying to get the people to function out of fear of God rather than love for God. And they were involved in a lot of ritualism. He objected to a lot of the different activities that go on in the temples. Rather than just being places of worship, there was a lot of merchandising, commercialism going on. And he felt that the people had strayed from their true relationship with God. His goal was to bring them back to that relationship.

J: Has he said why he decided to become a teacher? To dedicate his life to teaching?

S: He feels that is his purpose in his life. And I think he's just totally committed to that. It is his total ambition and commitment. Just as some people are driven by wanting to accumulate wealth or to living a life of pleasure or trying to just subsist, to survive, his commitment and his drive are to help people, to show people the way, to show people truth.

J: One of the beliefs that has come through the ages about Jeshua is that he is the son of God. Does he talk about that?

S: Yes. He says we're all children. We're all sons and daughters of God. We all are, and we all have God inside of us. A part of God. Most people don't recognize this or understand it at all. He says that we should get in touch with what's inside of us and have God become part of our daily life. It is my belief that what separates him from others is that he has done that. The part of us that is God, with him, that part is at one with his mortal life. It would be like two people having a great talent. One not recognizing, and the other recognizing it and using it in his daily life. I believe this is why he is so unique. His spirit-mind is at one with his mortal mind. It's like he's alive, and yet, as I would envision, a being who is also at the same time on the other plane, on the other side. He has needs just as we all do. But there's another part of him that—this is me saying this, not him—that's Godlike. Another part of him that's Godlike.

J: So you're saying he does not describe himself as a unique son of God, but a son of God more in touch with the God within him?

S: He speaks on a very personal basis of his relationship with God. Let me see if I can explain what I am saying. Take three people, blindfold them, [and] take them to a certain location. Two of the people don't know where they are, but the third is completely aware of where he is, understands completely what is going on around him. So it is [with] Jeshua. He's totally aware of his relationship with God and our lives. You see, he believes that God isn't the one that punishes. You punish yourself when you do things that are wrong or bad. You have to sometime atone for those things, whether it be selfishness, rudeness, greed. And by the same token, the law of God says that if you do good things, good things will happen to you. God and nature are one. It's the law of nature.

Natural laws exist because that is the way things are.
I think he has knowledge of who he has been in previous lives, although he doesn't say. He just laughs when I ask him about that.

J: He doesn't want to talk about that?

S: No. He just laughs when I ask him about it.

J: Does he explain why he doesn't talk about it?

S: No. He just teases me about wanting to know about it and asks me who I think I [was]. He and I talk differently than the people who follow him. They quarrel among themselves, and they're not very educated people. He has people that know him at places we stop—not every place, but some places. People know him, and those people are both affluent as well as others who aren't. And that's how we stay. They provide him sometimes with—depending where we are—lodging as well as food.

J: So he now has this route where people expect him, and take him in?

S: Sometimes they take him in. Sometimes we'll just camp out or we'll stay on their properties, outdoors, if the weather's nice. Some places he stops and talks to people, teaches. Other places he doesn't. Some places they pay attention to him. Other places they do not. It's going to take him a while, I think, to make an impact on people.

J: He seems to have patience.

S: He has patience? I don't think so.

J: No?

S: Sometimes he shares with me that he's frustrated over the people who are uneducated. A lot of them don't understand what he's saying when he's talking. A lot of them don't understand. And the ones who are brighter are usually more affluent, and it might be less important to them. So he's trying to find ... he's experimenting with the right level to be able to talk to these people so he can communicate with them, so they can understand what he is saying, and [he can] receive the response he's looking for.

J: So it must be a relief when you two are alone and he can be himself and say what's on his mind.

S: I know he enjoys talking to me. And I certainly enjoy talking with him.

J: Move forward to some point on your journey that you felt was interesting or important.

S: Well, I don't know if it's important. There was one place where he couldn't get the attention of the people. He was talking to them. We were around a well. They were just not interested in staying. They would do what they were doing, draw the water and leave. He couldn't get their attention, and he finally stopped trying. I felt some anger. He didn't say anything. He got quiet, and we just walked away. But I felt some anger. I mean, not his anger. I felt my anger. I didn't feel anger from him. He just got quiet.

J: And what was your anger about?

S: I felt angry over the situation. I wasn't angry at the people because I realized they didn't know. They didn't know him. They didn't know him at all. I don't know how many other people have traveled through there so many times, that the people have a lack of curiosity. But I felt what he had to say was so important, and I was angry that there was no way to get these people to come around and listen to what he had to say. But I understood the situation. They don't know who he is or if what he has to say has any substance to it.

J: Do you ever speak?

S: No. I just speak with him. I occasionally just have small talk with his followers, but not too much.

J: What was the outermost place you visited on this trip?

S: I went up to the sea with him. Some people call it a lake. It's really a lake more than a sea. It's about twice as long as it is wide. They call it the Sea of Galilee, but some people call it Lake Tiberias. Which is also the name, I think, of the first town we came to when we reached the lake. The town's name is Tiberias, too.

J: What are your impressions of this place?

S: It's not like Jerusalem. Most of the people there make their living from the sea, fishing or transporting people [by boat]. So you have smaller populations. People are less educated than the ones in Jerusalem and more similar as far as their backgrounds and personalities.

J: How is Jeshua received there?

S: He has a lot of friends up and down the coast. But he doesn't preach as much there. He's more conversational than teaching.

J: How long do you stay there?

S: Once we get there, to Capernaum, I just stay a few days, a little less than a week, and then I go. I leave and go back by myself.

J: Anything else you'd like to relate about this trip?

S: I visited several times when his family was there. They live in Capernaum. I could feel and see his sister's love for him. I think his two brothers, who are younger than his sister, have some resentment towards him. I believe they think that he should work and live in one place, like they do. They don't understand what he's doing, and they kind of resent the fact that he's not in some form of commerce. They don't understand what he's about, and when he tries to explain his philosophies to them, they're not interested in hearing about it.

J: Do you remember his sister's name?

S: You would call her Ruth.

J: OK. Thank you. And the brothers?

S: They both begin with a "J." One's Judah. The other

one begins with a "J" sound—James. James, or something like that. I just thought of something. The father was Joseph, and the three sons all began with a "J" sound.

J: What do you think of his mother?

S: Very sweet, loving person. She's still a young woman in the sense that, you know, she was young when Jeshua was born.

J: How old was she?

S: Sixteen. His father was a lot older. He is dead now, though.

J: Yes, you've mentioned that he died when Jeshua was fifteen or sixteen.

S: No. He would have been around eighteen.

J: There's a story about his mother, Mary.

S: Yes.

J: People refer to Jeshua's mother as the virgin mother.

S: No. (Saul frowns.)

J: That Joseph's actually not his father.

S: I've never heard that. (Saul has an edge to his voice and a wary expression on his face.)

J: You've never heard that? Possibly a myth that's grown up later?

S: I don't know. Why would someone say that?

J: I don't know. (I decided not to get into possible explanations. Saul appeared upset at the question.)

S: Maybe someone is saying that because the father was so much older. I don't know. I don't believe that. You mean they're saying that as making fun of them?

J: Remember the question I asked earlier about Jeshua being a special son of God?

S: Which he is.

J: Some maintain that a special son of God wouldn't have a mortal father, and that Joseph did not actually participate in the conception. The story is that the Holy Ghost came down and helped her conceive.

S: I don't know what you mean.

J: OK. So that's not something that's discussed?

S: No. That's not something that's discussed, but ... no!

J: Nor does it make any sense to you?

S: No!

Saul is showing considerable irritation. I realized that again I was asking Saul to comment on something that made no sense to him. In fact, the only sense he could make of it was to think that it was a story created to mock the family because of the difference between Mary's and Joseph's ages. I decided to drop this line of questioning.

J: Well, we'll let that go. So you spent some time with his family. You see that the sister and brothers don't understand what he's doing?

S: The sister loves him. She's sympathetic. She's very sensitive to him. She has a tremendous respect and love for [Jeshua]. It's his two brothers. They're younger brothers. They don't seem to ... well, I can see the resentment. So that's fine. He doesn't let that bother him. Oh, it probably bothers him, but he doesn't fight the issue.

J: Anything more you'd like to discuss about his family at this point?

S: The only other thing I see is that almost all of his followers come from that area. The ones who travel with him are from that area. But he performs differently when he's down in the Judea region, in Jerusalem or Bethany, than he does when he's up here. It's not that he acts differently. It's that he's not trying to teach and lecture and philosophize. He gets a much better reception from the people when he's in Jerusalem than he does up here. And I think it's partly because they're more educated and more receptive in Jerusalem. And also because these people know him personally, so they're having a hard time, I think, having one of their own people lecturing to them, someone they've known since childhood. You know, his family was originally from Nazareth, and then they moved to Capernaum when they came back from Egypt. So he really spent most of his time in Capernaum.

J: What do you know about why the family went to Egypt? What has he said about that?

S: The king was threatening to kill the young boys in the family between certain ages, and a lot of families, for fear of their children's lives, left—the ones that could afford it. But then the king died. He died shortly after that—about four years later. The new king had the same name as his father. The king had several sons, and his several sons ruled in different areas. One son took over Judea, and another son the Samaria region. [The king's] name was Herod. One of the sons was named Herod also.

J: Why did the older king Herod want to kill the young boys?

S: Well, he had—(Saul laughs) this is stupid—he had astrologers that were advising him that, according to the astrology and alignment of the stars—I guess, I don't believe in astrology, so I don't know—but that a baby, a boy was born during that period of time of Jewish faith, a Jewish baby, that was a threat to his throne. But his wife the queen didn't believe in that. So they were fighting among themselves over his paranoia about it. It didn't make a difference. He was an old man. He died shortly afterwards, anyway. But there was a lot of rioting and fighting going on over that— families rising up to protect their children. There were civil riots in different places where hundreds of people ended up getting killed. I don't mean babies. I mean adults. I wasn't living there then. That's what I'm told. I didn't live in Israel [at that time].

J: You would have been just an infant.

S: Yes.

J: Did it go on for a few months?

S: No, no, no. It went on for a couple of years as I understand it. But I'm not from that area.

J: This is what you've heard?

S: Yes. They didn't know if their sons—their children—were going to be killed. So some left. Some of those that couldn't afford to leave rioted, thinking that their children were going to be killed. But more people got killed in the riots. I don't even know if any infant boys were killed. That was just the rumors that were going around, from what I understand. [But] Herod's wife didn't agree with him. She thought he was crazy for listening to that kind of advice.

J: OK. Now, let's talk for a little bit about what's going on in your life. You continue to acquire shops, getting your financial affairs in order?

S: Yes. I have the rights to rent out the shops. I purchased the rights. Yes, stalls to merchants to sell their products. I'm involved in other commercial transactions so I'm fine financially. I'm self-sufficient now.

J: Do you go home to visit your parents from time to time?

S: When my father was dying I went home to visit him. That was about a year later, after my trip to the Galilee.

J: So right around this time, twenty-four, twenty-five, your father is dying?

S: He died when I was twenty-six. I haven't seen him in a long time. I didn't feel very close to him. But I did go back to see him when I heard he was very sick. I got word he was very sick, and he died while I was there.

J: And how is your mother doing?

S: Not too well. She's old. She's not too well, but doing OK. As well as can be expected.

J: OK. Move forward to the next time Jeshua and you are together.

S: He comes to Jerusalem for the holiday season and he's staying for a while. So we see each other quite often this time. We visit together and he's preaching, teaching and he has more and more people listening to him—larger crowds gathering for him to talk.

J: And how are you participating? Are you still watching?

S: I just watch when he's talking except when he and I are alone. Rumors are going around that he is the one who is ... that they said would be coming to be the Savior, the Liberator, the Messiah. And that's also what John is saying now, evidently.

J: So John has been saying that Jeshua is the one?

S: Yes. That's what I'm told.

J: And does Jeshua agree with that?

S: He's evasive about it. There are people in the past who have claimed ... It was written about 400 years ago or so that a prophet was going to be reborn again. And that he would be the Liberator of the people. And every so often there are people that claim that they're that person. But they're just crazy people that no one takes seriously. People are confused as to whether that person is supposed to be like a soldier who is going to lead them into battle to liberate them, or whether it's to be a spiritual type of liberation. And also the predictions were that this person would come from the province of Judea.

J: So that part fits?

S: No, I'm not sure. Jeshua's family was from Nazareth, although he was born in Judea. What was your question?

J: The real question is, does he agree that he is the prophet who was predicted?

S: He doesn't give a direct answer. He's evasive.

181

J: You're saying there is some evidence of the prophecy?

S: Depends on how you want to interpret the prophecy. But I asked him, and he was evasive. He said that ... let me think for a minute. He threw it back at me and simply asked me what I thought. (Laughing) I told him I didn't know. But there are rumors that he's doing things that are—how should I say?—supernatural.

J: Like what?

S: Oh, that he can make things appear that aren't there. Or make more food than there is. There are rumors saying that he was in Galilee preaching to a group of people—a large group of people—and there wasn't enough food. It was time for the noon meal and he was able to manage somehow to make food appear to feed all the people. So there are a lot of people coming to see him now because they hear these rumors, and they're in awe to see the person that supposedly can do these magical things.

J: Do you think that he does do magical things?

S: I haven't seen him do any of them. I don't know if it's true or not. I didn't ask him because I wanted him to know that I loved him and was impressed by him regardless if those things are true or not. So I didn't ask him. Whereas a lot of the people now are joining him or identifying with him for that reason.

J: They feel like rumors to you?

S: They might be true. I don't know. There is something ... I know there is something mystical about him. He has told me before that if we could become at one with God inside of us, that we have the ability to do a lot of things that we otherwise can't do. So it wouldn't be inconsistent with what he's told me before, although I don't know if it's true.

J: Thank you. Are there other rumors about him?

S: There are some people that claim [Jeshua's] the

Savior. He's also becoming much more critical of the priests. He's very angry over what is going on in the temples with the merchandising and the commercialism. And he has gone [inside] and preached in the temples—as though he were a priest himself—against what was going on. The hierarchy is getting very upset. They feel he is a threat to them.

J: So he's just going right in there and ...

S: Well, the temple is open. Right outside the temple is where we usually meet and talk. It's a large open area. But inside the temple, they're selling birds and animals, exchanging currencies from Roman coins or silver. And this shouldn't be. He's saying that shouldn't be done in the temples of God.

J: And the priests are condoning this kind of merchandising?

S: Well, they're allowing it to happen. They haven't been doing anything about it. He's saying it's wrong, and he's saying that people shouldn't bring sacrifices to the priests—food and things of that nature. Of course, the priests are telling them that they're sacrificing to God. But Jeshua is saying they're really not, they're really not sacrifices to God. If they want to give the priests money, that's one thing. But they shouldn't give them animals to kill that they end up using for their food. He doesn't have respect for them. And the priests resent him also because he's preaching on the Sabbath day. They said he's not supposed to be doing that on the Sabbath.

J: So are they speaking out against him? How do you know they resent him?

S: That's what I am being told by other people. I don't have any contact with the priests. But I'm told by other people that this is going on—people who are exposed to both the priests as well as to him. The ones who go into the temples and listen to the priests preach, and also listen to Jeshua, are saying that it's controversial.

And thus begins the emergence of the Messiah through Saul's caring eyes. Early on, Saul senses that Jeshua may be in danger. Not only from the priests, but also the zealots who are looking for a prophet. The only group that seems not to care, at least for now, are the Romans. Saul, who walks through the marketplace each morning exchanging pleasantries, finds himself in deep contrast to his loving friend Jeshua, who now walks through marketplaces causing quite a stir.

184

Chapter 12

A TIME OF MIRACLES

As I reread my notes from the earlier session, I can picture in my mind's eye the events as Saul related them. The people are very real, the situations familiar because they are on a human scale. I remind myself that these are very young adults we are hearing about—both in their early twenties. My own children are twenty and twenty-one right now. They alternate between being wise and wacky on a regular basis. They are young adults, still deciding who they are, what they believe and what they want to be when they grow up. Saul and Jeshua, both evolved spirits, are nonetheless human, and, therefore, still going through a maturation process. It has been sobering to watch Jeshua and Saul mature throughout these sessions, too.

It is also sobering to realize that some of Paul's writings as a young, opinionated fellow—later mellowed by age and experience—have been construed as the word of God. It becomes apparent in later sessions that beliefs and prejudices Saul now holds are modified in his later years as Paul. This throws a different light on the near-infallible character that some in today's world attribute to his early writings. In the following chapter, we witness profound changes in Saul as he himself begins to witness the fullness of Jeshua's powers.

The next session finds us four years down the road with Saul telling me that life has been good—he has his own house now, not far from the Temple of Solomon, where the discussion groups have met. The house is in an area where many if not most of the merchants and business-people live. The property is co-owned by a man named Armainus. They each have their own separate quarters, with a few sections of the structure as common space. These are comfortable accommodations, though Saul makes a point of noting that these comforts are not a high priority in his life.

Saul has matured considerably in these last four years, wearing his twenty-seven years well. He reads many books written in different languages. In addition to shop space, Saul now acquires leasing rights on land, subleasing it to farmers. This generates substantial wealth for him. He has extended his area of operation to include Damascus, in Syria.

Jeshua is now staying in Bethany, a short walk from Jerusalem. He has more followers with him. There are about fifteen people staying at his friends' house in Bethany. Chickens and other animals wander the yard. Jeshua and Saul agree to meet alone the next day. It has been more than a year since they have seen each other.

J: So let's move forward to tomorrow and the time that you two spend together alone. Where are you?

S: [We're] in Bethany. We're saying good-bye to the people of the household so we can be by ourselves. We're walking along a dirt road and getting away from the other people so we can talk.

J: Are you just catching up now on things?

S: Yes. I've been hearing stories of what he's been

doing, and I wanted to tell him what is happening in Jerusalem [because of it]. There are rumors and stories that he's been healing people that are sick. I ask him about that—if it's true, and how he does it. Also, I want to tell him about the reaction to those stories in Jerusalem.

J: What does he answer when you ask him these questions?

S: He shares with me that he has been [healing people] because he's been disappointed that people haven't been accepting him and what he has to say as much as he would like them to. He found by doing healing he was able to have more and more people accept him and his relationship with God, and more importantly, *their* relationship with God. He's also going to do healing in the Jerusalem area, too, so people can see the power that they have when they are at one with God.

J: You also ask him how he does it?

S: Yes.

J: Has he answered that?

S: Yes.

J: What does he say?

S: That the people who need to be healed must believe that they have God within them. That the same power, the same force which has the ability to create life also has the ability to sustain health. That much of our sicknesses are caused from within through sin and self-infliction. And he shows them the way.

He teaches them that they have God within them and that they can forgive themselves for their sins. That they have caused the illness and they have the power through him and with his help, through God that exists within them, to cure that illness and be made well. They recognize through the healing that they can be at one with God. They [recognize]

the role that Jeshua plays because of his relationship
with God in that process of healing themselves.

J: He's saying he's helping people to heal themselves.

S: Yes. And he says that they're healing themselves
through his ministering with them. But they must
believe that they are able to [bring about their own
healing with him]. If they won't believe that, then
they can't heal themselves. [My] understanding is
that it requires both him and them in order to accomplish the healing process. They can't do it without
him, and he can't do it if they don't accept what he's
saying.[2]

J: What else do you talk about?

S: I tell him the reactions of the people in Jerusalem to
these stories. He's becoming more well-known, and
the people want to see him. People want to see him
heal, and others want to be healed by him. They're
becoming very excited about him, and his name is
spreading throughout the area. But at the same time
the Sanhedrin, [their] people and the authorities, religious authorities, are really concerned about his
influence on the people. They're afraid that he's a
threat to their power. Some of them are saying that
these stories are false. At the same time, they're concerned that he might have too much influence on the
people—more than they have. They're concerned
they'll lose their relationship with the Roman authorities because of that, because the Roman authorities
look to them to control the people.

---

2. During conversation after the session, Nick said it was apparent to him
that Jeshua made a deliberate decision to heal the sick to establish his
credibility with the populace. Had he not decided to heal the sick publicly,
he might not have achieved his goals. In that case, the world might never
have heard his teachings.

J: Did I understand? I believe I heard you call them the Sanhedrin?

S: That's the council, the religious council in Jerusalem. They make the decisions in the management of the temples and the priests of the Church. There are seventy of them when they are all present. Most of them are Pharisees. Some of them are Sadducees, since the temples are for all Jews regardless of which sect they are. There are no Essenes on the council. The Sanhedrin makes the decisions regarding which priests will preach and teach at which temples. They manage the tithings and make all the major decisions, particularly in the Judea area.

J: How does one get on the council?

S: You are appointed by the other members when there is an opening.

J: Then they all have equal power?

S: No. There is a chief of the council whose name is Caiaphas. Caiaphas and his father-in-law are on the council and have a lot of power. And some of them, called elders, have been on the council longer than others. The longer you've been on the council, the more influence you have on the council.

J: Is it a lifetime appointment then? Once you're on the council, you stay on?

S: Not necessarily. You can be discharged either because of health or if you've lost favor with the council. But most of the time, they're on the council until they die.

J: Do you know Caiaphas?

S: Do I know him personally?

J: Yes.

S: No. I have been places where he has been, and there were one or two occasions where we met. But he wouldn't remember me. They were just passing moments.

J: What do you think of him?

S: I think he has more power than he deserves, than he is warranted. I think he is concerned about his position, and in wanting to maintain favor with the Romans. Of course that's the biggest fear they have regarding Jeshua.

J: How is that connected with disfavor with the Romans?

S: The Romans want stability among the people. They feel that stability is accomplished through religious control and religious relationships. Stability for the Romans represents their ability to continue to collect the taxes, rather than having people refuse to pay the taxes. There is a relationship between the religious leaders and the Romans. The Romans look to the religious leaders to control the people and to assure that they continue paying their taxes. The council realizes that if they lose control over the influence of the people, and instead the people start looking to Jeshua as their leader, they will lose their position with the Romans. They'll lose their authority with the people as well as their relationship with those who are basically responsible for governing the area. So the threat to the council is twofold from Jeshua. One is in the religious authority, and the other is in terms of the Romans looking to the council as being the leader of the people.

J: Thank you. Do you give Jeshua any advice about this?

S: First, I'm telling him to be very careful. I'm concerned about his welfare. The reason he's been doing healing in the Galilee area is because he's safer there. The Pharisees and religious people are located mainly in the Judea area where they have their power. That's where the Roman authorities are mainly located. So I tell him to be careful in Judea because I'm concerned they might take action against him. And I tell him to be careful and not to alienate them.

J: And is there anything else that you tell him? Does he

now ask you questions, or is this frightening to you?
(Saul looks very worried.)

S: He understands that, and he's indifferent.

J: He's indifferent?

S: Yes. He jokes about it. And he plans to stay for a
while. He says he'll teach me how to heal, also.

J: He'll teach you how to heal?

S: He wants to teach his followers. I don't know if
they'll be able to. They're not very bright. But they've
become a lot more committed to him since he started
healing, and it seems to me as if they're arguing
among themselves for position—particularly the ones
from Galilee arguing with the ones from Judea. But
there are more from Galilee than from Judea.

J: Are they all familiar to you now? Have you gotten
acquainted with all of them?

S: I know who they are. Yes, I know who they are, but
they're not friends of mine.

Saul is certainly aware throughout these sessions of
his relationship with the disciples. It is obvious he does not
relate to them nor want to identify with them. He does not
spend as much time with Jesus as they do, since they travel
with Jesus and are with him constantly. Yet, at the same
time, his relationship is singular and personal, whereas the
others appear to have a group relationship, such as the relationship between a group of students to their teacher.

J: But you've seen them all before?

S: Oh, yes. Well, some of them are new. He has some
new ones. I mean new ones in addition to the ones he
had before. But I think they're—oh, how can I say
this?—I think they're competing with one another to
try to be closer to him and be on his good side, to win
favor with him now that he's doing these healings.

J: So that impresses them as well?

S: And they want others to be impressed by them because of their relationship with him. (Saul laughs.) But I ask him why he has a need for them. I know they perform functions for him as well as give him security and take care of some of his requirements. But I ask him why he doesn't—well, I don't want to offend him. They're just not very impressive people to me.

J: So you're not saying everything you're thinking?

S: No, I don't want to hurt his feelings. I understand why he has them with him.

J: What are you thinking that you're not saying?

S: They're just not people of very high quality. But I realize that he would have difficulty, probably, getting people of high quality to leave their families and travel with him like these people do, because they're not working. They're getting the benefit of his relationships, too, in terms of being taken care of, by getting food and places to live while they're traveling. I guess it's necessary, so it's OK.

J: So you don't respect them much?

S: Yes, it's not a question of honesty. It's just a question of their motives. I don't consider them very bright or very spiritually mature people. But he speaks to them often, and they can hear what he's saying and doing. From a spiritual standpoint, I'm not sure they understand who he is. On the surface, they certainly know who he is, in terms of the influence he has on people's lives, being able to heal. I think they're not sure in their minds who he is from a spiritual standpoint.

J: What else did you talk about on your walk today?

S: I told him about the things I've been doing, and he says to me that he would like to see me spend less time in those areas now and spend time with the things that he is doing. He knows I'm not going to travel with him, but he would like to see me get involved with his activities when he's not here.

J: How do you respond to that?

S: I'm not particularly enthusiastic about that because of the other people he has around him. I don't want the people to think of me as one of those other people. I enjoy spending time with him alone. I enjoy being in groups when we're having intellectual conversations, when he's talking to us and we're asking questions back and forth. But I don't want to be identified with the other group of people [who] are his followers. So I don't stay with them overnight or get involved in activities in which they're involved.

The Scriptures say Saul persecuted the disciples. I wondered if he would do this, and what would transpire to cause this young man to take such an aggressive action. As I have gotten to know him, it seems he observes and even judges—but to actually campaign against his close friend's companions? I decided to not ask, but to wait and see what would come up in its own time in later sessions.

J: Anything else you'd like to add about your walk and your talk today?

S: We're talking about what he's going to be doing for the next few days in Jerusalem. So I'm making plans to be there when he comes. We're not a very far distance apart. We're only about, maybe a twenty-, twenty-five-, thirty-minute walk from where he's staying to the temple grounds.

J: Does Jeshua always stay with the same family in Bethany?

S: No. There [are] two or three different families that he stays with, and two of them are related.

J: Do you know them?

S: They're not friends of mine. I know who they are. I visit them while he's there, one [family] in particular—two sisters and a brother who live together.

193

J: What are their names, or the family name?

S: Magdalene. The brother is the head of the family. He is older than his two sisters. He's fairly well off. They don't live in affluence, but he has a lot of property and land, a lot of animals.

J: Are you aware of whether Jeshua has a special female relationship? A romance? A marriage?

S: He's not married; he has female friends, and I don't know what their relationship is. If you're asking me if their relationship is carnal, I don't know. But he has female friends as well as male friends.

J: So he keeps that part of his life more private, or would you know?

S: I've never asked him, and I believe it is private. When he goes into fasting, he does so both with the body and mind, in which he will avoid pleasures of the body, as well as go into deep prayer and meditation at the same time. I've seen him do that before.

J: You've seen him do that?

S: Yes. He'll eat very, very little, spend a lot of time in solitude, deep thought, and deny himself pleasures, physical pleasures, social activities. Other times he is very socially active in life, being at festivals and activities, and being around a lot of people, laughing a lot, enjoying life. It's like two people. I mean, he has two different transitional personalities, depending on when he feels he has a need to be spiritual as opposed to when he puts that aside, [when] his needs are to be very outgoing and social.

J: All right. Thank you. So you've spoken of several days of activities. Please move forward. You said that he was planning to do some healing.

S: Well, in the morning he went to the temple and preached there. A lot of people started to congregate. He's preaching with a much stronger demeanor than he did before. He's speaking with much more authority, where before he was soft-spoken and quieter. He's telling the people that God will forgive them for their sins if they're sincere and that they can be at one with God—that they're being taught wrong, told wrong things by their priests and rabbis in the temples. And they're asking him a lot of questions which I knew they were going to ask him because I've heard the questions asked before he came to Jerusalem.

J: What questions are they asking?

S: They're asking him what his relationship is with God.

J: And what does he answer?

S: He says things like, "God's love is like sunshine," and that there are too many people that prefer to stay in the shade rather than standing in God's sunshine. He has stood in God's light, and having stood in God's light he speaks the word of God—that God speaks through him. And (Saul is laughing) that frightened some of the people.

J: It frightens them?

S: Yes. It frightens them. Those who are frightened of God would be frightened of him. Those who love God would instead find great solace and pleasure and comfort in that. I'm saying this now. (Saul means he is injecting his own opinion here.) I guess, depending on their relationship with God and how they feel about themselves, they would know what God thinks of them. They would think of Jeshua either as a threat or as a wonderful opportunity for them to be exposed to Him. So you have all kinds of mixed reactions in people.

J: You seem amused by this.

S: I didn't realize that was what would happen. Their reaction to him reveals what they think of themselves—who they are in relation to God.

J: Are you watching from the side? (Saul motions with his hands as he paints the picture in midair.)

S: I'm standing. I'm facing Jeshua at an angle. I'm to the left, to his right, but not alongside of him. I'm in the crowd, standing on the stairs so I can see a lot of different people, because I'm at a higher level than most of the people.

J: What other questions are asked?

S: [There are] some questions that are hostile and some that are very loving questions. The hostile questions they're asking are if he is claiming that he and God are one and the same. Others are asking if he is a prophet of God.

J: How does Jeshua respond to hostile questions? (Saul's face lights up.)

S: The same way as he does to the loving questions, friendly questions. He doesn't get hostile back if that's what you are asking. He tries just to have them understand what he's saying. He says he doesn't proclaim to be God. But he says that we're all children of God, and that he has stood in the light of God. He wants them also to come with him and stand in that same light—in an example he gave—to get up, to remove themselves from the shade and stand in the sunlight of God. But he means that figuratively. He doesn't mean that literally.

J: Are there any more questions or answers that you would like to recall?

S: Some of them are asking him to heal, and he's saying he will do it later in the day, in the afternoon, away from the temple grounds. The crowds keep getting larger and larger as the word gets around; and he's grown a lot in stature, in the way he delivers his messages—much different. It's much stronger, and of course he's speaking to larger crowds, so he'd have to speak louder too, wouldn't he? But his personality has changed somewhat. He's speaking with much greater authority and confidence, and he's aged a little bit. He's not quite as thin as he was before. But I think that's probably because he hasn't been traveling as much in the last year or so as he was before. I know the traveling takes a lot out of you, the stress of always moving. But he looks good.

J: Shall we move forward then to the afternoon and the healing?

S: It's not quite midafternoon yet, and we're in an open area in a part of the city, not the busiest part of the city, but where there are some shops. We're in the middle of this area. There's a lot of people, as well as sick people who have come, who want to be healed.

J: So the word is really getting around about this?

S: Yes.

J: What happens?

S: We're all walking over towards the well. They follow [Jeshua]. He's standing on the stone wall that surrounds the well because there's no other place he can stand to be taller. He wants to explain to them what their frame of mind must be for him to heal them. [Jeshua's] telling them that those who have sickness caused by themselves, even though they may not realize it, must acknowledge it, and forgive themselves as God would forgive them. Their sicknesses might have been caused from greed, anger, jealousy, or intolerance. Those who have sicknesses that might be self-inflicted can't be healed if they don't acknowledge that they are responsible for their own sicknesses, and to understand what caused [them]. If they're willing to acknowledge that they caused their own sicknesses, he can pray with them. And as God forgives them, they will forgive themselves, and then he can help them heal themselves.

He separates them. He tells them to move over to the right, away from the rest of the people. Some of them do, and some of them won't—are reluctant—won't admit it. (Saul is laughing hard.) I'm just thinking that if they won't admit it, they're not going to be able to be healed. And then there are others who are sick, and it was not brought upon by themselves. [Jeshua] says to them they must have incredible faith in their love for God and God's ability, and their own ability from God within themselves, to be able to heal themselves.

I'm saying this now—(Saul is reminding me he is giving his own opinion) that unlike those who inflicted their own sickness upon themselves from sin, I'm thinking that it's going to be a lot harder for the others to heal themselves who were either born with an affliction or through accident or injury.

Jeshua's telling them that it's going to have to be through incredible faith and belief in God that is within them, that God and they together have the power to heal. And it may take a longer period of time for them to heal themselves than those who can be healed by forgiveness and self-acknowledgment.

Because of Saul's powers of observation, his curiosity, and the fact that he always can be counted on to have an opinion, I ask the following:

J: Is there a way to know which is which?
S: Yes. They all know, but some won't admit it. Some won't admit that they need to be healed at all, and others don't want to acknowledge that it's because of their own fault that they're sick. So they're going into the wrong groups, where they won't be healed even though they want to be.
J: You can see that?
S: Well, yes. Some of the people are even saying things to them like, "You should be over in the other group. You weren't born with that disorder." Some of the sicknesses are involved with the intestinal areas. They

get sick when they eat, or they can't eat. And some people have physical injuries like lameness.

J: So you're saying that people know if they've caused their own illness?

S: I'm saying that. Jeshua described the first group and told them to move over to his right. And then he described the second group and told them to move to his left.

J: All right. What happens next?

S: [Jeshua] talks to them for a long time, maybe more than an hour. He then steps down and goes over to the group on the right and starts working with each one of them individually. He places his right hand on their forehead and his left hand sometimes on their shoulder, sometimes on their arm. And he's praying out loud for them to forgive themselves, and for God to forgive them, that they won't sin any longer. That evil—only he's not using the word evil, he's using a different word. When we speak of evil spirits, we don't really mean literally spirits. We mean that which causes sin, such as greed, jealousy, and anger, are an evil spirit. So [Jeshua's] asking God and the God within to drive out that evil spirit (attitude) so it's no longer a part of their being, whether it be immorality or stealing.

But he knows they won't admit what it is, so he does not name it by name. He just says, Drive out that evil spirit, whether it be greed, or anger, or hostility, or dishonesty which caused the sin. And to forgive, forgive this individual for having in the past committed that which is evil or wrong. He's making them feel better. [Jeshua's] healing them one by one— almost *all* of them. There are a few that he wasn't able to [heal]. He tells them, "It's up to you. You must first acknowledge and then forgive. But you can't forgive unless you first acknowledge."

Acknowledge, forgive and accept—I'm saying this now. He didn't say accept. But it's apparent to me that they have to accept that they have the ability. They first must acknowledge that they are guilty of the sin. They must then ask for forgiveness. And I'm saying that they have to go beyond that and accept the fact that God's within them, that they have been forgiven, and to ask for the healing. (Saul was very emotional and intense as he spoke. He was clearly moved by what he was witnessing.)

J: So this is the first time you've seen this?

S: Yes.

J: What do you think?

S: It's very dramatic. Particularly the reactions of the ones that he healed. I mean, Jeshua just goes on to the next one, but the ones that are being healed are very dramatic in what they're saying, thanking God and telling the others in the crowd that they feel better.

J: Does one particular person stick out in your mind?

S: A number of them do.

J: Tell us. Choose one or two.

S: One had a speech problem, and he could barely speak. When he did, he kind of stuttered. And now he's speaking perfectly. Yelling at the top of his voice. You know, like cheering. (Saul is laughing and tears are coming down his cheeks.)

J: So you're very moved by this? Very excited?

S: I'm realizing [that] I'm coming to terms with Jeshua—of who Jeshua is. I'm coming to terms with myself. I have been trying to make my own evaluation as to who he is. I realize that he is the one they predicted that would come and be the Savior of the people. And I know that his life will be taken from earth sometime in the not-too-distant future, as the predictions say. So I'm feeling both happiness and sadness at the same time.

J: And today it really hit you? (Saul is showing deep emotion.)

S: I ... I realize. Yes. Watching him heal people, I now understand. I'll talk to him about it when we're alone. But I understand now. I understand his frustration in the past, and I understand now why he's doing healing. He had to. He had to do healing to make the people believe in what he is saying. (Saul is still very moved.)

J: All right. Any other healings that you would like to share?

S: Well, then [Jeshua] started healing the other group of people after he finished with the first group. And there were some people who wanted to be healed whom he told [there] was nothing wrong with them. But he prayed with them anyway, and told them they were fine. He understood that they wanted to be healed anyway, in case there was something wrong with them. But [Jeshua] then went over to the other group, and of course the crowd was just following him every second. They were standing. He had to keep asking them to move back a little bit. His followers kept saying move back a little bit and give him some room. [The crowd] wanted to touch him and be next to him. I can understand that. Thinking that whatever his relationship is with God, that some of it would rub off on them by standing next to him and touching him—touching him.

Well, [Jeshua] just continued using the same tone. He went over to the other group and told them that their healing process might take days. It might take months. It could take years, or it could be immediate. It was directly related to their belief and love for God, as well as that within them. And he started the process with each of them to help heal them.

I could see that some of them were showing

immediate improvements, physically. And some weren't. But they all were feeling better for having done it. He told them that they must continue the healing process on their own. But some had immediate results. I think some of them were going through the process [though they] really didn't believe. But they felt they had nothing to lose. I thought to myself that they're not going to be healed, and then they'll blame Jeshua because they didn't get healed. But everybody understood that. Not just me. It was obvious to others who was being sincere and who just wanted to be healed but didn't have the real spirit and feeling that was required.

J: Any particular person that you'd like to share with me? Any particular healing on that side?

S: There was a boy, a little boy, I think maybe eight or nine years old, and his mother was with him. He wasn't blind, but his vision was impaired—I gather from an accident. Anyway, he believed and his mother believed, and he was healed. His mother was crying. That was very touching. (Saul is very emotionally moved.)

J: Thank you. Is there anything else about this healing that you'd like to talk about today?

S: I'm just conscious of the fact that it's going to have a tremendous impact on the people in the city when the word gets around—in many different ways. Some of it very positive. Those who might consider him a threat are going to feel even more threatened. That's just in the back of my mind. But that's not very important at this moment right now.

J: So you're just making some predictions?

S: It just crossed my mind, that's all. Particularly when we were leaving—the crowd's breaking up. You could see they were going to go immediately, which I wanted them to, and Jeshua wanted them to. Jeshua didn't say that, but I know that they would spread the word of what's happening.

J: And is there another healing planned?

S: Yes. He is going to continue doing it almost on a regular basis for the rest of the time he is here in Jerusalem. He's coming back tomorrow.

J: Do you have any time with Jeshua alone today?

S: No.

J: After this?

S: No. There are too many people around. I say good-bye to Jeshua, and I tell him I'll see him tomorrow when he comes to talk again at the temple.

203

Chapter 13

JESHUA—THE TEACHER

The next session took place on June 6, two weeks later. Nick indicated he wanted an extra week between sessions to process what he was experiencing. It was apparent he had been very emotionally moved during our last session. I wondered what it was like for him to be re-experiencing these powerful events. I wondered what effect these memories were having on his business and personal life now that they had moved into his conscious mind.

J: Good. Where do you find yourself today?
S: I'm in the portico of Solomon's Temple.
J: And what's going on?
S: There are a lot of people there, and Jeshua is going to be teaching at the temple and talking to the people. The crowd is very large.
J: Is this after the first healings?
S: It's after the healings that he did here in Jerusalem. The people are excited.
J: The people are excited? How are you feeling today?

S: I'm feeling very good about what [Jeshua] is doing. I am concerned for him. But I'm feeling very good.

J: Is Jeshua here yet?

S: Yes. But he hasn't started. He's going to start talking very shortly. The people are all talking among themselves now. There is quite a cross-section—men, women and some older children—not any young children, but children, people that I have not seen before.

J: New people are coming now?

S: Yes.

J: Do any of the Romans come?

S: No. I don't see any Romans. No. Just Jews.

J: Thank you. Please recall for us if there's anything regarding the teachings today that you would like us to know about. Please remember that now.

S: Yes. He's telling the people that even though he's preaching in a temple, it does not require a building to pray to God, or to be in communication with God—that our temple is within each one of us, and we can pray in the fields, indoors or outdoors. And even though it's fine if we want to pray in the temple, the temple doesn't have any priority or any special environment in which to pray as opposed to wherever we are, since God is always with us and we have our temple. Our being is our temple.

J: Our being is our temple?

S: Yes. Our body is our temple because it houses the God that's within us—that part of God within us. And it doesn't require an individual, such as a priest, a person who is preaching to us, in order for us to be able to communicate with our God. And I know that's not going to make the officials very happy.

J: Jeshua's saying they're not necessary?

S: He's saying it's OK to pray with the priests also, but

it's not necessary. The priests have tried to persuade the people to believe that [the priests] are the [way through which they] communicate to God, and only in the buildings [of the priests]. Jeshua's saying that's not necessary, that's not so. And he's saying that he will act as an intermediary to God and them. That he will function as a means of being able to communicate and get in touch better with that part of God that is within them, as well as with the divine God that we're all a part of.

J: Thank you. Is there anything else he said today that you would like us to know about?

S: He's speaking of love. The importance in our lives of all of us loving each other because he says that not to love, to feel anger, hatred, jealousy, or animosity, all of these things, cause harm to us, harm to us physically as well as mentally. Jeshua says that he can show us the way, show the people the way, to cleanse themselves of these ... well, he refers to them as evil spirits. But not literally. He refers to things such as greed, jealousy, and selfishness as evil spirits. And he said he can help cleanse us of those evil spirits which will not only heal our minds and our bodies but make us at one with God. And he can play that role.

J: Isn't that the same sort of thing that a priest might say? That he could be the intermediary? How is that different from what the priests are doing?

S: I don't think the priests have the understanding that he has. For they say they can do it by our giving them tithings and physically being in the temples, praying with them. [Jeshua] says that he can do that by our accepting in our hearts that he [Jeshua] has the ability to do it, and for us to let him come into our hearts and our minds. He asks us nothing in return. And he doesn't say it has to be done in temples. I don't remember the priests saying that, or the priests saying

that they could heal the people. They're more
involved in rituals, praying in rituals, [rather] than
what Jeshua is saying.

J: All right. Thank you. And what happens after the
      teachings?

S: In the afternoons, the latter part of the day, before it
      starts getting dark, he does healings in different parts
      of the city.

J: Is he doing this on a regular basis now?

S: Yes.

J: Teachings in the mornings and then healings in the
      afternoon?

S: Not early mornings. It's almost at noontime when he
      starts his teachings. He starts talking to the people,
      and then later in the day he tells where he's going to
      be, and he does healings. But the crowds are getting
      so large.

J: Word's really spreading?

S: Yes. And he's starting to talk to them more specifical-
      ly now that they've seen his powers and are accepting
      him as being a person of God who has a special rela-
      tionship with God. He's now being more specific in
      his teachings.

J: Is there something about today's healing you would
      like to share with us?

S: I wasn't there this afternoon.

J: You didn't go to that one?

S: Not today. I've been to a lot of his healings, and I've
      spent some times with him alone. Just the two of us in
      the mornings and in the evenings and some suppers.

J: So you're getting to know him even more. I have
      some questions for you. Would this be a good time to
      ask them?

I came to understand that I could ask Saul to remember events in addition to asking him questions and he would

express his own opinions. This means we can tap into more than memory in regressions but also into personality and judgment.

S: It's fine.

J: Now, I believe that you said Jeshua is an Essene.

S: Jeshua is Jeshua.

J: Are there any parts of his philosophies or beliefs that are in opposition to yours?

S: Opposition to mine? They may have been before I had an opportunity to spend so much time with him. But I accept everything he has taught me. I have learned so much from him that I don't have any conflicts in my beliefs now with his, although some of them might have been at some earlier time.

J: In talking about reincarnation, or rebirth, did Jeshua believe that the dead rise again?

S: Pardon me? (Saul sounds incredulous.)

J: Did Jeshua believe that the dead come back to life?

S: Not the body. But the spirit never dies. When the spirit leaves the body, it still exists in a body form that we cannot see because they're in a different ethereal vibration. But the spirit will be born again in a new body. Not in the old body.

J: Reborn in a different body?

S: In a new body because the old body can no longer function for one reason or another. Also, the spirit would want to experience different environments and different conditions in order to continue the process. That is the law of God and the law of nature. If you are being reborn in order to compensate for some sin or evil that existed in a previous life, then you would have to be born under different conditions to compensate for that, to atone for that particular shortcoming or sin that had been committed previously. Just as you also will be rewarded for the things that you did that deserve reward.

J: Have you and Jeshua spoken of how this process happens in the spirit?

S: Yes.

J: So something happens after death?

S: Yes.

J: And there's a decision made to come back into a body? Where does that come in?

S: You speak of death, but it is the physical body that dies. Not the life. The life is continual. That which makes us one with God. It is that power, that energy which is part of God, which cannot die. When that energy leaves the body which is no longer functioning, it then is in another plane, another vibrational existence with other spirits who have also left their physical bodies. During the time that we exist in that plane, we have knowledge that we do not have during our mortal lives. And we spend time understanding what transpired in our last life, preparing ourselves for our next rebirth.

J: How is it decided whether you will be atoning or being rewarded?

S: We have guides. We have guides that we work with. The same guides who help us and work with us when we are living as mortals also participate with us when we leave this plane. We have other guides also, but it is another entire realm, which is much more real than this one we live in. This one is artificial and temporal [while] the other is eternal. The closer we are to returning to God, the longer period of time we generally stay on the other plane, rather than returning again to this plane. In some cases, when the body of the spirit has died at a very early age, either through accident or war, there is a need and desire on the part of the spirit to come back as quickly as possible.

J: All right. One of my questions is regarding spirits. What has Jeshua told you? What do you now understand? You've mentioned that spirits seem to be qualities within people.

S: We use spirits different ways, but you mean the spirits within us? Are you talking about our spiritual guides?

J: I would like to understand the difference. You seem to be saying spirits are qualities within us. Are you also saying there are spirits that are separate from us?

S: Perhaps I used the wrong word. Jeshua says that we all have spiritual guides who help us. They can't alter things physically, but they can help us by giving us encouragement even though we might not be consciously aware of it—while we're sleeping, while we're praying, while we're meditating. But they are like us—souls, entities who are not on this plane now. For they're in spirit. We can't see them, even though they have form, because they're in a different ethereal plane, different ethereality. What word can I use? Let's say different vibrations. Rather than the material vibration. So we cannot visibly see them. Just as when the soul leaves the body, when one passes over, they're still in form, but now they're in a different ethereality. And as a result of that, we can't visibly see them. But our spiritual guides are constantly with us and helping us, even though we're not aware of them. I asked Jeshua who his spiritual guide was, and he said God. I realized that's one of the things that separates him from me and the others. His spiritual guide is ... (Saul is moved) his spiritual guide is God. The rest of us have spiritual guides who are like us— souls that are sometimes mortal and sometimes in spiritual form.

       When people say that Jeshua, when he is healing, is driving out people's evil spirits, what they mean is that he's helping them rid themselves of bad thoughts, bad traits, and bad emotions. But we all have free will. We all end up doing that which we want to do. Spirits can influence us just as our parents influence us when we are children. Or our friends can influence us when we seek guidance. God doesn't directly control our lives in this life other than our becoming at one with Him, in atonement with Him, by internally being in tune with that part of God that's within us. And that's where Jeshua can play a very important role also, by helping in that connection—by our accepting him into our hearts and our minds, as well as his connection with the Lord, with God, and that part of God that's within us.

J: Do people have a choice about the spiritual guides? How are our guides chosen? How does one come to have certain guides?

S: No. We have no choice. We have no choice of that. And some people don't even recognize they have spirits. Some people call them guardian angels. But they are really spirits that are on another plane than we are [on] right now. The only spiritual guide that we do have the ability of having become part of our lives is Jeshua. That's why he's here. And he told me that when he's gone from this plane that he can come back, by people accepting him in their hearts and minds so that he would still be here with us.

J: That he would come back as their spiritual guide if they accepted him?

S: Yes. He would come. Yes. That he was always able to do that—be available to those who are willing to open up to him and accept him. I realize now that Jeshua is the Christos. That he is the Christ. *Christos* is Christ in Greek. He is the Anointed One. Jeshua is here to help people understand and to teach them. He is willing to continue to guide them even after he leaves this plane, providing they're willing to accept him. He's trying to establish that.

J: Is there anything that you'd like to add?

S: I don't know if I'm explaining it right. It's complicated in some ways, even though it isn't. It appears to me that he's providing us an easier way to be in communication with God and to get in touch with that which is within us, which is a part of God.

J: And he's saying an easier way. Is it the only way?

S: I don't think it's the only way. There are people that I think have that ability of being at one with God. But for most people it's extremely difficult. So he's making it clearer to them as to the role that God plays in our lives. And I believe that as we become better people on this earth, then we become closer to perfection, not having to keep coming back and being reborn. The reason we keep coming back—well, that's another area.

J: That's an area of interest. Shall we go into that now, or would you like to leave this?

S: No. It's OK, I can talk about it. Jeshua says that God controls that which is nature. Nature responds to the laws of God. The reason man came on this earth plane was to experience material sensations and emotions and experiences. But having experienced that, they also separated themselves substantially from being at one with God. And now we go through cycles of being reborn until we can become at perfection again with God. But as we commit to being reborn in order to improve in one area, we sometimes fall back in some other area. If we can understand better the true importance of life, then we will achieve more quickly the perfection necessary and not have to come back again, but finally to be at one with God again in a true sense and not just a spiritual sense.

J: So you're saying that in some lifetimes we move

ahead, achieve a closeness. In some lifetimes we move back and we lose some ground?

S: Well, that's possible. But that wasn't what I meant. We might solve one problem, but form another one at the same time. Time is irrelevant. Time has always been and always will be irrelevant. It may seem long to us, but it can also seem very short. Those things in life that we seem to enjoy seem to pass by very quickly. And the things in life that we don't seem to like, seem to appear longer than they actually are.

J: You've spoken of being separated from God. Could you speak to who is God or what is God?

S: You mean as a Pharisee, or do you mean as Jeshua sees, as Jeshua tells me?

J: As Jeshua tells you, please. Then I'd like to know if you agree with that.

S: Oh, I accept what he says. I believe him to speak total truth and knowledge. Jeshua says that even though we often refer to God as the Father, that God is both the Father and the Mother. And that God has no single gender. That God is a force, an entity of love and life—that all of us are a part of that. Think of a body of water—like a lake. And that lake, for purposes of understanding, is an energy force of love and wisdom and knowledge. Each drop of that water, of that lake, is part of the whole. And then we take a jar and dip it into the lake, which was made up of thousands and thousands and thousands of little drops of water. These are part of the whole of that lake. We then scatter the drops in different places. Each little drop is put into the body of a newborn. Inside each of those people would be a part of that lake, even if they didn't recognize it. And that little part of that lake is eternal, is everlasting, and is part of the total, is part of that lake. It is what gives us life. And when that little part of that lake leaves the body, the body no longer has

213

Now if we equate that lake, instead, to being
d, a different form of energy, rather than a lake,
then we have a better understanding of why Jeshua
says that we are part of God, just as that drop of
water was once part of the lake. And if that drop of
water were to return eventually to that lake, it would
then be again at one with the rest of the lake. So it is
when our spirit becomes at one again, someday, not
only in thought, but physically with God, that we
[again are one with] God.

J: Thank you. There are people who believe that God
gives favors and that God also punishes. Can you say
whether that's true or not?

S: No. It's not. God never punishes. Are you speaking of
the God inside of us or are you speaking of God that
is on the other plane?

J: Actually, I'm speaking of what I think people's conception of what God is.

S: No. God does not interfere with our lives, not in the
physical sense. Only in the spiritual sense in terms of
giving us inspiration, love, hope, understanding, or
creativity. But on a physical sense, he does not punish
us in terms of taking things away from us, or causing
us sickness, any more than we would come home one
day to our house and find gold in it and think that
God gave us that gold as a gift. We ourselves create
our own punishments and our own rewards by our
actions. As Jeshua says to the people in his teachings,
if you put an onion seed into the ground, you grow an
onion. If you give love to people, you get love in
return. If you are generous to people, you also shall
receive generosity. But if you give anger to people,
they respond in anger. If you injure people, they
respond by injuring you. So in that sense, we are
responsible for that which happens to us, whether it
be punishment or rewards.

J: Are you familiar with the story of Moses?

S: Yes.

J: The story as it is told today is that God did punish the Pharaoh in Egypt by killing his son. Have you heard that?

S: Yes.

J: What do you think of that?

S: Those are just fables. They are fables. The Sadducees take them literally. But I don't take them literally. Most people do not.

J: Most people don't?

S: No. They're stories to explain that people who commit evil receive evil in return. Our people at that time were held in bondage by the people who lived in the area, which is now considered the Egyptian area. But anyway, the story tries to explain that they in turn brought bad things upon themselves in the way of sickness and death and injuries to their own minds and physical beings. And they were exaggerated in order to make a point.

J: I'm fascinated to hear you say that most people don't believe the fables are literal.

S: Well, what stories are you talking about? Some are true and some aren't. They did travel away from that area and went to the desert looking for a new place to establish themselves. And we are the descendants of those people. But sometimes stories are exaggerated in order to make their point.

J: One that comes to mind is the story of the avenging angel who came to kill the firstborn of each house. That if the blood of a lamb were seen on the door, the child would be saved.

S: You're talking about why we celebrate the holiday of Passover. The angel passed over the houses of those who were Jews, and that's why we have that holiday, which is a very big holiday. What is your question?

215

J: I was wondering if that was one of the stories that had been magnified to make a point, or is that one true in your belief? Is there an angel?

S: Yes. I understand. No, I don't believe that story. God doesn't take life away. People bring harm upon themselves. God does not take life away. He gives life. What we're really celebrating in our holiday and our festivities is that we were liberated. Our ancestors were liberated from slavery, and they use the story of the passing over as the focal point of the celebration. And it's part of the ritual of putting out food during the ceremony. You put out a plate of food outside your door for the angel to eat from. We know that the angel is not there eating from it. It is just a ritual.

J: Saul, do you still practice some of those rituals yourself?

S: The rituals are important for a number of reasons. They are practiced throughout all of the lands by Jews, which allow us to have a common understanding of our heritage, whether we are living in Peraea or in Tarsus, where I was from, or in Judea. We are all practicing the same thing, and it keeps us bound together. Other rituals have different meanings. But of those rituals that have to do with the celebration of the holy days, by continuing them as they were, it maintains the bond between all of us even though we may be separated by long distances. It also maintains the respect to our heritage and to those that have lived before us, who are our forebears.

J: And does Jeshua practice these rituals as far as you know?

S: Yes.

J: And do you know whether he would recommend that people continue to practice the rituals even if they were having him be their spiritual guide?

S: I'm not talking about the rituals that take place in the temples. I'm talking about the rituals that are part of our religion. Yes. He practices them. With one exception. Many times he'll do things during the Sabbath that more religious people say he shouldn't be doing.

J: For instance?

S: For instance, teaching, traveling. The ones who are more pious and religious say we're not supposed to travel during the Sabbath, and we're not supposed to work. That's one of the areas that the ones who are in religious authority are saying he's violating, that he's blaspheming.

   Blaspheming is a very serious offense—even more so if it's true—more so than stealing or doing other crimes against people. They claim that it is actually a crime against God. So therefore it has greater consequences if one is truly guilty of blaspheming.

J: Who determines if one is guilty of blaspheming?

S: Those who are in authority of the religious people like to believe they determine [guilt]. Sometimes they accuse people of blasphemy [but] the people don't [agree]. But it's not a crime that is controlled, let's say for example, by our civil authorities, or by the Roman authorities, because the Romans don't care about our religious beliefs. But the authorities are constantly claiming when Jeshua heals on the Sabbath, he's blaspheming. But do you think the person who's been healed is going to accept that? (Saul laughs.)

J: That well may have been the most spiritual experience they've had.

S: Yes. So complaints of blasphemy against Jeshua are not being accepted by the people as being valid.

J: Yes. It's understandable. Well, thank you. You've answered many questions regarding his teachings. I'm wondering if you'd like to move forward to a

time that you're spending together. If you have any
questions for him that you'd like to tell us about.

S: We spent a lot of time together in this last visit.
Which one do you want me to relate to?

J: Please, you choose.

S: He didn't want to heal that day; he was tired. He and
I went away from the city to the area where there are
big rocks overlooking the river. We spent almost the
whole day together up there. And we talked about
many things. He taught me—I don't know if it's the
right word, "taught" me. He explained to me in detail
how I may also heal people. He's also been teaching
his disciples. The Romans call them *discipulus,* his
pupils, the followers from his group, his old group.
He's been teaching some of them how to heal. He
told me the importance of the necessary elements to
heal. How the people must believe first, and if they
don't believe, you cannot go through the rest of the
process because it won't have any effect on them. But
they must totally, absolutely accept and believe that
you can help heal them, and that they can heal themselves with your help. Otherwise it won't have any
effect on them. We talked about that at great length. I
asked him many questions. He answered my questions and shared information with me. He told me
that he's leaving soon because he's going to go to
other areas and other regions to do healings and
preach, also.

But, I'm really concerned for him. I'm concerned that he's become such a threat to the authorities, not the Romans, but the religious authorities,
that they might try to have Jeshua killed while he's
traveling. He told me that he would have many people with him when he was traveling. They would be
able to provide him protection since he has many
more people now that follow him and keep company

with him. But I told him that I really believe that he [is] in danger, and he knows it. He acknowledges it. But he doesn't seem to be concerned about it.

And I asked Jeshua about his purpose. It surely is not to correct sins that he'd done in the past. For he is, *I* say he is, perfect in spirit. His purpose in life is that which he has been telling the people. It has been prophesied for several hundred years that a person would be born, a soul would come back, a soul would be reborn who would be the Christos—the Messiah. And from time to time, individuals have claimed to be that Messiah. And from time to time people have attributed to individuals—who did not claim to be the Messiah—that they were. There are some people who go around preaching all the time, who claim to be the Messiah, who no one takes seriously. They are just fanatics. But I believe that Jeshua is the Christos. And when he is asked that by the people, during his last trip, now that he's been doing these healings, he never says yes or no. Instead he answers them by saying, "I am here to help you understand the way you can become at one with God."

If we were just to understand that was what the Messiah was trying to do, or that's what the predictions were that the Messiah would be, then we could not help but come to the understanding that Jeshua is the Messiah the Jews have been waiting for. Our people have been waiting for him for several hundred years now.

And it has been prophesied that the Messiah would be born in Judea. Some have said, "How can he be the Messiah when he's from the Galilee region?" But he was born in Judea. His mother was in Judea when he was born. So I don't see that as a conflict. Not that I think it's important anyway. So I am convinced. I totally believe that he is the Anointed

One. He's the Messiah. And I believe he matured, as we all do. It is like a seed of a beautiful flower. And as that seed is put into the earth—as he was born unto this earth—it takes a while for that flower to bloom. He has now bloomed into the Messiah. Even though he was the Messiah at birth, there was a growth period that had to take place.

J: Do you feel he's now in full bloom here?

S: Yes.

J: As the Messiah?

S: Yes. And I love him dearly. He generates love. Even though at times Jeshua must be austere in his teachings, he generates love. I have learned so much from him. And I have concern over those people who are his followers. Whether they understand, whether they have the ability to understand all that he's trying to teach them. And whether they'll be able to pass on to others Jeshua's teachings as he meant them to be. I shared that with him.

J: And what did he say?

S: He said that he hopes that they can, that he will try to continue to influence them even after he leaves the earth plane.

J: Saul, is there anyone you know of who is writing down what he is saying?

S: Some of them can't write, but some of them can. The one who's the twin takes notes. I believe he writes sometimes. One of his followers that's a twin—Thomas, I believe.

J: OK. So you've expressed concern about him possibly being killed. Are you aware of others who have been killed for their teachings?

S: Yes. There have been others before him.

J: Tell us about that.

S: There have been some that were killed because their followers were—as they were also—militant. They carried weapons and ended up fighting with the soldiers, and getting killed. Some were killed by the people for blasphemy. They stoned them. You hear stories. You hear stories about somebody that might have appeared in some other area of our land. None of them have done like Jeshua. None of them are of the same stature. Jeshua has traveled and taught, and now he's healing. These people didn't have the same credibility that he has. They were either single individuals who made the claim that they were the Messiah, who no one took seriously, or they were individuals who only a few believed were the Messiah. They were trying, maybe for their own purposes, to promote the feeling they were, in order to get a position of influence or power. But it didn't happen. They either would have lost their following after a while, or they were killed in physical fighting with others that were against them.

J: Did you ask Jeshua whether he knows what's going to happen from here on?

S: He told me.

J: What did he say?

S: He told me that there would come a time when he would leave, in the not-too-distant future. That he would leave the earth plane.

J: You've spoken about Jeshua instructing you on healing. And I'm wondering if you are beginning to practice that yourself?

S: No.

J: What are you deciding about that?

S: I don't believe that Jeshua wants any of his followers that he's taught, or me, to practice it while he's doing it. And I think to do so would lessen the impact he's having on the people. And for that reason I know he's not intending for us to do it now. Maybe someday he'll want his followers to do it. But certainly not now.

J: I see. So he's passing on the information, the knowledge of how to do it.

S: Yes.

J: So that he might ...

S: To use at some future time.

J: Anything else you'd like to tell me about your day alone together?

S: He's leaving soon. This is probably the last time we'll see each other, just the two of us, during this period of time that he's been here in Judea. I had the opportunity to spend much time with him during this visit, listening to him preach and watching his healings, as well as alone, so that I don't feel the sadness that I have in the past when he was leaving. I feel very blessed that I was able to spend so much time with him. He'll be leaving in a couple of days.

Saul describes to me how Jeshua continues his travels around Samaria and Galilee, continuing to teach, continuing to heal. Even though Saul is aware of Jeshua's eventual "leaving," Saul is calmer about the idea after coming to the conclusion that Jeshua *is* the Messiah. As we leave this time in Saul's life, in his twenty-ninth year, with Jeshua now thirty-two, we begin to realize the profound impact that Jeshua has had on Saul, and how great Saul's love for Jeshua is.

Chapter 14

THE CRUCIFIXION

*B*ecause of Saul's concern, and Jeshua's prediction of his own imminent death, I assumed that would be the topic of the next session. Since the core belief of modern Christianity is that "Jesus died for our sins," I approached this session with a great deal of anticipation about what our eyewitness would report.

Saul tells me of Jeshua's fame growing with each passing day, and along with it Saul's fear for Jeshua's safety. Rumors are like sand in the wind. Religious authorities now want Jeshua killed. Saul tells me about his next meeting with Jeshua and his concern for Jeshua's safety. I ask Saul if Jeshua is in danger.

J: You've said this to him several times, that you're worried about his safety.

S: Many times, but more so now than ever. Because he has many, many more followers now since he began his healings, and is perceived as a greater threat now by the council and the religious leaders.

J: Saul, how do you know? Is this just your assumption

because of the culture, or have other religious leaders been killed? Are you hearing the rumors? How do you know?

S: Well, I'm a Pharisee, and I know some of the people [who are] on the council, and it's common talk among all the people of what is happening. We are all aware of it. It is the most talked about activity going on right now in the city.

Jeshua and Saul spend many hours together in conversation before what will be Jeshua's final trip. More time is spent explaining how to heal. Philosophies are exchanged between these two men of great heart and intellect. Neither Saul nor Jeshua knows how long the ensuing trip will take. Circumstances will dictate the length of this last journey.

J: Shall we move forward then to the next important event of Jeshua's life as you know it?

S: He has been gone now for almost a year. I hear many stories of his healings and of more and more people accepting him and following him. His friend has become very ill.

J: Which friend is this?

S: His friend in Bethany. His friend Lazarus has become very ill, and he's dying. They are sending for Jeshua. Jeshua often stays with Lazarus and his two sisters in their home when he is here visiting Jerusalem because it is a very short distance to Jerusalem from Bethany. Martha is the oldest, and Mary.

J: I want to be sure I understood his name correctly. Would you say it again?

S: Lazarus.

J: Is this the Magdalene family?

S: Yes.

J: So Jeshua has been sent for because Lazarus is dying?

S: Yes. So people are saying he'll be coming back to our

city to see Lazarus before he dies. There is much excitement, as well as concern, from the authorities over what will happen when he comes back because of the rumors that there are some people that want him killed. And they're trying to convince the Romans that he's a danger to the peace in the area.

J: *They're* trying to convince them?

S: The council is.

J: All right. Now move forward to the next event.

S: He is coming back with his people, with his followers. And it's my understanding that Lazarus is in a state of unconsciousness and that he could die at any moment. I am told two days later that Jeshua has come back. Some people are saying that Lazarus had died before Jeshua had returned, and that Jeshua brought him back to life. Others are saying that he was in a state of unconsciousness and Jeshua brought him back to consciousness. But there is much excitement. Many rumors are flying around. People are going in big crowds and repeating the story that Jeshua brought [Lazarus] back after he had died. I don't know which one is true. It doesn't make a difference.

J: It doesn't matter to you which?

S: Well, it matters to the people. I meant that to me it doesn't matter. But to the people it seems to be very important to them as they argue—those who believe that [Lazarus] had died and Jeshua had brought him back to life, and those who believe that he had not yet died. There are many people who want to believe that he had died.

J: What are the sisters saying? Do you have a chance to speak to Martha or Mary about this and hear their opinion of whether their brother was dead?

S: No. There's so much confusion going on right now. So much confusion—large, large crowds, people coming from all over. Jeshua and some of the people leave. I didn't see him. They went in a direction toward Peraea, I am told. I didn't see him. He left because of the big crowds and confusion—too many people who were coming down from all over. So [Jeshua] and some of his people left before I could see him, and they went across the river, towards Ephram—in that area.

J: What time of year is it? What's going on?

S: It's not too far from Passover holiday. The hot weather has not yet started. It is several months away from the real hot weather.

J: All right. Move to the time when Jeshua returns.

S: He returned with his followers, and they went back to Bethany to visit Lazarus. Huge, huge crowds were following. Everybody was talking about Jeshua coming the next morning from Bethany to Jerusalem to preach in the temple. And thousands of people are gathering and lining the way along the road to Jerusalem. And I did not see him. But the next day people were lined alongside the road, cheering for [Jeshua] as he rode a donkey into Jerusalem. Large crowds. It was so crowded—so many people trying to get to hear him speak. There were thousands of people there, thousands as he was speaking on the top of the temple stairs overlooking the portico. I was in the crowd. I couldn't get to him—so many people. He spoke with such wonderful words. Many of the people were moved. Others were angry at him because they didn't believe. They believed it was a hoax, particularly those who felt he was a threat to Herod and to the council. So there were a lot of emotions and feelings going through the crowds. But I didn't feel he was in any danger because there were just too many people there. So I was not concerned about that.

J: But you are worried about something? (Saul looked very worried.)

S: I'm always concerned over his safety. The holiday will be starting in another couple of days. During the holidays, things will be able to quiet down a little bit, and I hope to see him then.

J: Do you get to see him during the holidays? Do you get to see him?

S: No. No. (Saul now appears close to despair, and tears are running down his cheeks.)

J: Are you very disappointed?

S: (Long pause.) He's arrested before I see him—the day before the holiday, that evening before the holiday. He's arrested. (Saul is very distressed. He is emotionally upset, and is physically and mentally experiencing great anguish.)

J: That has been your fear?

S: What?

J: That he would be arrested?

S: No. I feared he was going to be killed while he was traveling. He was arrested in the early morning. He was taken before the council. They made accusations against him.

J: Tell us everything you know about this.

S: Well, I hear that [Jeshua] has been taken before the council, and that they questioned him for hours. Tomorrow they're going to bring him before the Roman authorities, for they don't know what to do. They have accusations they're making against him. But only the Roman authorities can make decisions regarding these accusations.

J: So the council can make an arrest?

S: Yes. But they can't try him. Only the Roman authorities can do that.

J: He was arrested then at Lazarus' house?

S: No. I hear so many stories. I'm told he was outdoors

when he was arrested, that they were sleeping out-doors, and that he was taken. Then later in the day, in the morning after, it was sunlight, that they had a special council meeting, that he was taken before the council. There are some people on the council who are not enemies of his and not afraid of him, who respect him, although they're in the minority. But I don't know what happened at the council meeting. All I know is that I am hearing stories that he is going to be taken the next day before the Roman authorities because of the accusations that are being made against him.

J: And you know now what the accusations are?

S: I've been told that they're telling the Roman authorities that [Jeshua's] inciting the people not to pay taxes and to rebel against the Roman authorities. I know that's not true. I've never heard him talk about taxes. He doesn't care about that, but that is what they're saying.

J: And what are you doing as you're learning this? Is there anything you do? Anything you try?

S: I can't do anything. I'm talking to other people who are closer to some of the members of the council than I am, trying to ask them to intervene and help. [Jeshua's] become such a threat to the council, now, since this Lazarus incident, that the council, from what I'm told, feels that something must be done to stop him. People are meeting in groups all over the city—some who are against him and some who support him. The supporters are afraid that they're going to be physically attacked by those who are against [Jeshua] because they believe he's a threat to those who are in authority—both in political authority as well as religious authority. Herod has a lot of followers, too. And there are still many people that have never seen Jeshua in person. So they never have

really accepted the healings and the stories about him
because they have never witnessed them.

J: So they're having opinions without knowing?

S: They think they know. They don't believe the stories.
There's a lot of chaos going on right now. But I'm not
concerned about that. I'm concerned about his welfare.

Again, Saul is experiencing great emotional distress.
I thought it best to stop at this point. Considering the time
of our session, I did not want to end with the crucifixion of
Jesus. I was concerned for the emotional state of mind that
Nick might experience if I ended with the death of Jesus.

We waited three weeks for our next session. These
particular sessions were extremely intense and emotional.
While in his hypnotic trance, it was apparent to me Saul
was experiencing trauma. I was very aware of his pain. I
instructed him to return to the memory of Jeshua's arrest.

J: What is going on at the present time?

S: (Long pause.) Last night Jeshua was arrested by some
of the Roman soldiers and was taken to the palace
where Caiaphas lives.

J: We talked some about why he's considered dangerous
both to the Romans and to the priests.

S: Yes.

J: Is any more information coming out about that now?

S: I already know why. The Romans don't consider him
dangerous. The council considers him a threat, as
well as the followers of Herod. They feel that they're
going to lose the power of the people to him. If they
lose the power of the people, then the Romans won't
look to them any longer as the controlling authority.
So the followers, the supporters of Herod and the
council, are the ones that fear Jeshua—particularly
since his healings and his having helped Lazarus.

J: Have you been able to speak today with any of the people who travel with Jeshua? Any of his helpers or friends?

S: Today?

J: Today, yes.

S: No, I haven't talked to them, but the rumors, the stories that are going around are that he was arrested last night while they were outdoors, sleeping outdoors. The Passover holiday begins tonight with the traditional ceremonies—supper ceremonies. So it is a holiday today.

J: Did you spend any time with Jeshua yesterday or the day before?

S: No, he had gone away after he had brought Lazarus back from his illness. He and some of his followers had gone to Ephram, away from the crowds, and then returned to Bethany to Lazarus' home. There were thousands of people who had lined the road when Jeshua went back into Jerusalem. He went back into the city, and there were crowds. He was preaching at the temple that day. But I haven't talked to him.

J: That must be very frustrating for you not to be able to speak with him.

S: Well ... I feel ... concern for his safety rather than frustration. I feel a great concern. I know that his enemies have become much more dangerous as they feel he's a greater threat. I don't know what's going to happen now. I know he's going to be going before the high priest, chief priest, today. It's what I hear. But I don't know what's going to happen.

J: Do you have any information about what he did last night? What Jeshua did last night? Who he spent time with?

S: I understand that ... last night that he ... he was arrested. (Saul is feeling the emotion of the moment.) Two of his followers, the brothers who are fishermen—John and James—their father has a house here in the city. He lives in the city even though he owns a number of fishing boats up in Galilee. His name is Zebedee. He has a house, and I understand that they all had supper at his house last night—he and his followers.

J: Do they often do that, or is this unusual?

S: No, they don't often do that. The holidays are starting today, so it might have been in preparation for the ceremonial dinner that would have been this evening, since Passover starts today. But I don't think that's normal for them to do that.

J: Is Zebedee one of the followers as well?

S: No, he's the father of John and James.

J: Thank you. Let's move forward now to the next event.

S: Well, all the information I'm getting is just rumor. There's so much going on right now with the holidays. And there's so many people in the city now that normally don't live here, who are here to celebrate the holidays with their relatives. I'm told that Jeshua met this afternoon with some of the top officials of the council, the Sanhedrin, and with Caiaphas; that they're going to detain him overnight, and then tomorrow morning he's meeting with the whole council. They're going to question him about his activities. They might be accusing him of blasphemy, which is very, very serious. People have been stoned to death for being found [guilty of] blasphemy, which [is an] act against God. And of course they've been saying that for years about Jeshua, claiming he has blasphemed.

J: Thank you. Is there anything else that you'd like to add about what's going on right now?

S: Tonight's the high holy day. Tonight's the ceremonial Passover supper ritual, so I imagine that's why they're keeping him over until tomorrow, to meet with the council. That's all I know about what's going on right now.

J: All right. Thank you. Please move forward to your celebration of the holidays. Where do you go? With whom do you celebrate tonight?

S: I celebrate it with some friends of mine who are Pharisees. And I have a friend, a lady friend with me, and we go to her family's home. There are two other families, plus myself, and my companion.

J: Who is your companion?

S: Well, she's a lady that I see. A friend. Her name is Leah.

J: Is there anything you'd like to tell us about the Passover celebration tonight?

S: It was very solemn because of what is going on right now in Jerusalem. But once the ceremony starts, we don't talk about that, since the ceremony is programmed in terms of how it's conducted and what is said. So we just talked about it before the ceremony started.

Saul is experiencing great sorrow. His sorrow is coming from deep within. I hear the hurt in his voice and see it on his face.

J: Has your companion Leah been attending some of the teachings and the healings? Is she acquainted with what's going on with you and Jeshua?

S: She hasn't been to the healings. She's heard him speak several times. I don't discuss with her my relationship with Jeshua.

J: I see.

S: Although she knows that we're friends.

J: How did you pass the rest of the evening then?

S: We spent almost the whole evening there—to attend the supper ceremonies. What did I do afterwards?

J: Yes.

S: I don't want to talk about my private life. (I never was successful in getting Saul to talk about his private life.)

J: All right. Let's move forward then to the next day.

S: OK. Yes.

J: You said that Jeshua would be going before the whole council today?

S: In the morning.

J: Are you going to be allowed to observe? Is this closed to the public?

S: It's closed to the public. Almost all the council were there. When all of them are there, there are 70 members. I'm told most of them were there.

J: So you're talking to someone who was there or has the information now?

S: I'm hearing information secondhand.

J: All right. Tell us what you're learning about what went on in the council meeting.

S: I'm hearing they accused Jeshua of blasphemy. And they asked him specific questions about his activities. There was uncertainty. There wasn't total agreement among the members of the council in terms of how to interpret his actions and his answers. Some of the members of the council were adamant that he be turned over to the Romans, that the Romans take action against him—that's what they're going to do.

J: Turn him over to the Romans?

S: To Pontius Pilate, the governor of Judea. But they're charging him with certain allegations that they want the Roman authorities to hold him responsible for. I hadn't heard what those allegations are, but that's what they're doing.

J: All right. Move forward to the next event.

S: There are thousands of people surrounding the government building where Pilate is, where Pilate lives.

Some of them are supporters of Jeshua. Many of them aren't. Many of them are outsiders also, from outside of Jerusalem. They're here visiting for the holidays. People are yelling.

J: Are you among this group?

S: I'm there.

J: Is Jeshua inside now?

S: Yes, he's inside. I'm told he's inside. Some of the members of the council have made formal charges against him to Pilate and his advisors. I'm told they're charging him with—which is not true—trying to incite the people to not pay taxes any longer.

J: So you know that's a false charge.

S: He never talked about that. The Romans don't care about Jewish religious matters. So I know that they must be saying that to try to get the Romans to take action against him because [the Romans] would care about anybody [who] was inciting the people to rebel against them and not pay taxes, since that's what their purpose is for being in our land—to receive a portion of our wealth.

J: All right. Continue. What happens next?

S: Well, there's so many rumors going around. People are yelling and screaming. Some of them in support of Jeshua ... some of them against him. It seems to me like the ones [who] are against him are organized, in groups.

J: Organized? This is not spontaneous?

S: There's ... there's supposed to be ... early this evening ... there's supposed to be ... up on ... on top of Golgotha ... a crucifixion of some ... criminals who ... and there's a rumor ... some people are saying that ... that the Romans ... that Pilate is ... going to have Jeshua ... taken with them to Golgotha. I don't know what to believe. There's so much confusion going on.

J: Then we'll get more information as we go.

S: Yes. (Saul is very sad and despondent. He speaks very slowly and softly.)

J: Continue please.

S: Well, apparently ... apparently it has been decided that ... they have traded ... one of the criminal's place with Jeshua, and that Jeshua is going to be taken to Golgotha, also, this afternoon ... and that he will be ... and that he will be placed on ... be placed on the ... the wooden cross ... in place of one of the criminals.

J: This was Pilate's decision? Is that what you're hearing?

S: Pilate and his advisors. They must have believed Jeshua's accusers, that he had been trying to incite the people not to pay taxes. Jeshua had told me previously that he felt his life was going to be culminated soon. And he didn't seem concerned. I have to assume that he's allowing this to happen ... for I ... I just can't believe otherwise, that he couldn't ... have shown the Sanhedrin ... the council ... and proven to them that he is the Christos ... that he is the Messiah.

J: You feel that he could have defended himself and proved ...

S: Yes, I feel he could have. I don't know what took place at the council hearings. But I have to assume that he allowed it to happen. There are members of that council that believe in him even though they're a minority.

J: So, with their support, possibly he could have ...

S: Well, he wouldn't have been sent to the Roman authorities. He wouldn't have been sent to Pilate if he had persuaded the council, the majority of the council, that he was not a blasphemer, that he instead was the Messiah.

J: So it appears that something is proceeding as Jeshua expected, he predicted?

S: I don't know that. I don't think it was predicted, but I believe he expected [it], I believe he realized that after the Lazarus incident it would come to some sort of point of resolution.

J: You mentioned what takes place on Golgotha. Is this a usual manner of dealing with criminals?

S: Not all of them, only those who commit crimes that are punishable by death.

J: It seems so severe. (Saul is deeply upset. Tears are running down his cheeks and his voice is almost inaudible.)

J: Let's go forward to this afternoon then. You've heard that it's been decided.

S: Yes. I've resigned myself.

J: You've resigned yourself?

S: That it's true.

J: All right. Let's move forward then. And please relay this in as much detail as you're able to.

S: I don't want to be there. I think I'll walk on the road to the mountain. I was told that Jeshua, along with the other two, were led by the Roman soldiers, and he carried the wooden stake on his back. There was a big crowd, and they were following Jeshua, that Jeshua was smiling, and he ... he showed no fear, that he talked to the crowd on his way up.

J: He talked to them?

S: He talked to them. And several of the people that saw him said that he seemed light-hearted. They saw him smiling to the crowd. He ignored the ones that were taunting him, and talked to the ones that were supporting him—yelling, yelling things, that they cared for him. I was told that they got to the top ... they got to ... Golgotha, which is where the ... stakes are placed into the ground. I have always stayed away from there. I have never gone to any of the ... crucifixions and ... I feel just so sad inside I don't ... I don't want to go, and I'm not going to go.

J: Where do you go instead?

S: I ... went ... I went by myself. I walked a long, long distance by myself ... so I could think and pray. I didn't want to be a part of it. I can only envision in my mind right now ... what it must be like—the pain he would be experiencing, and what must be going on in his own heart and mind.

J: All right. Continue with what you have heard about what took place in Golgotha.

S: Well, I couldn't sleep that night. I didn't sleep ... and ... I returned to the city, in the morning after the sun came up. It was very, very quiet in the city—a sort of quietness when people are either afraid or very sad over some event that took place. People seem very, very sad ... as each has its own thoughts.... He died during that night on the cross, I'm told ... and that his ... family and supporters ... then removed ... removed his ... removed Jeshua. I just find it so hard to believe that he isn't here. They removed him, and took him near the city—on the outside of the city where Joseph Arimathea's property is located. And that they were going to have their ritual ... burial there, which they do for special people, where they have the body rubbed in ointment, and then wrapped in cloth and linen.

J: Did you participate in any of this? (Saul is despondent.)

S: No. No ... I ... don't want to be ... I ... he has his followers that do that.

J: Who of his family is here?

S: You mean in Jerusalem?

J: Yes, you said some family was ...

S: His mother.

J: His mother is here?

S: Well, she's been living here for a while now. And his brother, the oldest of the two brothers—his brother James.

237

J: He has a brother named James also?

S: What do you mean also?

J: Well, he has a follower named James.

S: Yes. Two different people. The other one is James the fisherman whose brother is John. I don't know if [Jeshua's] other brother is here. But his sister, Ruth, is here. And there is another woman. I've met her a couple of times. She lives with them and helped raise Jeshua since he was a little child. She's like a sister to Mary, a member of their family. She's lived with the family, always, as far as I've known. She came with them when they moved here from Capernaum. But I'm told that they're going to be placing Jeshua's body, after the ceremonies have been completed, in the family tomb, of Joseph Arimathea, which is in a cave on his property. But I don't know if they're going to bury him there or not, but just keep him there for a while—several days, three days, I'm told.

J: And then what's the plan after that, do you know?

S: I assume they're going to bury his body someplace. I don't know. I'm not in contact with them, I want to be by myself. I'm very, very ... very, very disturbed and sad. I feel I've lost ... somebody ... who was so important to me, and to ... to everybody. And it all happened so fast. I had always feared that he would be killed, or attempts would be made on his life while he was traveling between Jerusalem and other cities and towns. I ... I just didn't think it was going to happen this way. It all happened so fast.

J: Yes.

S: I almost feel like I'm not able to relate to it. I feel like my mind's just not accepting it yet.

J: You're in shock. It's a shock to you. (I have witnessed individuals in shock. Nick was experiencing the physical and mental effects of the shock of Saul.)

S: So, I've been by myself for the last several days; just

occasionally coming in contact with people whom I've asked if they know anything more that is happening. It just doesn't seem real.

J: Go on to the next event, please.

S: Well, there are rumors going around now. Oh, several days have gone by and there are rumors now that ... that Jeshua is ... well ... that Jeshua has appeared, has reappeared, that he's reappeared to his people, to his followers. That when they went back to get him, to get his body, that it wasn't there. And that he has reappeared to them physically, that people have seen him.

J: That people are seeing him?

S: Well ... that's what ... that's what the rumors are.

J: Do you try and find out?

S: Yes.

J: Where do you look?

S: I don't know where his followers are right now. There is so much conversation going on. I mean, that is what everybody is talking about. That he has reappeared, that he is not dead now.

Saul's demeanor is depressed and solemn, and he appears to be puzzled. You can only imagine what he is feeling and thinking regarding these traumatic and now confusing rumors and events that are unfolding in his life.

J: Are they saying this is similar to what happened with Lazarus?

S: No. No, I'm ... I don't ... I don't ... no one's equating it to Lazarus. I don't know what to make of it. I don't know if it's true or not. But that's what I'm hearing, that he has reappeared. I have to find somebody that has seen him because there's so much confusion right now. So many rumors going around.

J: And do you find someone?

S: Not right now. It took me awhile. I finally was able to come in contact with one of the followers several days later, one of the two brothers, Peter. (Saul often in the past also referred to Peter as Cephas.)

J: Peter? Let's move forward to that, and then we can come back. Tell us what Peter said.

S: Peter says that he has reappeared, that he's come to them several times now, but that he's flesh. Not just in spirit. That he had flesh. That he has the wounds where he was pierced when he was placed on the stake.

J: All right.

S: Peter is [exultant]. He's excited. He said that Jeshua came to them the evening before and supped with them, actually ate with them. That he is in physical ...

J: You mean, after his death? And now in his reappearance he was eating with them?

S: That he joined them the evening before and actually supped with them. I'm trying to understand this, what this means. He's not staying with them. He just appeared. He gave them information and instructions to carry on his teachings. There are some people, there are many people that are claiming they saw him, and I don't believe some of them. I'm not talking about Peter. I'm talking about others. There [are] also people claiming that he never died. That, rather than reappearing, they just hid him for a while. I know that's not true, though.

J: They're saying he's recovered?

S: And that he hadn't really died, that he'd been removed before he'd died from ... well, I know that's not true.

J: So Peter is telling you from his own observations, his own experience?

S: Yes. Peter has seen him, and that Jeshua instructed them to carry on his teachings. [Jeshua] told them he wants them to go, to travel to Galilee, and that he will meet them there.

J: How does Peter explain what has happened?

S: Peter seems changed. I never really felt close. I never liked Peter. Peter was always, to me, boisterous and argumentative. He seems changed. It seems like a peacefulness has come over him. (Saul's demeanor is also changed, now—it's gentle.)

J: You must have had many questions for him.

S: (Long pause.) I had questions. He answered all my questions that he could. Peter seems at peace with himself. He said that he is going with some of the other followers. They're going to go up to Galilee and meet Jeshua up there, near the sea, a place that they have agreed to meet. I asked him where Jeshua is staying. And he said that Jeshua's just appeared, and that he doesn't think he's staying. It's hard to explain. It's as if he just reappeared. But as I say, there are many people who are claiming they saw him, that I don't believe. But there's so much confusion going on. I mean this all happened so fast with Lazarus, and then Jeshua being sent up to Golgotha, and being dead and now—his reappearances!

J: It's a lot to take in.

S: Yes, all this happening, too, during the holiday period. All these events are just happening so quickly. I'm trying to absorb them and understand what's going on.

J: Had Jeshua said anything to you about this? That he would die and reappear? Had he said anything to prepare you for this information?

S: No. Not about the reappearance. He never told me that. He had told me at different times, most recently, that he anticipated that his stay on earth would come to an end very shortly, and that he wasn't concerned about it. I never argued with him about that.

J: So the reports of his behavior suggest that his attitude was what he said it would be: Not concerned?

S: Yes. That's correct. I still find difficulty in accepting the fact that he did not take a stronger position before the council and prove to them that he was the Messiah. I have to believe that he could have if he wanted to.

J: You're wondering why he didn't?

S: I found out more information about what took place at the hearing.

J: Oh. Please share that.

S: Well, they asked him questions specifically regarding their concerns as to whether or not he was claiming to be the Messiah. And I'm told that he left them with the impression that he was, but that he chose not to do anything to prove to them that he was at one with God. So it basically, from my own analysis, was giving them a confirmation of their claiming that he was blaspheming. If one claims to have a certain position, with that position would come certain powers. And if one chooses not to show those powers, but instead just to claim the position, it could be interpreted as blasphemy. Then you're basically giving confirmation to the accusations against you. That is my own analysis.

J: So, by claiming it, but not proving it, they have a stronger case?

S: They charged that he was claiming to be the Messiah. By his answering them in such a manner, he is allowing them to think they are correct. But by his not showing them that he has certain powers, he left himself vulnerable to their accusations.

J: And in your analysis, why do you think he did it that way?

S: I've tried to figure it out. I've tried to analyze. He must have known. He must've known what was going to happen. Perhaps he thought that he could make a greater impact allowing these events to take place, and this reappearing after his death. It's got to have a tremendous impact on the people. I mean, there are so many people that never saw him, that only heard of him. How is it going to touch their lives? When added to everything else they've heard? Now his reappearance from his death in flesh. It's got to have a great impact. And maybe that's why he wanted it to happen this way. He was not afraid of death. He always said that death does not exist, that it's an illusion, that we live on. Our spirit is always there.

J: Did Peter have anything else to add during this visit?

S: Peter had a calmness. No. He was very believable. He was very, very believable, very credible in what he was sharing with me. I saw something. There was something different. I imagine the way Jeshua has touched his life. There was something different about his personality. There was a quiet strength there that I had never seen previously.

J: His calmness seems to have calmed you, too. (Saul is now appearing less agitated.)

S: Yes. I believe it now. I believe that Jeshua has reappeared, where before I'd only heard rumors, but I hadn't talked to anybody that I had believed had actually seen him.

J: Do you have occasion to ask Peter any more about the supper the night before he was arrested or the night he was arrested?

S: No. I didn't ask him anything about that.

J: OK. Do you have plans to journey to Galilee as well?

S: No.

J: Have you thought about it?

S: No. I wouldn't do that unless Jeshua had ... I wouldn't do that. I hadn't been invited.

J: Oh. I see.

S: By them or by Jeshua.

J: I'm trying to understand how you fit into this.

S: I'm not a part of that group. My relationship with Jeshua is mine. I'm not a part of that group. They have always resented me because of my relationship with him being different than theirs. I have accumulated a substantial amount of wealth. I am educated. I have different social friends and associates. And I've never been impressed with those people. They were always arguing among themselves. Also, his followers from Galilee were always arguing with the ones from Judea. I've never held them in high regard, and they know that. As I say, there was something different about Peter this time.

And thus we come to the end of Saul's walking with the Master. In one sense, this could be the end of the story. But not unlike what Jeshua taught about life, the end of this story creates the beginning of another. This thread of connection with Peter will later be woven into another story that will ultimately change history.

Chapter 15

THE EARLY "CHURCH"

Our next session took place two weeks later, on July 22. We began after the death of Jesus. Saul obviously had been affected by the events he had witnessed. He appeared very somber.

J: Would you go back in time and tell us how many days it's been since Jeshua was killed?

S: It has been many months since he reappeared.

J: Saul, would you tell us your age right now?

S: I'm almost thirty-two.

J: All right. Thank you. Many months since his appearance? As I recall, you did not, at that time, see him.

S: I did not.

J: What's been happening in Jerusalem since that time? With his followers and ...

S: His followers have established quarters in Bethany, and they are recruiting other people. Others also are becoming *discipulus,* which means pupils, learners. They're soliciting others to join them, and they, his original followers, have become teachers. Some of them are doing healings. They appear almost daily at the temple. At the porches of the temple where Jeshua used to preach, they now preach. They refer to their teachings as the "Good News" and themselves as Witnesses of the Good News.

J: Do you go and listen sometimes?

S: No. I pass by there at times, but I'm not interested in listening to them. I know what Jeshua had to say.

J: Which of the disciples is doing healing?

S: Some of them are.

J: More than one?

S: Yes. Peter, the one that Jeshua called Cephas, is doing a lot of healing. He seems to be the leader, since Jeshua is no longer here. Phillip is doing healing, and Bartholomew. I don't think all of them are, but some of them are.

J: Part of the story that has come down about the events before the arrest and the crucifixion was that one of the disciples took money to show the priests or the Romans where Jeshua was. Have you heard of this?

S: I've heard that one of his followers had turned him in to the authorities, as to where they were the night that Jeshua was arrested. Yes.

J: Are you able to provide us with some details of this?

S: I'm told that it was Judas Iscariot, and that he had not been getting along with the others for quite a while. He had not been accepted by the others. He was a person who had a bad reputation.

J: A bad reputation?

S: Yes. He had a bad reputation in terms of his character and honesty, and he had not been well received by the others when he joined them in following Jeshua. I'm told that he was the one that, out of resentment and anger with the others, had turned [Jeshua] in to the authorities that evening. But they would have found him the next day, anyway. Jeshua wasn't hiding.

J: All right. After the crucifixion and the reappearances, there was a very difficult time for you. I know you went through a period of not being able to grasp that it had happened. How are you doing now? How are you feeling about it?

S: I'm feeling a great loss, and I'm disappointed at some of the things the followers are doing. So I have some sadness about it. But I'm going about my business and not becoming involved in their activities.

J: Have you considered carrying on the teachings yourself?

S: No. I had come in contact with Peter that one time when Jeshua had appeared, and Peter had suggested I might become involved. But I do not want to be involved with those people. And I'm not too enthusiastic about what they're doing right now and the way they're going about it.

J: What are some of the things you are unhappy about?

S: For one thing, they're saying that unless you accept Jeshua as the Messiah, you cannot have salvation. But there are many, many lands, many places far from here where the people will never come in contact with Jeshua or with his teachings. Are we to believe that these people will not have salvation even though they have lived a good life, as far as honoring the laws of God? I'm talking about places such as where I came from, in Cilicia, or other lands, such as the area of Pisidia, Cyprus and other areas. So I have a hard time. They're putting fear in people's hearts and alienating the Pharisees even more. I also understand that they're having people sell all their possessions and donate it to their cause. I understand that this is providing them with the wealth they need to continue spreading the teaching of Jeshua and what they refer to as the Good News.

       But what is happening is that a lot of people

who are undesirables are becoming members of their organization so that they can have the benefit of the redistribution of this wealth. So I'm really concerned about the quality of some of the people who are becoming members, or Witnesses.

J: Do you think that Jeshua had this type of organization in mind? Something as formal as this?

S: I don't know about formal. I can't answer the question regarding formalities. But it appears to me that there is going to be a new sect of the Jewish religion, of Judaism, along with the Pharisees, Sadducees and the Essenes—one in which Jeshua would be accepted as the Messiah. Hopefully they would all accept him, and he would become the Messiah of all of us. But they are branching off and telling the people not to go to the temples and pray any longer because the temple priests are not saying that Jeshua is the Messiah. So it's separating the Jews who are accepting Jeshua from the rest of the religion. Also, they have a ritual they're using that is somewhat similar to what Jochanan Ben Zachary [John the Baptist] was doing with water years and years ago—immersing the people in water. They're using this ritual as the point of significance in which the person has accepted Jeshua as the Messiah, which is fine. I don't have any problem with that. There is much good that is being done, but I have a problem with some of the fear they're instilling in people to get them to accept Jeshua as the Messiah and become one of them.

J: Thank you. Is there anything else that you'd like to add about what is going on with the disciples right now?

S: They also made Jeshua's brother James the figurehead of their organization. And I realize why they did this. They did this in hopes of giving greater credibility to their efforts, even though I realize he really doesn't have leadership capabilities.

J: In an earlier discussion of James, if I'm recalling cor-
       rectly, he wasn't very supportive of what Jeshua was
       doing.

S: No, he wasn't, until Jeshua started doing healings.
       I've thought about that. Not about his brother, but
       I've given a lot of thought in terms of how the popu-
       lace has accepted the teachings of Jeshua. For so
       many years he was trying to make inroads, and it was
       so difficult. I was thinking about events that took
       place which so dramatically changed the people
       accepting him. First, when he began to do the heal-
       ings, which they referred to as miracles—which in a
       sense they were. Then the incident of Lazarus, where
       people believed that Jeshua brought him back from
       the dead—although some people say he was in a state
       of unconsciousness—but regardless, this had a
       tremendous impact on the people. And then after
       Jeshua died, his reappearance, in which hundreds of
       people claimed they saw him, those three activities,
       coupled now with his followers creating these com-
       munal environments—where they're having people
       give them all their wealth and redistributing it as well
       as telling people that they won't receive salvation
       without accepting Jeshua—I believe all of these
       things have contributed [to the numbers of people
       becoming followers]. But mainly, [it was] what Je-
       shua did.

J: Would you go back to the few days after the reap-
       pearance? Is there anything more that you can add to
       those reappearances and the messages he was deliver-
       ing then? And the nature of the last of the reappear-
       ances?

S: I don't know how much to believe and how much are
       false rumors. I'm told that he appeared a number of
       times to his followers. I'm told that he appeared in
       many different places throughout not only Judea but

also Samaria and Galilee and that he was seen by many, many people. This has had a tremendous impact on the population in terms of anger and fear from his opponents—on the other hand, excitement and enthusiasm on the part of his followers. I believe he reappeared because some of the people that had seen him are people that I not only have a great deal of respect for, but there were many witnesses. Not just one or two. So I believe it to be true. I know it to be true.

J: And was there any particular ... I'm trying to ask you a question about his last appearance. The story that's come down is that he did have a last appearance in which people saw him go up into Heaven. Does that sound familiar?

S: No. I've not heard that. I heard stories of appearances very strongly for, oh, perhaps a month and a half from the time that he was crucified. Then occasionally after that you hear some story of somebody claiming to have seen him, which I don't believe.

J: There are also stories that he made appearances in other parts of the world. Did you hear anything like that?

S: I wouldn't have. I wouldn't be able to know that. I wouldn't have any way of knowing that.

J: Well, I thought you might know or that you might have heard or spoken with someone who had heard Jeshua say that he was visiting other places.

S: I've heard that he visited other places. Some of the stories are outlandish. You have to assume that he'd have no reason to show up someplace where people didn't know him and had never heard of him before, where he'd never been before.

J: Saul, even if in your judgment it is outlandish, would you mind repeating the stories just for our interest?

S: Well, somebody will tell me that they heard from

somebody else, who heard from somebody else, who heard from somebody else that [Jeshua] appeared in some obscure place, or someplace far away from our land. And the assumption, when we hear these stories, is that it's just people looking for recognition that are saying this.

J: There are some questions I'd like to ask you. Would it be all right if I ask them now?

S: Yes.

J: I think you answered this to a certain extent already. You talked about three reasons why people were converting. Are you seeing any other reasons why people are converting?

S: I don't recall saying three reasons why people are converting. I said there were three different activities that Jeshua had been involved in which created a lot of believers that weren't there before.

Although it was not my intent to misrepresent what Saul had previously said, it is apparent it would be very difficult, if at all possible, to get something past Saul that was inaccurate.

J: Yes. Yes, that is different than what the disciples are doing to convert.

S: I'm concerned. The disciples are telling people that God is going to punish them if they don't accept Jeshua as the Messiah, agree to become a Witness and give up all their personal wealth. They're telling stories of people who held back and hid some of their wealth but told them that they were giving it all and that God struck them dead. And I resent this terribly. (Saul is angry.) To me, one of the worst crimes a person can commit is to violate the laws of God in the name of God. And I believe that even though their intentions might not be malicious, they are doing that.

251

If they are lying and using God's name in their lie in order to have these people give them wealth—all their wealth—I believe this is wrong. Jeshua would never suggest for people to do this. Jeshua objected to tithings in many cases because he felt the priests were corrupt in coercing the people through demands and threats, spiritual threats. I cannot believe Jeshua would condone threatening them with punishment from God.

J: Please continue.

S: They're not saying that Jeshua taught them that. They're saying that it's necessary that they give up their wealth in order for the Witnesses to continue their activities. But where the lie comes in is saying that God has punished people who held back. It's totally inconsistent with our belief system.

J: Do you make your anger known to any of them?

S: I don't come in contact with them. I make my anger known to others. Others who are considering becoming part of their organization, suggesting to them to accept the beliefs of Jeshua without becoming involved in their organization.

J: What have they named the organization?

S: They refer to themselves as the Witnesses. Sometimes they refer to themselves as Witnesses to the Truth or Witnesses to the Good News. Sometimes other people refer to them as—well, I've heard some people call them Nazarenes, but that's only because that is where Jeshua's family originally came from.

J: Speaking of Jeshua's family, have you seen his mother, Mary, or spoken with the family?

S: No. James, his brother, is involved, as I indicated. They've given him a position of authority. His other brother, I'm told, stayed in Galilee, in Capernaum where he works. And Mary lives in Bethany, as she has for several years now. She must be fifty or fifty-one years old by now.

J: How is she doing? Have you heard?

S: I don't know. No, I haven't.

J: All right. Thank you. I'm curious about some of the practices of the Jews. I want to ask you some general questions. Why are the dietary laws important to Jews?

This is the first time I deviated from spontaneous questioning of Saul, for I had written down some questions even though I had not told Nick that I was going to do this.

S: Dietary laws. Well, throughout our history we've always been concerned about our health. And oftentimes we connect the rules of good health to our religion in order for the less-educated people to believe it's a sin, a spiritual sin to disobey those particular laws which are designed to give us better health. The heathens eat certain foods that we know aren't healthy, and oftentimes makes them sick. It can even cause them to die sometimes, for the food may be infested with disease or worms. So, we do not allow our people to eat those foods. So we say we've entered a covenant with God in agreeing that those foods are unclean and that we'd be violating one of the laws of God if we eat those foods.

J: Thank you. Is there anything else you'd like to add about foods? For instance, do all of the sects, the Essenes for instance, have the same dietary law as say one of the other sects?

S: All Jews have one religion, and all of our laws are the same.

J: All the laws are the same?

S: We don't have different laws for Pharisees as opposed to Essenes.

J: The next question is why is circumcision important?

S: For the same reason. Heathens do not circumcise

themselves. They contract many diseases. It causes uncleanliness of their bodies from lack of circumcision. So we have incorporated it as part of our religious beliefs and our commitment to God to have our bodies, as well as our minds, clean. Every male child that's a Jew goes through a process of circumcision after they are born.

J: Thank you. Did you ever ask Jeshua, or did he ever mention whether he would be coming back in body again?

S: Yes.

J: What did he say to that?

S: He said that, first of all, he would be here continually in spirit for those who accepted him as an intermediary between him and God. God does not interfere with our lives on this earth. But through Jeshua we can have a contact with God. As far as returning in body, he said that it would be a long, long time from now when all on earth have accepted the truth—even those who were not given the Word—that did not have an opportunity to accept him and God, since many people in our world are heathens and do not believe in God. But even those who do not believe in God, if they live their lives as if they had been taught the Word of God, when that day comes, it is only then that he would return.

J: When all the people are like that, he will return?

S: Yes. But again, I do not say that they all may have heard the Word of God, because some of them will have not. But they may still lead a life that would be at one with God even though they may not have [heard the Word of God].

J: I have some more questions. Talking about spirits, our spirits, what is your opinion about a beginning and an end of spirit? Is there a beginning and an end?

S: I don't know what you mean.

J: Is the spirit also born? Or is the spirit always?

S: The spirit is always a part of God. We originally came onto earth because we wanted to experience physical emotions and feelings that can be found on earth that are not on the other plane. We came onto earth wanting to have that experience but recognizing too that we could not return to be at one with God unless our spirit was pure, as it was before coming onto earth. We would continue to be reborn on earth until such a time—no matter how many births it takes—that we became pure again and could be at one with God and not have to be reborn again.

J: Is it possible for the spirit to die or be destroyed?

S: No. The spirit is part of God. It cannot be destroyed.

J: In your opinion, was there ever a time when there was no God?

S: (Long pause.) I have thought about that. And perhaps in my spirit-mind I would understand and know the answer to that question. I do not know that answer. I do not know, that other than as a mortal, I would believe that there always has been God. And yet I do not fathom the understanding of "always." As to whether there was a time before always? I am not able to give you an answer to that. Again, I will know for sure on the other side.

J: Thank you. Would you explain what a heathen is?

S: A heathen is the same as a gentile—one who does not believe in God. They either have no beliefs, or they pray to idols or mythical powers. Some of the people who were heathens at one time have become Jews. We have Greek Jews as well as some Roman Jews as well as Jews that live in Peraea, Syria—and of course, where I was from—Cilicia, and other places; even though they came from a region in which basically the people were gentile.

J: Do you know in your own family how far back your Jewish line goes?

S: I believe that we were always Jews, for we were not converts. I am guessing that my forefathers might have left Israel and traveled to the region of Cilicia as opposed to the other way around—of having been natives there and then converting to Judaism. My parents were Pharisees even though we were Roman citizens, for Rome governed Cilicia.

J: All right. Thank you. Now we are several months past the crucifixion. You are now age thirty-two.

S: Yes. That's accurate.

J: OK. So, let me ask you if anything else happened during your thirty-second year that you would like us to know about?

S: In my own private life?

J: In your own private life, or in the community.

S: Not really. We have a number of people who, as time goes on, are moving here to Jerusalem from other places who want to join the Witnesses.

J: How is this impacting the Roman government?

S: Indirectly, there is some concern, because the Roman government looks to the religious authorities in Jerusalem to keep order and control of the people. And there is some conflict and confusion. There is conflict and animosity existing right now between the followers of Jeshua and the religious leaders, the Sanhedrin council. So there is some problem in that area.

J: Do you hear anything more? Was there much impact from Pontius Pilate's role in the crucifixion?

S: I understand the Roman authorities are concerned about his decision and that it is under question. Right now the Romans seem mainly concerned about maintaining order.

J: All right. Thank you. Let's look at the year in which you were thirty-three. Report events both in your personal life and in the community. Take your time.

S: I'm doing a lot of reflecting on my life. I've become wealthier from my activities. But I'm doing things I'm doing almost by habit, for they're not particularly challenging. They're relatively simple, now that I have substantial wealth to basically accumulate more wealth. I've come to realize that you can measure people by their knowledge, their wisdom to use that knowledge, and the direction in which they wish to use their wisdom and knowledge. There are many, many people who do not have knowledge. There are many people who do not have wisdom. There are many people that do not have motivations. So I am blessed in that sense, that I am able to separate myself in that respect from most people. I've developed many skills and abilities. But I also spend a tremendous amount of time thinking of the words of Jeshua, his teachings and discussions that we had.

It is more difficult now to talk about them with other people because some people have become very incensed over what is taking place with the followers, and others have become tremendous supporters. So you have great intensity on both sides. It's difficult for me, from the standpoint that I believe so strongly in his teachings. I have so much love for Jeshua, as well as his beliefs that he shared with us. At the same time, I find a sadness with some of the activities and some of the methods of his followers.

J: Had you written down any of Jeshua's teachings for your own use? Have you recorded any of his teachings yourself?

S: I haven't written them down for my own use. But prior to his—I find it difficult saying the word "death," because I know he hasn't died. So I'm going to say prior to his leaving, I had written to other people about some of his teachings—to acquaintances that I had outside of Judea.

J: So you've written to your friends?

S: My acquaintances. Some are friends. Some are just people I know. But I'm a prolific letter writer. I write a lot, and I'm known to express my views very strongly, things that I feel (Saul is laughing), both verbally as well as written.

J: You seem pleased about this.

S: No. I'm laughing because many people feel that I express those views too strongly. And when they challenge me, I enjoy having them try to present their views in conflict to mine. If they are successful in convincing me differently, I will accept their views. But it's very rare that they are successful. Perhaps I give more thought than they do to those views, as well as have greater skills in presenting my views.

J: Do you still go to the Temple of Solomon for meetings?

S: Not for meetings. I go for ...

J: Discussions?

S: No. I go for Sabbath. I go to observe my religion. But I don't go to listen to the preachings of others. How can I, when I ... well, I shouldn't say how can I. Of course, I could. But I have little motivation, incentive to, after having had the opportunity to hear them firsthand from Jeshua. So many times there were just the two of us. My information that I received was of much greater depth than what these people are saying now. But they have recruited some other people who are very good people, people with character, and people of standing who are now apostles also, as opposed to being disciples—pupils. They're now teachers. They're now what the Romans call *apostulus*.

J: The Romans call them *apostulus*?

S: Well, a pupil and a teacher. A pupil is a *discipulus* and an *apostulus* is a teacher. So many of the pupils have now become teachers.

J: Who are those outstanding ones? Name some of them
      that you consider good teachers.

S: You mean since the original ones?

J: Yes, since the original ones.

S: Well, my very dear friend Lucius has become part of
      them. He's become one of their leaders. Lucius is not
      from Israel. He is a Greek Jew. I think his family
      must have converted, for he looks Greek and he acts
      Greek, except that he is a Jew. He came here from the
      region of Cyrene, and he is one of the leaders now.
      He is a friend of mine. I enjoy him. He is a very, very
      bright man. And also they have accumulated so much
      wealth now that they have had to appoint people as
      caretakers and officials to manage the activities and
      the wealth. And these are people of fairly high educa-
      tion and character who have the ability to do this. So,
      they have, in that sense, brought in some very talent-
      ed and educated people who are now part of their
      association. Stephen was appointed as their treasurer.
      He's a very articulate and bright person also. I like
      these new people actually better than I liked the origi-
      nal followers. Although some of the original follow-
      ers now have grown in stature with the responsibili-
      ties they have taken. Barnabas is another one. He's
      from Galilee. But he was fairly well-to-do, and he's
      now also one of the apostles who is teaching the
      Good News.

J: Did they try and recruit you to join them?

S: The ones I just mentioned?

J: Yes.

S: No. They know I was here before them. They have
      not tried to recruit me, and I've shared with them my
      reasons for unhappiness towards what is happening,
      and they understand. They had not met Jeshua. They
      had not known Jeshua personally. So they respect
      what I have to say, both because of my own back-

ground and skills, as well as the relationship I had with Jeshua. But the one thing that I am fairly concerned about, also, is the wealth that is being redistributed, and their living communally. They have attracted many people who are not Jews. They are specifically told that to become part of their organization, to become a Witness, they must accept Judaism. They must give up eating unclean food, and males must be circumcised. I don't believe some of these people are sincere. I believe some of these people have become affiliated because they did not have the financial means to support themselves, so they become part of the organization. I'm very concerned about that.

J: They're not sincerely converting to Judaism?

S: That's what I'm concerned about. They are accepting the Word. They're accepting the teachings of Jeshua. But I question their sincerity. They can't come into our temples. They want to come into the temples now, and the temple keepers are saying that they're not Jews, that it's all a pretense. I understand that. And as a Pharisee I agree with that. So there is that element that I'm concerned about—of people with questionable motives.

J: Another personal question, please. Can you look into your future and see if you marry?

S: I don't marry. I have women companions. But I do not marry.

J: OK. Thank you. There is a rumor that you became so angry with the disciples that you persecuted them. Can you say something about that rumor?

S: That I persecuted them? (Saul has become indignant.)

J: Yes.

S: How could I persecute them? I'm not an authority. I have no power to persecute them. I can disagree with some of the things they're doing. I can disassociate myself with their activities and try to discourage other people from becoming part of their group, even though I want them to accept the teachings of Jeshua. But I am in no position to persecute them. Nor do I have any interest other than as I indicated: to discourage others from becoming part of their activities.

J: Did you ever do anything to disrupt the organization? (In truth, I have grown so fond of Saul, and find him so reasonable and honest, I felt ashamed to even ask.)

S: No. I don't know if you mean physically or otherwise. But since the answer is no in any form, I have not.

J: All right. Thank you. I feel like I should apologize for the question, but there is a story that it happened. Anything else in your thirty-third year?

S: There's a lot of things going on. I have some friends who have become active members of the Witnesses. And by the same token I have other friends who have more responsible positions within the activities of the religious leaders of our area. Because of my wealth and business activities, as well as my intellectual pursuits, I have made a lot of contacts now—more so than before, in Jerusalem, as well as outside.

J: Are you speaking of your own sphere of influences?

S: Yes.

J: You have spoken of this year as a year of reflection. How does that fit your increasing sphere of influence?

S: Unrelated.

J: OK. What is your intention in increasing your sphere of influence?

S: I have no ambitions.

J: It's just occurring because of your wealth and your intellect?

S: And my personality.

J: People are attracted to that?

S: Attracted, and sometimes also intimidated. Sometimes those who are intimidated want to befriend the intimidator. Even though I'm not intentionally intimidating people, I'm aware of the fact that it happens, that many people are intimidated by my demeanor.

J: Does an incident come to mind of this? Can you give an example of this?

S: There is no one isolated [event]; it happens all the time. I can tell when I meet people that they're concerned they might say the wrong thing in front of me, which could embarrass them or make them look foolish. It's just the way it is. And sometimes I don't make the effort I probably should to allow them to feel more relaxed and at ease.

J: So you're aware that you can be intimidating, or that people are intimidated by you, without your intending to be intimidating?

S: You are what you are. And if you evolve into a certain person that people are intimidated by, but you are comfortable with who you are, you accept it. I don't consider myself a person who tries to intentionally make other people uncomfortable, unless I think that they have done something to deserve that. But because I appear as a very strong, physical individual, and at the same time an attractive individual, that in itself, to some people, would be intimidating. But I don't try to use it for negative purposes, unless you consider business transactions, where those skills are used.

J: If I were to ask someone who knows you very well, say one of your dear friends, how to describe you physically, what would they say?

S: Physically?

J: Yes.

S: You mean as to what I look like?

J: Yes.

S: They would say I have black wavy hair which curls up at the ends. I keep it cut above my shoulders. I have a black beard which I keep fairly short. I have very strong features, although I do not have a large nose. I dress very well, consistent with my position. I have a tendency to stand with my two fists on my hips while I'm talking. I got in the habit of doing that. That might be considered arrogant or intimidating to some people, but there are some people that stand with their arms crossed when they talk, in front of their chest, others by their sides. This just happens to be my posture. I have strong teeth. And my eyes are greenish in color. I'm above average in height and strong in build.

J: Do you do anything to retain or to increase your strength?

S: I'm not sure what you mean.

J: Exercising? Walking, lifting things?

S: I take walks up the sides of some of the large hills that we have on the outskirts of the city to maintain the strength in my legs and my endurance. I don't lift things, but I have a natural strength which came with my being, as a person.

J: Thank you. Anything else you'd like to add about the way you look?

S: I would say if I were born at another time or another place or to another family, I would probably look like a military leader and be a person that was physical in nature, although I have not had to use that aspect of myself.

J: You haven't talked much about your personal life, your social life, your relationship to women. Do women say you are attractive, too, or is that something that women of your day are not allowed to talk about except among each other?

S: Are you asking me what they tell me privately?

J: Yes, that would be a good way to ask.

S: I have no reason to share that. I have had many lady friends with whom I've had close relationships, and I find that increases also in direct proportion to my increasing my wealth. But that's not unusual. I've had opportunities to marry, and I chose not to.

J: If you want to keep this private, I will certainly understand, but I would be interested to know why you decided not to marry.

S: I have the ability to receive the benefits that one would have in a marriage contract without having the marriage contract. Therefore, I have no motivation for having a marriage contract. I would prefer being able to change my relationships when I choose to, which is what I do. And I'm comfortable with that.

J: Do you have children?

S: No.

J: Thank you. How would your best friend describe your personality? The way you are with people?

S: Hopefully my best friend would have kind things to say about me. I would believe that my best friend would say that I am very opinionated, but my opinions are not without logic. That I have tremendously strong convictions, but that my convictions have been [reached] after substantial thought. That I am generous with some people and not with others. That I am very articulate and interesting to talk to and share thoughts with, providing that we do not get into confrontations.[3]

---

3. In regression therapy it is common, or even expected, that a spirit-mind takes on different personalities in different lifetimes. It is occasionally evident that a client possesses almost exactly the same personality that existed in a previous lifetime. It has become quite obvious that Nick's traits and life experience mirror those of Saul 2,000 years ago.

Like Saul, Nick had absolute confidence in himself at a very early age.

J: And then?

S: I have little patience with people who don't agree
     with me, which then affects the relationship for that
     moment, although not permanently. I am confrontive
     and blunt, stating how I feel about things. And I enjoy
     many things, which I keep to myself, and I do not
     show that enjoyment on the surface.

He had always been a risk taker, very independent, and was accused of
being intimidating, as Saul was, even though it was not his intention. Nick
appreciates that the challenges Saul faced could not have been met if he
had been meek in character, had not totally believed in himself and his
skills in meeting those challenges. He also voices a growing realization
that he may be required to face many of those challenges and obstacles in
this life.

Chapter 16

THE ROAD TO DAMASCUS

During the session in which Saul was describing Jeshua's appearing to the disciples for weeks after the Crucifixion, I asked him if he saw Jeshua, himself. He said not then, but years later on a business trip to Damascus. I was eager to discuss the trip; I couldn't wait. Saul was in such grief from the crucifixion, and I was so anxious to hear the real story about the trip, that I moved out of chronological order to the event. I felt it would comfort him as well as satisfy my curiosity. We have moved that part of the story back into chronological order to keep the flow of the story intact.

J: Let's move forward into the future to the next time you see Jeshua again.

S: Well, I was going to Damascus on business, traveling with a caravan, which [is what] I do whenever I go there. I would not go by myself on that trip through the desert. So instead, I always would wait and then pay [a caravan] so I might travel with it, thereby having its resources available: safety, as well as food and transportation.

I [was feeling] at odds with what [Jeshua's] followers had done, holding a lot of sadness and anger within me. It was evening just before we reached Damascus. [We had stopped] and were sleeping off to the side of the road.

I woke up and felt as if I was compelled—I walked away from the others, who were all asleep. And I felt this incredible presence ... and (Saul begins to weep) ... I looked up, and Jeshua was there.... He had this brilliant light around him. As I looked into the light—it was so brilliant ... I couldn't look into it. I felt blinded ... I fell to my knees. He talked to me. He told me that I should help his followers, that I should join them and help them because he wanted my support. I told him that I was sorry that I had not helped them. He said he understood, but he wanted me to accept their shortcomings and to do the best I could in helping them. That it was more important that I help them even if they had made mistakes.[4] And

---

4. I told Nick that theologians refer to the experiences of Paul on the road to Damascus as his point of conversion. Nick's recollection suggests this interpretation is not accurate. Nick said that Paul fully understood the Messages of Jeshua but chose not to become an apostle before his experience on the road to Damascus because he disagreed vehemently with the activities and methods practiced by Jeshua's followers. Nick was particularly concerned about two instances in which the Scriptures are inconsistent with the actual experiences of Paul and Jesus.

The first is the scriptural account of Paul's persecution of the early members of the Jewish Christian faith. When I asked Paul if he had persecuted the early Jewish followers of Jeshua, he responded that it was absolutely not true. He was not in a position of responsibility that would enable him to persecute anybody. It would be totally inconsistent with the customs of the Jews. For the practice of persecution of dissident religious

I told him that I would—that I loved him. And he told me that he would always be with me, that I should turn over my commercial activities to others, I should become a part of what his followers were trying to do and take a position of responsibility with them. We said good-bye to each other, and then he left.

But I didn't have all of my vision back. I could barely see because I had been almost blinded—not completely, but almost totally blinded when I looked at him and the light that surrounded him. But that's OK. I'm OK. There would have been no one else that had seen him. I didn't know if they had all slept, or whether they would have seen him if they had been awake. I don't know.

Then I went back to the campground; I just [lay] there and prayed for the rest of the night until the sun came up. I didn't tell any of them what had happened. (Awestruck is the only way to describe Saul's reaction to seeing Jeshua. It took him several minutes before he was able to continue.)

---

groups is unknown in Jewish history, particularly the persecution of groups that were made up of Jews. It is even told in Scriptures that Paul was on the way to Damascus to punish, persecute and possibly imprison Jews there who had accepted Jeshua as the Messiah. It is beyond logic to think that the Syrian governmental authorities would allow a Jew from Jerusalem to travel into Syria to persecute and imprison other Jews who were Syrian citizens. Under hypnosis Nick recalled that Paul was traveling to Damascus for business reasons, not for purposes of persecution.

Although I did not ask Nick about certain details during the session, he later revealed the fact that travelers arriving at the gates of Damascus had to be counted and pay a toll. After daylight hours, the gates were closed, and latecomers were required to camp in the desert until the following morning, when the gate would be reopened. Jeshua appeared to Paul during the encampment of the caravan, outside the locked gates of Damascus. Nick was totally confident that his spirit-mind had correctly recalled what actually transpired during this tremendously important moment in history.

I needed help because of my difficulty in seeing. The next day, we arrived in Damascus. My sight was starting to improve, although I didn't have it all back yet. But it was starting to get better. I stayed with a friend of mine in his home, which I do when I go to Damascus. I didn't tell him what happened. He is a heathen. He's a gentile. He has no religion. So I did not share with him what happened. It took me another two or three days to get my sight back completely after I got to Damascus. Then I was fine.

J: Your sight has completely returned?

S: Yes. And I have spent the last several days collecting my thoughts about what I must do. Jeshua also told me that I should do healings as he had taught me, so that I might help people, as well as establish my own credibility in terms of getting people to accept Jeshua as the medium between the part of God that is within them and our Creator. Jeshua is to be the messenger between that part of God which is in all of us and God who is the Father and Mother of us all.

I understand all that because he and I talked many times about what his role would be after he was to die, or after his physical body was to leave earth, for he is never dead. And my responsibility, along with his other followers, is to get other people to accept him as their Messiah and the messenger between them and God.

I have decided how I'm going to turn over my commercial activities to others. I will give [others] a larger part of the profits that we receive in return for their taking over my responsibilities in Jerusalem as well as here in Damascus. They're very willing to do that in Damascus. Why wouldn't they be? I don't go there that often anyway. And I've decided that I'm going to visit the temple. I'm going to stay in Damascus for a while and teach them the Word.

J: Your life has been changed?

S: My life is totally changed.

J: Please continue.

S: I send word back to Jerusalem that I'm going to stay in Damascus for a while. And I go to the temple. I am a Pharisee, so they accept me readily—more so than if I were one of [Jeshua's] followers in Jerusalem, or one of the new people who had joined them. And I start preaching to them the Word of Jeshua. They call it the Good News back in Jerusalem. I start preaching the Good News. I find it comes easy to me. I start doing a little bit of healing, but not in groups or crowds. I want to do it first on a basis of just one individual at a time until I am comfortable with my ability to do it, as well as what to say. I can't do it unless I can convince them that they are able to heal themselves, with my help, using Jeshua as the medium between them and God.

J: Just as you described it when you first saw Jeshua healing?

S: There is a difference because now I'm acting as the intermediary between them and Jeshua. It's one additional element that Jeshua didn't have to deal with. So, I want to make sure. I want to be comfortable with [the healing] until I feel that I can perfect it. Others have always accused me of being a perfectionist. I assume they're correct. I'm feeling very comfortable with it and I have substantial speaking abilities. I have known that I was a good speaker, very articulate in front of large groups of people. I had several times represented myself in legal situations in front of the courts, in front of judges. They are very impressed with what I am saying. I can see that I'm going to make a substantial impact on the progress of having others accept Jeshua. I'll have to deal with how I'm going to handle this when I get back to

Jerusalem, with his disciples and the organization that exists there now.

J: Yes. It would appear to be complicated.

S: I don't think they'll think me a threat. I think they'll be very pleased to have me become part of them. But I disagree with some of the things they're doing. I have to be careful I don't alienate them by becoming a part of them and immediately challenging some of the things they're doing. I have to learn to have patience, which is not one of my stronger points, in having them accept me, first, before placing myself in a position of leadership, before I start challenging some of the things they're doing, and the way they're doing it.

J: Thank you. There is a story that's come down that this was about the time you changed your name. Can you tell us about that?

S: I didn't change my name. They changed it. People started calling me Paul later on. I didn't change it.

J: It's not something you did?

S: No. The other supporters started doing that after I came back to Jerusalem. They did it first as a joke, teasing in good nature because of their interpreting me as having changed.

J: Yes. That makes sense.

S: But that was their doing, not mine.

J: And would you please let me know how old you were on that journey?

S: (Long pause.) I'm thirty-six years old; approximately five years since Jeshua has left.

J: And during those five years you've been telling us about the struggles of the early organization and your disappointment. Would you please look at the organization of the Witnesses. How is it doing in this fifth year?

S: There have been retaliations by the authorities. They

have tried to impose different rules about meetings and collective preaching in groups. In many cases there have been times when the Roman soldiers have had to disperse the people. There have been some people who have been killed when there was resistance against the soldiers. So it is getting more tense, and the numbers of people who have joined have increased more and more. Some of the followers have become very proficient at healings and at preaching. They have developed skills in addressing the people regarding the words, the teachings of Jeshua. As the numbers have grown, so has the tension grown. That's basically the status at the time that I left for my trip [to Damascus].

J: So now I'm going to ask you to move back to the trip to Damascus, or to Damascus. You talked about spending a week getting your affairs in order, following Jeshua's appearance to you in the desert. Is there anything more that you would like to tell us about that week of getting things in order, and the decisions you made?

S: No. I stayed there after that. I stayed and preached the Good News, the teachings of Jeshua in the temple. I wanted to get comfortable with what I was going to say and how I was going to say it. I knew some of the temple leaders there from previous visits to Damascus. I wanted to take it slowly, become comfortable with what I was saying and how I was presenting Jeshua's teachings so as to not alienate them. Unlike some of the followers in Jerusalem, I didn't want to alienate them. I wanted to have them accept Jeshua, and to not be a threat to the authorities. It made sense to me to approach it differently than they were doing it in Jerusalem, outside of the religion, as though it was almost a separate one. I want to do it inside the religion.

J: Yes, that is a different approach. Is that part of what Jeshua wanted?

S: We never discussed it. It never occurred to me that it [should be] any other way. I don't recall our ever discussing it. I had always assumed that was his intent, and it was consistent with his actions.

J: So during his appearance to you in the desert, he gave no details about how to help with the work? He just knew you knew? He had a sense that you would be in tune with it?

S: He just told me to do the best that I could—to accept and be tolerant of their activities [in Jerusalem], and to provide leadership and to become active. He asked me, he didn't order me. He asked me. And I said that I would, with all my heart and soul. So, I experimented in Damascus as to how I could teach his words, his thoughts, his philosophies without being a threat to them (the local elders). And I felt very comfortable with that.

J: How long do you stay in Damascus this time?

S: I stayed there about another five-and-a-half, six weeks, in addition to those first few days that I put my business affairs in order. I was able to persuade several of the people to willingly commit to continue preaching in the temple what I taught them.

J: So you trained others, so to speak?

S: Indirectly. It would have been hard not to. There were some who were concerned. But I assured them that I was not a threat, and that what I taught was not a threat.

J: Who were you assuring?

S: Those who were some of the leaders, some of the elders of the temple. I assured them that what I taught was not a threat to the temple or to them but was consistent with our Judaic laws, and consistent with

273

what had been told to us by our forefathers, what was to happen. But more important than that, was that the philosophies and the teachings that I shared with them could only make us all better people and help us lead better lives.

Chapter 17

THE TRAVELS OF PAUL

*T*hree weeks passed before our next session on August 12. I was very interested in seeing Nick's reactions since our last meeting. We proceeded where we had left off at the last session.

Saul returns to Jerusalem eventually to find that he has been given a new name, Paul. News of his work in Damascus has preceded him, we are told. Word has spread of his effective manner and persuasive talks. Two days after Paul's arrival in Jerusalem, he ventures over to Bethany to meet with Jeshua's followers. He enters Bethany with confidence but aware that he will have to be careful not to seem a threat to the followers, nor to be seen as having ulterior motives.

Julia (J): Please describe your first meeting with the leadership in Bethany.

Paul (P): I go up to the second floor, where most of the people are located. I'm meeting with Lucius, who is my friend. Peter and his brother Andrew, along with several others, are there. James is there—not Jeshua's brother James, the other James. He's John's brother. And some other people I don't know.

J: Thank you. What do you tell them?

P: They had already heard that I had been in Damascus preaching at the temple, so it was not a surprise to them. But they didn't know what my intentions were, or what had motivated me to do it. I told them that Jeshua had appeared to me on the way to Damascus. But I didn't want to discuss that too much because I was concerned there might be jealousy, which could cause disbelief. So I did not make much of that. I told them that I was now committed to teaching the Good News with them, that I wanted to help them teach the work of Jeshua, and to help also, through my friends in Jerusalem, to relieve some of the pressures, tensions that were being applied towards them.

J: And how was this received?

P: They were very joyful. They had received good reports from others, when I was in Damascus, [about] what I was doing. So they were very enthusiastic. (Paul laughs.) They did ask me if I was going to donate all of my money and wealth to them and sell my properties. I told them no, but I would make a donation.

J: It's one of your objections as to how they're operating, and I imagine that's one of those areas in which you will have to be tactful.

P: Yes. But they're doing less of that now. It has been about five years [since the Crucifixion], and they have accumulated substantial wealth during that five years. So they're fairly self-sufficient now.

J: How old are you now, Paul?

P: Thirty-six.

J: Thank you. Would you like to tell us more at this point about the early organization, or would you like to move to the first of your journeys?

P: They are very well organized, and some of the disciples who have now become apostles are healing. Phillip has become very proficient in healing. But Peter has become the most proficient. And they have many others they have solicited who are now part of the organization, who are more educated and more sophisticated than the original followers. They've come from other parts of the land, even outside of Galilee, Samaria, and Judea. They still have problems in Judea, in particular with both the Pharisees and the supporters of Herod. I'm going to help them in that area to stop being such a threat to the local religious authorities.

It is apparent from what I hear that Paul begins to make his mark in spreading the teachings of Jeshua. His skills in diplomacy and oratory are effective tools in reaching people who previously felt threatened. Paul reverses earlier exhortations from his colleagues who asked the people to stay away from the temples, even if the priests were not teaching that Jeshua was God's messenger. Paul also reverses demands that temple tithings not be paid. In short, Paul works within the system, where his predecessors worked against the system.

J: So you're educating the followers and meeting with the friends in high places? Do you start preaching in the temples as well?

P: Not in the temples. I start preaching in small groups at first. I want them to listen to how I [preach] without offending them, for I'm being less controversial, more persuasive and less dogmatic. I think they can learn from me as I learned for myself when I practiced in Damascus. Daily we preach at Solomon's porch outside the temple. The weather is slightly chilly, so we're on the other side of the portico.

J: Would you please give us a sample of the things that you're saying to the people, the way you're modeling this.

P: I have my own style. I walk in front of them, pace in front of them, standing at a higher position than [they]. I don't talk until I have their attention, no matter how much time goes by, even if some of them start getting uneasy wondering why. And after I have their attention, completely, I look at them and tell them that I am bringing them Good News, that I'm sharing the Good News with all of them, every single one of them. And how fortunate we are to have this Good News. I try to get them excited about what I'm going to share with them before I start talking about it. What is particularly helpful for me is having seen firsthand many of the things we're talking about, which some of the followers have not.

J: You mean because you saw Jeshua healing and teaching in this same manner?

P: Yes. But he didn't use that style. The style is my style. He had his own style. I'm not ... I can't be Jeshua.

J: Go on.

P: I slowly get them to recognize the need for the Good News and how it can change their lives. How we all have a tremendous need to communicate with God. Then I talk about how it was predicted many years ago, 400 years ago, that God was going to send his perfect son to provide us forgiveness for our sins and to become a conduit between that God which is within us and our Father-Mother God. Then I show them how Jeshua came during our lives, the wonderful things he did, and share with them his Messages and his purpose. I change from talking very strongly to talking very softly in a quiet, emotional manner so that they can feel his love through me. I start doing healings too. And it's very effective.

J: You are doing healings in public now?

P: Yes, but I'm very careful in terms of being able to recognize people in the audience who I feel are the most receptive to what I'm saying, to select [whom] to heal, so I don't have an experience of trying to heal someone who is not prepared to be healed.

J: Thank you. Please move forward now to the next important event.

P: There are still persecutions going on, and we're finding that we must travel from Judea to other places to avoid the persecutions and, at the same time, to spread the Word—spread the Good News to other people who otherwise are not going to hear about Jeshua. So some of the people are leaving. Phillip has left. He's going to Samaria. Some of the others have gone to the Mesopotamia area.

J: Who goes along with you?

P: I go by myself right now. I'm first going to Caesarea, which is on the coast of Samaria. Then I'm going home to visit there for a while. So I go to the Cilicia region of Tarsus.

J: Tell us what happens in Tarsus.

P: I'm just visiting right now, just seeing where I grew up. I don't know any people there any longer. I only know a few families by name, so I only stay there a short while. Then two of my friends came and got me—Barnabas and the younger boy, Mark.

J: Mark?

P: Yes. And we left and went to Antioch and started preaching in Antioch and doing conversions.

J: And how is the work going?

P: It's hard, but it's going well. We appointed Lucius as the chief minister of the Samaria area, Caesarea and Laodicea. I stay there a long time. I use Laodicea as my base, going back and forth between Laodicea, Caesarea, and Antioch. And we do very well. Over a long period of time we had a lot of people become Witnesses. Many were gentiles that we brought into our fold. They had to accept Jeshua as well as Judaism, and stop eating unclean food. [They] had to become circumcised, although I think some of them lied about that, probably most of them.

J: Do you think that's important that they are circumcised?

P: I think that to become a Jew you have to be circumcised. I understand why it would be difficult for many of them as grown men to do that.

Paul relates the advantages of being a Roman citizen when it comes to facing the different problems that confront him. He has the security of not worrying about being persecuted by the Romans when the local people complain of his public displays. However, there are other problems that being a Roman citizen cannot help. And Paul changes the topic readily to this other kind of problem.

P: ... but I'm having some problems with Lucius that are creating a very serious [situation].

J: Tell us about that.

P: Lucius is married to Mariah. But he has become involved with a Roman woman named Vesta.

J: Vesta?

P: Yes. And he has had two children by her. It's causing a tremendous amount of controversy because many of the people who accept Jeshua through his apostles look up to these people. And some of these new officials are women, as well as men, and they're getting involved with each other carnally. So we have a serious situation to deal with. Barnabas doesn't agree with me. I want to change things, in that the head minister cannot be married and must be celibate to avoid some of the things that are happening in

Laodicea and some of these other areas. And Barnabas doesn't agree with me. We argue over it. He sides with Lucius. But I insist on it because it can destroy the credibility of what we are doing. The local people we're trying to have join us will lose respect for us and it will affect our mission.

J: So your proposal is that the head person not be married and be celibate? What happens with that idea?

P: I insist on it. Anybody I appoint from this time, if he is single, unmarried, he must commit himself to being celibate from that point on. Otherwise I won't appoint him. Also, I don't think we should have women in those positions of responsibility because they're coming in too close contact with the men. They're getting involved in relationships, and many of these women are married.

J: What was the nature of Vesta's position?

P: She was just a citizen there. She didn't have a position.

J: Oh. Your concern then is just in general that women ...

P: It's happening in other places in the Laodicea area. Then, to make matters worse, Mark got involved with Mariah, and we had a big fight about that. I'm really upset at him.

J: Mark got involved with Mariah?

P: Yes.

J: That's Lucius' wife?

P: Yes.

J: What is the outcome of that?

P: He cannot see her any longer. It created quite a conflict in the area because of all these happenings. But not many people know about Mark's involvement with Mariah. That's more privately known to a smaller group.

J: So you're worried that these relationships between

the men and the women are going to hurt the movement, hurt the work?

P: Yes.

J: It sounds as if you feel rules are needed.

P: There absolutely has to be rules. Otherwise it's going
to destroy our efforts. (Paul was obviously agitated
and he sounded adamant.)

J: So what is the rule regarding women holding positions?

P: I won't appoint any more women. Women will no
longer, as far as I'm concerned, hold positions of
priesthood.

J: Up until then, what kind of positions were women
holding?

P: The same as the men. There wasn't any deviation or
selection based on gender.

J: Thank you. Anything that you'd like us to know
about that? About these problems?

P: Just that I have to get control of them. I've sent word
back to Jerusalem to Peter and the other administra-
tors on the activities that are taking place. I've been
keeping them very informed by letter writing. I don't
anticipate they're going to argue with me over these
issues because I'm the one out here doing it, and I
feel they'll allow me to make those decisions.

J: It sounds as if you're really the major policy-setter
then. Would that be accurate?

P: I am as far as the activities outside of Jerusalem.
Enough years have gone by now that my position is
strong enough that I can make these decisions.

J: When you made the decision to prohibit women from
being priests, priestesses, because they were getting
into relationships, did you think about perhaps having
women and prohibiting men from being priests?

P: No. Our society is one which generally looks to the
men for the major decision-making. If we had said

that women could be the leaders rather than the men, this would have deterred many, many men from becoming followers and joining us as Witnesses. So I did not consider that as an option.

J: Were women priests in other groups at this time? Are women holding positions in the Jewish tradition? Are there women priests as well?

P: Only [among] the Essenes, but not with the Pharisees or Sadducees. In fact, they had to sit, as you know, in separate places in the temples. They did not hold positions within the traditional church. There were no women on the council either, the Sanhedrin council.

J: I believe that around where you were born and raised, there are still statues to some of the Greek goddesses. Is there still some goddess worship?

P: Yes, but not among the Jews.

J: Now you're telling us about your operations from Laodicea and Caesarea and Antioch.

P: Yes.

J: Move forward to the next event.

P: We start traveling. Barnabas and Mark go with me to Cilicia and we go across the Great Sea to the island of Cyprus. We stop in Salinas and spend some time there.

J: What was it like there?

P: It's very pretty. I like the scenery there—the ocean, the water. And the people are different than they are in Israel, of course.

J: Different in what way?

P: Well, Judaism is not their religion there. They don't have a religion. They're heathens. They're gentiles, with a few exceptions, a few scattered Jews living around there. But we're mainly converting people now into accepting not only the Good News about Jeshua, but also trying to have them accept Judaism with Jeshua as the Messiah. We spent a long, long time in Laodicea. I'm not going to spend much time anymore in one place because I won't get an opportunity to go to as many places. From Salinas we go to Pathos, which is also on the island [and] isn't very far away. We make conversions there. Hopefully the ones we convert and preach to will continue and will grow in numbers. We are selecting those individuals who are the most enthusiastic and seem to have the most capabilities to continue our work after we leave.

J: And do you find such people here?

P: Oh, yes. It's always easy to find people that are eager to hear and accept the Word, just as there are those who are offended by our coming, and offended by what we are saying. But we want to stay away from those who are against what we're doing and deal with those who are receptive to our work [and will continue with it] after we've gone. We will stay in communication with them.

J: Do you teach in the same manner here as you taught in Jerusalem?

P: No. No.

J: In what way do you change it here?

P: Well, I'm not talking to Jews. I'm talking to people who pray to a lemon tree; I have to get them to accept not only Jeshua, but God, and to stop praying to idols. There are those who are very receptive to having something stronger than a statue to pray to—or to not pray to anything. They don't take the statues seriously.

J: So in some ways you're finding people who are hungrier for the Word. Is that right?

P: Yes. In any group it's easy to identify those who are sincerely interested in what you have to say as opposed to those who have no intentions of being open-minded.

J: Thank you. Would you tell me about Barnabas? What is he like?

P: Barnabas was from Capernaum. He was a robust,

strong individual, physically as well as personality. He was fairly well-to-do. He had moved to Jerusalem after Jeshua's reappearances, and became involved fairly early in the activities. He's very committed. He had turned over his worldly goods when he became a member, when he became converted and accepted Jeshua, which would have been about twelve, thirteen years ago. Mark was with us. He was eight years old when Jeshua had healed him from a leg ailment. He walked with a limp. He was eight years old then, so he's about half my age now. He's a timid individual.

J: Mark is timid?

P: Yes.

J: What is his role in the missionary work?

P: He's supposed to be helping us, but he doesn't have a very forceful personality. He believes strongly. He just doesn't have a strong personality.

J: You were telling us why you're not happy with Mark.

P: He's not making very much of a contribution to what we're doing. And then he got involved with Mariah, which complicated matters.

J: And that's still going on?

P: No. No. But I'm still upset at him.

J: Is it your wish that those of you who are out teaching not be involved with women at this point? Have you decided to be celibate yourself?

P: I don't want to talk about that. What was your first question?

J: Have you decided that the men who are out teaching need to be celibate?

P: Only if they become the head minister of that area. But most of them are married. I only want them to be celibate if they're single. I don't expect them to be celibate if they're married.

J: And any future appointments, you would want them to be single?

P: I don't care if they're married. But if they are single, I want them to remain single, and to commit themselves to being celibate.

J: I think that I misunderstood. Only the head of the organization, you would have be single?

P: In each area we are appointing someone to be in charge as chief administrator. If he is married, I want him to maintain his relationship exclusively with his wife. If he is not married, I want him to commit himself to celibacy and not get married, not be involved in any carnal relationships.

J: All right. Thank you. What is the position then that Lucius holds? What is his title?

P: He's the chief minister of the Samaria area, of Laodicea and Caesarea.

J: All right. Thank you. Move on then. You're telling me now of your work in and around the island of Cyprus.

P: I visited there, and then we went across the sea to the region of Pisidia. Then we went to Atillia, and then to Antioch—not the big Antioch that is between Damascus and Tarsus—the other Antioch, the smaller Antioch in Pisidia. We go to Perga, and Mark leaves us at that point. I got into an argument with him. It hurt his feelings, and he left to return to Jerusalem.

J: You hurt his feelings?

P: Yes. That is OK. If he can't handle it, I'd just as soon not have him around. He wasn't making much of a contribution. And then from Perga we go to Iconium, then Lystra—stayed there for a while. These are all close to one another. Then to Derbe.

J: Do you encounter any difficulties here in any of these smaller places?

P: We encounter difficulties everywhere. Sometimes [the people there are] more hostile than others. They try to have the authorities evict us, throw us out of the area. That is when my being a Roman citizen is particularly helpful. Again, we identify with those who are the most receptive and appear to have leadership skills. Also, I do healings, which has a substantial impact on the people. But I have to be careful. It's hard to heal people. If they don't believe that they can be healed, you can't heal them. So, I have to be very selective. It is not the same as being in Judea and doing healings there. Many of them make a mockery of it and think that it's not actually happening. So, I have to be very selective.

J: How do you select?

P: By trying to ascertain if that individual has truly accepted Jeshua as the Messiah and believes that he can be forgiven for his sins and can heal himself, with Jeshua's help, through me. If I do not feel that he has that belief, I won't try it, because to try and fail discredits our efforts in converting people.

J: This sounds like very difficult and discouraging work. What keeps you going?

P: I believe what I'm doing is tremendously important to their lives. And I believe I'm getting my inspiration from my love for Jeshua, and my commitment to him. If it takes time, it takes time. But I know that it will continue to grow, and I have to plant the seeds. There is a saying, if you plant an onion in the ground, it grows an onion, and more onions. So I want to plant as many seeds as I can so they will grow.

J: At this point, Paul, do you have a plan of action? Do you have a master plan, so to speak?

P: No. I just plan to continue traveling for a while, but I have to return now to Jerusalem. They're having a problem.

J: All right. Let's move to that problem then.

P: When I was in Derbe, I got information that they're making a major decision to convert heathens to accept Jeshua without having them become Jews.

They are having a big debate about it. And it's become a controversy among the leaders in Jerusalem. So I'm going to leave here, Derbe, and stop in Antioch on the way back just to visit and see how they are doing. And then go back to Jerusalem so I can participate in the discussions.

J: Before we leave this, let me make sure I understand. The question is, can you be converted to the Good News without becoming a Jew. And your position is, this is a Jewish sect. Is that correct?

P: It has always been my position that you cannot accept Jeshua as the Messiah if you are not a Jew. I don't understand how they can have Jeshua be the Messiah with no religion, without having our Judaic religion as a basis. This is becoming a major, major issue right now, and I'm going to return so I can participate in the arguments and the decision.

J: All right. Thank you. Please move forward to those arguments now.

P: Peter is the main authority in Judea for the Witnesses. It is his belief, and he is supported by many of the others, that Jeshua's work and the Good News are too important to confine exclusively to people who are Jews, and that there are many, many people who can benefit by practicing the teachings of Jeshua who do not want to become Jews. He feels that they should be allowed to have the same privileges and the same beliefs and be able to have the same communion with God, even though they don't accept Judaism.

J: That's Peter's position, then?

P: Yes.

J: And we've heard your position.

P: Having been gone for the last several years in areas where the people were not Judaic, I understand the problem. I feel there are many, many more people who would have accepted our News, and Jeshua, if they did not have the requirement to accept Judaism also. And I find when I go back to visit those places where they are not practicing Judaism, they are still talking about Jeshua and his teachings. So I understand the rationale, and I'm willing to accept, with certain reservations, the fact that individuals can accept Jeshua as the Messiah and not be Jews.

J: So this represents a compromise for you?

P: A compromise for me. And I want them to accept my compromise.

J: How would this work in practice?

P: I want them to stop eating the unclean food that they eat. I'm willing to accept that the men do not have to be circumcised. This debate goes on for a long time. This isn't resolved in one day. This goes on for a long, long time trying to resolve this issue. It is a major, major issue.

J: Is there support for your position? Or are you the only voice for this?

P: No. No. There are others who support what I'm saying. And there are others who don't agree at all that people should be allowed to have Jeshua as their Savior and not have Judaism as their religion. So there are different factions. But the strongest faction, in terms of numbers, is with Peter. I've been gone a while, so I don't have as much influence on those who are in Judea, in Jerusalem, as I did before I left.

J: Who will make the ultimate decision as to how this issue is settled?

P: There is no one individual. We might end up with a situation where some of the apostles will still continue to only allow those who are willing to accept Judaism to become Witnesses for Jeshua. And others may allow people to accept Jeshua without any requirements at all. It will be basically the result of what the majority of us collectively agree to do. But there may be some inconsistencies still between us as we go on.

J: So this is still in process?

P: Well, some apostles are in Alexandria, some are in Mesopotamia, some in Syria, some in Peraea. So there [are] bound to be some inconsistencies because of the distances between us, and [because of] our personalities and our beliefs. I think that out of this will come a collective decision which will represent the majority. But it takes a while to get there.

J: OK. Please move to that point and tell us how it becomes resolved.

P: There is no specific point or day. But the consensus—which has taken us three or four years to resolve from the time I returned—is that a person benefits by accepting Jeshua regardless if [that person] accepts Judaism or not. And as we particularly travel to regions outside of Israel, we have to understand that these people can't practice Judaism. There is no one there who is capable of teaching them and giving them the foundation they need. We do agree, though, that we must do everything possible to get them to stop eating unclean food. At least do that, as part of having Jeshua as the Messiah, and accepting God Almighty as God.

J: All right. Thank you. Were there other things as well that needed attention when you got back?

P: Other things in my private life?

J: Whatever you would like to tell me about.

P: I stay here for a while. It's good to be home and to be able to rest and visit with my many good friends that I had left behind. I share in detail with my fellow Witnesses the experiences that we had, and develop a plan as to how we can continue going out on missions. We share information as to what were the most effective ways of having people accept our teachings

J: Yes. So, you now have the benefit of three-and-a-half years of your experience while being away from Jerusalem?

P: Yes. And I have developed some manuals of how it should be done, as we travel, to best influence the people we come in contact with. Also, I spend a lot of time writing to all these people while I'm in Jerusalem, to stay in touch with them, and encourage them to continue as well as to find out the progress they are making. I tell them the decisions we have made in Jerusalem regarding changing some of the conditions that they were working under. The condition about celibacy of non-married leaders. They agree with me in Jerusalem about those decisions I've made.

J: So that goes in the manual?

P: That becomes an accepted practice as part of the rules that we establish.

J: Who is participating in setting out the rules with you?

P: Peter. Stephen's dead now. Jeshua's brother, James, plays a minor role. John's brother, James, died also. Andrew is involved. Barnabas. Mark is involved. He doesn't have a strong personality, but he is a bright individual.

J: This is the Mark that was traveling with you?

P: Yes. John, Mark, and Bartholomew. Did I say John?

J: Yes, you did.

P: John is very much involved. But Peter is the strongest personality of them.

J: All right. Thank you. You mentioned Stephen being killed. Would you tell us about Stephen being killed? How that came about?

P: Well, Stephen was a very glib individual. He alienated a lot of the Pharisees because he was so adamant [that] Jews who accepted Jeshua discontinue going to the temples, and stop paying tithes. He preached that other Jews would not have salvation if they had not accepted Jeshua. I don't agree with that. I think it's very wrong. You have some very, very righteous, holy, God-loving Jews who, for one reason or another, don't accept Jeshua. To say that these people now would not have salvation if they don't accept him, I feel, is very wrong. Stephen was very whimsical in that attitude, in terms of repeating it over and over again—almost [as if] he [were] taunting them—that they wouldn't receive salvation even though many of these people were very good people. Then he was killed in a riot. He was killed during a demonstration against what he was doing. He appeared several times before the council. There were rumors that he was stoned to death.

J: Yes.

P: But it's my understanding he was killed by a sword during one of the demonstrations that got out of hand.

J: Were you there?

P: No. I wasn't there. This happened during the first few years after Jeshua had reappeared.

J: Were you in Jerusalem at the time he was killed?

P: Yes. But I wasn't involved with the Witnesses at that time. That was before I went to Damascus.

J: One of the stories is that you participated in Stephen's death.

P: No. (Paul gets very angry.)

J: Or stood by and approved of it.

P: That's absolutely false.

J: That's false?

P: No one said that. I have no knowledge of that. That is totally false.

J: Also one of the stories is that Stephen was charged with blasphemy. Would you think that might be accurate?

P: Yes. Blasphemy is using God's name, and saying things which are not consistent with God's law. He was accused of blasphemy by the Sanhedrin because of his being adamant, in particular over their not having salvation from God unless they had Jeshua as their Messiah. He shouldn't have been saying that.

J: All right. Thank you. Can you tell us about James?

P: Which James?

J: You said the other James got killed.

P: John's brother, Zebedee's son, got killed in a riot. I wasn't there. I was traveling then. He got killed in a demonstration, by Romans. When there were riots, the Roman soldiers would try to control them, stop them. They often used their swords, broadside. And sometimes, it could be by accident—maybe it wasn't—sometimes people got injured, or wounded, or killed. Even though, as a rule, they tried to use the broadside of their swords rather than the edges, in dispersing the people.

J: What were the riots about?

P: Some of the people would riot against the preaching. An apostle would be preaching [with] followers around him. Some of the people took exception to what [was being said] and got very angry when they were told they were not going to receive salvation. They would physically attack [the apostle], and then the soldiers would come and separate them.

J: Are there still riots that take place, or has that ceased now that there's a different way of teaching?

P: There's still a lot of animosity, but now there's much less physical activity. The apostles have become more sophisticated in being able to preach the Good Word without alienating other people. But of course, they are still considered a threat by the council. There are still occasional arrests of the leaders to try and persuade them to stop their activities.

J: Will you tell us what you've decided about the missionary plan?

P: Well, we decide geographically where we are going to go, and who's going to go. We agree on the methods we're going to use in terms of accomplishing our objective. We have changed the criteria. We try to select individuals who we feel can be effective, because of their own skills. I still feel I have a lot of energy, even though I'm getting older. I feel fine, so I can still go on the missions, and I prefer doing that. I think I can be more effective teaching and converting away from Judea, where we have pretty much reached our limits in terms of new converts. They have heard us long enough in Judea that they would have converted by now, if they were inclined to accept what we're sharing with them.

J: Thank you. I recall your saying when you were in Damascus that you worked out a plan for having other people manage your business.

P: Yes.

J: And how is that going?

P: It's going fine. I stay in touch with them occasionally by writing. I don't care about that anymore. They are retaining my share on my behalf, but I don't have a need. All my needs are taken care of, so I don't find that an important issue.

J: All right. Thank you. I do have one question about your business, though.

P: Yes.

J: One of the stories is that you were a weaver.

P: A weaver? (Paul laughs.)

J: Yes.

P: No.

J: What do you suppose is the basis for that story?

P: I own weaving establishments that people rent from me. They rent space from me to do weaving, and they sell their product. I have a number of them. But I don't weave. (Paul laughs again.)

J: When I heard that, I said that doesn't fit with the Paul that I know.

P: If one owns a farm, does that mean that he works the farm with his own hands?

J: Yes. That didn't fit. So I am assuming that you're making plans to go out again?

P: Yes.

J: And where is your next territory going to be?

P: I'm going to start again in Cilicia, and I'm not going to take Mark with me. Barnabas wants to take Mark again, and I refuse to have him come with us. So Mark is going to go with Barnabas and I'm going to take somebody else. I'm going to have Silas go with me.

J: Silas? I don't think I've heard of Silas.

P: He's a good man.

J: Is he a new convert, or has he been in the organization for a while?

P: He has been for a while, but he wasn't one of the originals. He came several years after Jeshua left the flesh.

J: OK. Thank you. You said that Barnabas was going to take Mark with him. That's John Mark?

P: Yes.

J: Do they get along well?

P: Yes.

J: Is there a relationship there?

P: There is a very strong friendship. Mark is young. He looks to Barnabas almost like an older brother. Barnabas is very supportive of Mark. He has more confidence in him than I do. Plus, I still never forgave him for what happened in Caesarea.

J: Do you have any other names besides Paul?

P: They refer to me sometimes by where I originally came from, which is Tarsus.

J: So when you're traveling as a Roman citizen you call yourself Paul?

P: My colleagues call me Paul, Paul from Tarsus. When a person comes from another area, they identify him from where he originally came from. And some refer to him as his father's name. They'll say, "Paul, son of," or "John son of so-and-so," in order to identify the person. I refer to myself as Paul of Tarsus rather than my father's name, since they would not know who my father was.

J: All right. We'll leave that then. Thank you. I think this will be a good place for us to stop today. We're talking about just making preparations to go out on your second journey, and you've selected Silas to go with you. I think that we'll begin here next time. Is there anything else you'd like to add about the questions we've been asking today?

P: I do not believe so.

J: All right. Thank you.

Chapter 18

THE BEGINNINGS OF CHRISTIANITY

*O*ur next session took place on August 19. Paul has traveled extensively teaching the Word of Jeshua. During this session, his personality has shown evidence of mellowing and he is now less intense, more philosophical than in his earlier years. We enter this next session with Paul reflecting on his own ways of doing things, reviewing the compromises reached regarding membership, and preparing for his next journey.

J: All right. Move forward then to the next important event.

P: We have a meeting of minds eventually. It has been over three years since I've been back. I've changed my way of doing things. I used to be very, very upset if I didn't get my way, and it was my belief that my way was the only way to do it. Now I have come to realize that, rather than demand that it be done my way, I'm better off trying to use persuasion. I guess that's part of growing older. I felt in the past I used to get my way through intimidation, at the same time

using my wit and my intellect. Now I am more
inclined to do it through persuasion, even though I
still feel the same fire inside of me that tells me that
I'm right and the others are wrong. So it is also with
this issue; I feel it's an extremely important issue. I
partially compromise with them.

J: And what is the compromise that's been reached?

P: We will allow the gentiles to accept Jeshua as their
Messiah, provided that they also accept there is but
one God. And they do not have to become Jews, nor
be circumcised. But they do have to give up eating
unclean food. So with those two conditions, regarding their dietary habits and there being but one God, I
am willing to accept the compromise that gentiles can
become Witnesses to Jeshua.

J: What problems do you foresee in the future? I know
you have a strong feeling that they should become
Jews.

P: I think there will be an alienation by the other Jews
who have accepted Jeshua. In the past, we always had
just one religion. Now we're basically creating another potential group of people who, although they
may have in common the acceptance of Jeshua as
their Messiah, will not have the same foundation and
background of the others who are Jews. This is of
great concern to me—that it will alienate the Jews
who have accepted Jeshua, as well as the people that
are Jews that we're going to try to persuade to accept
Jeshua, because they will not want to identify with
the gentiles.

J: OK. So, we've moved forward in time a couple of
years regarding this issue. We need to go back now to
the place that we started. You were preparing for your
second missionary trip?

P: My second missionary trip? I took many trips. I don't
know if I would think of it as my second trip. I've had

many, many journeys to different lands. Sometimes stopping for just several days. Other times stopping for many, many months. But I do take another trip, another journey after this decision is made.

Paul is in his late forties as he tells me how he prepares to leave Jerusalem and retrace his steps before his return. It has been a three-year stay filled with arguments and controversy. With a compromise having been reached, Paul sets out once again for Derbe, Lystra, Iconium, Antioch (in Pisidia), and Perga. He revisits his past contacts to see how they have carried out his instructions, even though his letter writing has been steady during his stay in Jerusalem.

P: It's during this journey that we're finding a separation taking place now, as I suspected. It was causing a lot of hostility among the Jews—our letting gentiles become Witnesses who are not becoming Jews at the same time. So, this is going to obviously have some ramifications. I'm not sure what the end result is going to be, but I must be careful and not anger those Jews who have accepted Jeshua as the Messiah. At the same time we are bringing many, many more people into our program, into our fold, who are not going to have that common basis with the others who are Jews.

J: Paul, do you continue to receive direct guidance from Jeshua?

P: It's hard to tell. You have an inspiration. Where does the inspiration come from? You speak in front of people and you move them, even though you may not know what you're going to say next. The words are there. I assume that much of my inspiration is of divine origin. Therefore it may be coming from Jeshua. I just do what appears to be natural to me. I don't spend time thinking of that. I know that I am inspired, and, now that you ask me, I have to assume [this] inspiration is coming from Jeshua. But I'm so busy, I really don't spend much time thinking about that. In my efforts to represent him, I don't question its origin.

J: When you are concerned, or when you have one of these difficult problems to solve, do you ask directly through prayer?

P: No. My opinions come very quickly, usually with very little effort. Of course, that's one of the criticisms said about me. And I try to temper that now by giving the appearance of being contemplative and wise, even though I'm basically the same person I was before. It's just a matter of experience and educating myself in terms of being able to reach more people and persuade more people to become part of what we're doing.

J: Is there anything more you'd like to add about prayer or asking for God's help?

P: Well, I fast often. And when I fast, both abstaining from food as well as abstaining from bad thoughts—I mean fasting mentally and physically—I find that I go through a transition. The fasting leads me to feel closer to Jeshua and God, because I'm cleansing my mind and my body. That is a time in which I'm most inclined to pray and look for guidance.

J: Thank you. When we met last time, you seemed to be recalling a time when you were physically attacked and injured. I wondered if you'd go back to a time when your arm was injured? Or maybe there's more than one time.

After the previous session, I noticed Nick's forearm was badly bruised. Nick was surprised as well, for he had no bruise when he arrived at my office. I wondered if Paul

300

had been injured during the time period we were working within, for at one point during the session, he had involuntarily grabbed his arm as if in pain. Remember, Nick is "seeing and experiencing" much more than I know about, for he only responds to the questions I ask him. Therefore, I assumed there must have been an injury he recalled, that I did not ask him about. This time, during the induction, I instructed him that he would not feel any physical pain nor manifest anything in the present-life (Nick's) body, even if he received injuries.

P: I was hit with a rod. Someone struck me. Someone was trying to strike at me, and I put my arm up for protection. I don't remember discussing that.

J: No. We didn't discuss it. I just saw the results.

P: There are many times I've been with groups of people hostile to what I'm saying. Just as there are times I'm with people who are very loving, receptive. Sometimes that hostility becomes physical, and I try to become aware of it before it happens, for I'll become less effective if I'm maimed, and totally ineffective if I'm dead. (Paul laughs. I also began to laugh with Paul.)

So, I try to be on guard when I feel that the hostility appears to be going in the direction of physical violence. And the time that you asked about is a time that it did. But it only lasted for a few moments before it was placed under control.

J: How was it controlled?

P: Others, other people were there. That was not a critical situation. That was just two or three individuals [who] had lost their temper. But others took control of them and held them back. There have been other times when it has been more violent than that. So the particular incident you're asking about was not particularly critical.

J: I think it would be important to round out this record, that we hear about those times when you were injured and persecuted. But I want to say to the body in the present life that, when we're recalling these details, it is not necessary to remember the injury in this physical body, in the present mind.

P: Yes.

J: All right. Would you be willing to tell us about some of the times when you're physically persecuted both by the authorities and by crowds?

P: Yes. I've been thrown in prison several times. There was a time when I was in—oh, that was a little later—but I was in Corinth, and the people there (Paul laughs), many of those people have strange ways there. There was a substantial amount of men mating with men. I say mating, meaning that they were carnally involved. And the morality of the people there—some of the people were much in need of correction. My instincts are to say the things that I feel. And I criticized them tremendously. There was a lot of anger and hostility there. But I am conscious of why they are like they are. I have my opinion very strongly as to why there are men who act like women, and occasionally women that act like men.

J: We would like to hear your opinion of that.

P: It is my belief that occasionally, in the rebirth process, an entity wishes to change genders. And an individual spirit who lived as a female for many, many lifetimes, who then is reborn into this lifetime as a man cannot make that transition in one lifetime. Therefore, many of the effeminate qualities remain, as well as their carnal desire for a man. And I believe this is also true when a woman has previously been a man in many lifetimes. But because it is less acceptable among women, they would be more inclined to be able to hide that, and it would become less obvious within their society. I feel sorry for those individuals. They have my sympathy. But it is not helping them make the transition by allowing them to cater to that perversity.

J: This is a perversity to you?

P: I believe it is. Yes. I believe it's sinful for individuals of the same gender to carnally relate to each other. We must do everything we can to discourage it and help them make the transition so that, as difficult as it is in this lifetime, it will be easier for them in their next lifetime.

J: Did Jeshua talk about this in some of his teachings?

P: No. That's my own opinion.

J: Did this ever come up in any of his teachings that you recall?

P: Jeshua was not a critical person other than with the priesthood. He was very much inclined to love people regardless of who they were, or what status they had in life. I don't, unfortunately, have those same qualities. I'm more inclined to want to change them than to accept them, which is my shortcoming.

J: Thank you. So, in criticizing some of this behavior openly, you were attacked or arrested?

P: No. I was attacked. I wasn't arrested. I was attacked there. I was attacked by those people when I would criticize their morals. I thought that's what you were asking me to talk about—other times in which there were attempts made to physically hurt me.

J: Yes. I was asking that.

P: And that's what I was responding to. Also in Ephesus, which I visited, they have the temples there of the goddess Artemis. There are many people that made their livelihood by selling statues of her and idols of others. And I criticized tremendously the worshipping of idols and statues, and their looking to them as holy relics. I created a problem with those people whose livelihoods were affected by it. That was another time when they acted violently. The Roman soldiers saved me that time, or I might have been seriously injured. They interfered with the efforts to harm me when I brought to their attention that I was a Roman citizen. They protected me. I was there for quite a while—both in Corinth, which is near Athens, as well as in Ephesus, which is in Asia (present-day southeastern Turkey).

J: In Asia?

P: Yes. I stayed there quite a while until (Paul laughs), until I knew it was better for me to leave.

J: Why was it better for you to leave?

P: I was very successful in healing there; people were converting and accepting Jeshua. There were many, many people. But I also had alienated a lot of people, too. Sometimes it's good, when people reach a certain point of alienation, to leave and get away from there, and give them an opportunity to release their anger and hostility by virtue of time.

J: In these travels, are you traveling alone or do you still have a ...

P: No. I have people with me. I don't have Barnabas with me any longer, nor Mark.

J: I remember they went together.

P: They went off together and, yes, I didn't want Mark to come with me. So Barnabas and he went to Alexandria, Egypt, and then to Cyprus. I have with me Silas, and then my very dear friend, whom I dearly love, young Timothy. Yes, he joined me too.

J: Tell us about Timothy.

P: Well, his mother is a Jewess. His father is Greek, and he was not born a Jew. But he accepted Judaism when he accepted the Messiah, and also was circumcised. He is a wonderful young man who is tremendously helpful in my endeavors.

J: Have the others also been attacked or injured at times?

P: Well, only when they're around me. (Paul laughs.)

J: Paul, do you sometimes walk into situations without being as cautious as you might be?

P: Oh, I know what to anticipate. What I do is in spite of the potential response. So, it's not a question of naiveness. It's more a question of willingness to move on in spite of the circumstances. You know, I have many friends in these places. And many of these places I'm going to, I've been before. So it doesn't bother me. The controversy doesn't bother me.

J: Are there any other times when you are attacked or in danger that you'd like to share with me today?

P: Well, I was in great danger when I was arrested and held in captivity for a while in Jerusalem and then was sent to be judged in Caesarea. This was when I was older.

J: Tell me about that.

P: I was in Jerusalem after one of my long trips. I thought I would not travel any longer. I thought I had traveled enough, perhaps, and I had some very serious accusations brought against me. The accusations were accurate. I was doing that of which I was accused. But I did not feel it was wrong. I was taking those [who] we now call Christians, who've accepted Jeshua, but have not accepted Judaism—I was taking them into the temple. It is my feeling there is only one God, and Jeshua is our Messiah. And as long as they had accepted the Almighty God and Jeshua, [I felt] they were entitled to the use of the temples also. The Sanhedrin got extremely angry at me, as did many, many of the Jews who felt I was defiling the temple by bringing these gentiles, who were uncircumcised and were not Jews, into the temple. The mobs—I call them mobs—these people were very,

very angry and shouting and yelling. I tried to reason with them. And I did well in reasoning with them until I got to the point where I tried to justify that these people (Christians) were entitled to use the temples. Then they got out of control again. I was taken into protection, as well as custody by the Roman soldiers. They knew I was a Roman citizen. I had showed them evidence of that previously. And as I understand it, there was a plot to kill me. First I went before the Sanhedrin and gave my arguments. Some of them agreed with me, but most of them didn't. They were arguing among themselves. Then I went back into custody of the Roman soldiers who took me from there. Then I was told that a group of fanatics had said that they were going to kill me, and they had notified the Romans that the Sanhedrin council wanted to visit with me again. They were going to kill me on my way back to the council. The Roman soldiers had discovered this plot. So instead, they decided to send me away from Jerusalem to Caesarea where the governor of Israel was now living. So, under armed guard, we went to Caesarea. There I was placed under custody. I wasn't placed in a prison. I was placed in a home, which I enjoyed. Had a wonderful view overlooking the sea. Felix was governor. I met with him a number of times. Representatives came from Jerusalem—high priest Anonus, his chief council Tertulus and others—came to Caesarea and made their accusations against me to Felix and his advisors. I presented my position to Felix and his advisors. He said he would make a decision. But he didn't. There was a change of governors, and the new governor, Festus, came into power. He also wanted to have information so he could make a decision. Many, many months went by. I was there for quite a while. Festus went to Jerusalem where he heard the charges against me again, directly. Then he returned. He eventually asked me if I would go to Jerusalem, and be tried there, and be judged in Jerusalem. I said no. I am a Roman citizen. The only ones that had the right to try me would be Roman judges, under the jurisdiction of the emperor.

J: The Emperor Caesar?

P: No. Not Caesar. I think Claudius was emperor.

J: The Emperor Claudius?

P: Well, Caesar Claudius, if you want to call him that. No. Claudius was killed by his wife, they told me. Tiberius had died a few years ago. I think it might have been Claudius then. They told me that I would be sent to Rome along with other people that were held by the Romans for other reasons, to be tried. As I indicated, I was not a prisoner. But I could not leave the area. I was confined to the area. But I had the freedom to move around the area. And I enjoyed Caesarea, which is where I had visited when I first came here many, many years ago as a young boy. This is one of the places I had stopped. And I have friends in Caesarea.

J: Thank you. Go on.

P: Eventually there were enough people to be taken to Rome to justify assigning a ship. And we left. The weather was hot. We sailed not too far from the coastline so we could stop for provisions. After we got past ... oh, I think it was after we passed Cyprus. As we sailed between Cyprus and the coastline north of Cyprus, we had some terrible, terrible storms. We all thought we were going to die. Some of us were so sick we wanted to die. The storms were just terrible and we had to abandon ship. I believe it was near Crete that we abandoned ship and swam for shore.

J: You swam to shore?

P: Well, washed ashore. We were hanging onto things. Some of the people didn't make it. There were some people experienced with the sea who said we shouldn't have been sailing at that time. And then we found a ship, a Roman ship that had come from Alexandria. They took us on board to continue our journey. We stopped at Malta, went on to Sicily, stopped in Syracuse, then went through the straits, along the coastline—the western coastline—stopped along the way several places, but finally made it to Rome. It was a terrible journey. I never want to go on the sea again (Paul laughs).

J: It sounds like a terrible journey. There are a couple of stories I'd like to ask you about.

P: Yes.

J: One was a story about a snakebite.

P: What's that?

J: Do you remember a story about a snake biting you?

P: What about the snake biting me?

J: They talk about when you were making a fire and you'd gathered a bundle of sticks and a snake came out ...

P: Yes.

J: ... and hung on your hand and bit you. Some thought that you would die, that it was a judgment that you would die.

P: Yes.

J: But you didn't.

P: It didn't hang on my hand. It bit my hand. I remember I was sick for a few days. But I recovered. And you say some people said that it was a curse on me?

J: Someone said, "No doubt this man is a murderer. Though he has escaped from the sea, justice has not allowed him to live." But then when you did live, they decided that you were a god.

P: (Paul laughs.) Well, I don't recall their saying that to my face. And I don't recall being called a god. But I was pretty sick for a while. But I survived it.

J: This is how some of the stories get told and retold.

P: I don't know. I hadn't heard that story. But I remember the snakebite. I don't have many years left in me anyway at this stage. A lot of the fire has calmed down.

J: Before we leave this very important time that you spend in Caesarea, I wonder if you'd talk about some of the things that happened with Festus?

P: Yes. I presented my case to him several different times as well as to other dignitaries [who] would be passing through Caesarea, [and] who wanted to meet me. And I was a very persuasive person. They didn't feel I did anything justifying harm coming to me. It was pretty well recognized that if they sent me back to Jerusalem, I would be tried by people and judged by people who might be partial towards the position of my accusers. And that was why they let me stay in Caesarea so long before they sent me to Rome. They sent me to Rome because I had requested to go to Rome if they were going to judge me and try me. They were getting tremendous pressure from the authorities in Jerusalem. When you're well-known, there are many people who want to meet you, whether they agree with your position or disagree with it, so they can tell others they met you. I found, usually, I could find favor with them even if they didn't accept what I believed in. I could still have them like me as a person and not want to see harm come to me. That was the situation with Festus as well as with Felix before him and their advisors.

J: Did you meet with the king there?

P: Yes, and his wife.

J: And what was their position?

P: [As] I described to you. They were sympathetic to my position and felt there wasn't justification for any harm coming to me.

J: How long were you in Caesarea altogether?

P: Oh, I think I was there two years—I'd say a little over two years.

J: Did any of the apostles come and visit you?

P: Yes. Phillip didn't live very far from there. So Phillip used to visit with me, and other apostles also. Barnabas came, as well as Mark, who had matured tremendously. Mark was no longer the young Mark that I was critical of. He had done nicely for himself since then. And I have many friends that come visit with me. I actually enjoyed my stay in Caesarea. I wrote many, many letters while I was there to friends that I had developed throughout all my journeys.

J: Did others write about that time also?

P: I know that Mark wrote about the life of Jeshua while he was visiting in Rome. That was probably about twenty-five or twenty-six years after Jeshua had left earth in the flesh. And Matthew, years later, also wrote his perspective on the life of Jeshua. But many of our people, many of our colleagues have died and are no longer with us. And I sorrow for their company. Even though I didn't agree with them all the time—and in the beginning I didn't accept them—as years went by I truly developed a brotherly love for them, and sorrow for their having passed.

J: Who are you thinking about?

P: Peter is gone. James—not Jeshua's brother James, the other James, John's brother—and others. Bartholomew and others have passed away from afflictions that take us as we experience the last years of our lives. And some died in violence.

J: Did you have occasion to read any of the accounts of Mark or Matthew? Their recollections of Jeshua?

P: Yes. I did. I read some of them. Mark wrote with the help of John and some of the other apostles because he was only a boy when Jeshua lived on earth. He was probably about eight or nine years old when Jeshua left.

J: On what is he basing his writing?

P: On what he's been told by the others. Years can change your memories, but others wrote also.

J: Did you feel that those accounts were accurate or reflected the way you knew Jeshua?

P: I believe some of those accounts were the perception of those individuals who either knew him, or that those who knew him contributed to the person who was writing it. And some of them might have been accurate as far as the events, but not in terms of the philosophy that existed.

J: You feel that the philosophy was not represented accurately?

P: Some of the things that I objected to were either not understood, or were omitted, or were given a different presentation in the writings. I don't say they did it dishonestly. They did it as they perceived the events happening. But I don't think that one who is writing the accounts would necessarily want to talk about some of the acts that I thought were in violation of the laws of God, that were being done in the name of God. Particularly in the early parts, after Jeshua's reappearance, when they were recruiting others.

J: Thank you. I'd like to take the opportunity sometime to read to you some of the translations that have come down and have you comment on them. We'll do that another time, perhaps?

P: That would be fine.

J: So I interrupted your telling us about your journey to Rome. Please continue.

P: Well, as I said, after we stopped for provisions in Syracuse, we proceeded going north along the coastline. We would stop along the way until we got as far north as we wanted to go on the sea, and then from there we went inland until we got to Rome.

J: Have you been to Rome before? Is this your first ...

P: This was my first time in Rome.

J: And are there Christians here by now?

P: Oh, yes. Many Christians.

J: Who brought the Good News to Rome?

P: A number of us. People had been here before, and
     some had been persecuted tremendously in their ef-
     forts. We had many, many [who] gave up their lives.
     Peter had been here, and he died in Rome.

J: Peter died in Rome?

P: Yes. And Mark had been here, and John had visited
     here also. Many of them had been here. They had
     been very, very critical of Roman lifestyle. I have
     learned through the years that you do not gain by crit-
     icizing the pleasures of others. All you do is create
     enemies when you try to take away their pleasures or
     tell them they're not entitled to their pleasures. It is
     easier to deal with the mind, the intellect than how
     people recreate and enjoy themselves.

J: How do you feel about being here in Rome?

P: I enjoy it. I rented quarters here. I have many people
     come to visit me. And I do not get into controversy
     with the Roman authorities. They allow me to spend
     my days as I wish, for I no longer (Paul laughs), I no
     longer am considered a troublemaker. I preach and
     continue to tell the people how I feel. But most of
     them are my friends who come visit with me, who
     have already accepted Jeshua.

J: Were you still under arrest at this time?

P: I don't know if you'd call it arrest. I'm told to stay in
     Rome and not to travel. But it would be like telling
     someone who is lame in their legs that they can't
     dance anymore. I have no desire to travel. I enjoy my
     peace. I write a lot still to those who I have met on
     my journeys. And I enjoy the companionship of my

J: friends. I cannot leave Rome, so I will spend the rest of my time here.

J: The rest of your time here?

P: The rest of what little time I have left on earth, I will spend in this lifetime here.

J: So you die in Rome?

P: Yes.

J: We won't ask you about that today. We'll save that for another time. Would you tell us about your trial? Would you be willing to do that?

P: I never had a formal trial. I presented my position at different times to those who were interested in hearing it. But my accusers never really came here to make their charges against me. Perhaps they were just happy to have me out of the country, out of Judea, or out of Israel. So I never had a formal judgment, if that's what you mean. And I really don't think of myself as having been under arrest. I was not held in captivity such as a prison. I was given freedom to live as a citizen in that community as long as I did not physically travel to another community. I was not treated as an arrested person. I was treated more like a celebrity, a captive celebrity.

J: Well, you said you didn't have a formal trial. What informally took place?

P: There wasn't an environment in which a verdict of guilt could have been placed against me that could have brought penalties to me. It was more of my presenting my positions. There was not going to be a formal decision made against my positions as to whether I was right or wrong. Have you been told differently?

J: No. What the scholars have said is that we don't know about his trial. It's not mentioned, but ...

P: Well, how could you envision the Jerusalem accusers traveling all the way to Rome? And I'm a Roman citizen. They're going to charge me with desecrating the

313

J: temples in Jerusalem? And expect to get sympathy from Roman judges?

J: It seems that you were in a good place, a strong position.

P: That was why I had said that I would not be tried in Jerusalem. A Roman tribunal is not going to find judgment against a Roman citizen in favor of an occupied group of religious zealots from another country. So I never had a formal trial.

J: What were the strongest Jewish sects in Rome? Were there Jews in Rome?

P: There were some Jews in Rome, but those who accepted Jeshua in Rome were gentiles. Very few Jews had. Most of the Christians in Rome were gentiles. The number of Jewish Christians would have been insignificant compared to the number of heathens who had accepted Jeshua. Many of them were underprivileged people, poor people who were looking for comfort in the Word, in the Good News that we brought them, because their lives were under strain. But again, that was before I came. I didn't have the energy any longer to do conversion. I mostly dealt with those who had already accepted the Word.

J: How old are you now?

P: In my sixties. I traveled for many years, and I have done my best to bring Jeshua to the lives of as many people as I could. And hopefully they in turn will share it with other people.

J: Who are the strongest leaders now in your eyes?

P: Oh, there are new people who are younger. They are spread throughout the Roman Empire: Asia, Mesopotamia, Greece, the islands. They're all converts. They're all new Messengers, new Witnesses to Jeshua. And they fall into three completely different categories now. You have those who are Jews who accepted Jeshua, you have those who were heathens that accepted Judaism and Jeshua, and now you have the Christians who did not accept Judaism, but have Jeshua as their Messiah, and believe in one God. So they are splintered. There is a lot separating the Jews who have accepted Jeshua from the Christians who did not accept Judaism.

J: Are you thinking now that it would have been better if the early apostles had followed your advice? That everyone be converted to Judaism first?

P: That was idealistic.

J: It was idealistic?

P: There would have been so many people who wouldn't have had the benefit of Jeshua as a Messiah if we had retained that restriction. There are more gentiles now who have Jeshua as a Messiah who have not accepted Judaism than there are those original Jews who have accepted Jeshua as the Messiah. I do question what is going to happen in time, since they are so far apart in the foundation of their belief system. The important thing is that there are many people who used to pray to a lemon tree who now have Jeshua as a savior.

J: You used that term "pray to a lemon tree" before. What does that mean?

P: It's a saying that we have. That's all.

J: What people are you describing when you talk about those who pray to a lemon tree?

P: Oh, we joked about those who did not believe in God, and while we pray to God they pray to a lemon tree.

J: Does that mean they worship nature?

P: No. It doesn't. It just meant that a tree cannot answer their prayers. All a lemon tree can give them is sour fruit to eat as opposed to the wonderful blessings that we get from our beliefs in the Almighty God and in Jeshua.

J: So, it seems to me as we're talking that this is a time when you've been reflecting on your work?

315

P: Yes. I have ever since I left Jerusalem, while I was in Caesarea as well as now. I have peace and substantial time to reflect, to write, and not have the requirement of energy that I had to put out when I was journeying from one place to another, meeting new people, and repeatedly having to prove myself. I enjoyed that. I reflect back that those were wonderful, wonderful years. But, as time moved on, it was no longer my role.

J: To whom will you be passing on your major responsibilities?

P: Well, Timothy is my beloved assistant. So if there were one individual ... but there isn't one. There are many, many, many people who now must take the seeds and continue to sow them and continue our work. It's going to be difficult because you can stop at Macedonia and listen to the people there, whom you left behind, what they are saying and practicing. And then you can go to Antioch, where you gave exactly the same messages and find that they are practicing differently than the ones in Macedonia. And that is true throughout, whether you go to Perga or Lystra. It doesn't make a difference. They all have their own slight interpretations. The ones that I have greatest concern for are the ones [who] still pray to idols who have accepted Jeshua and God Almighty, yet still have retained some of their old practices which are in conflict with our belief system.

J: Where is that most common?

P: In those lands which had not been exposed to Judaic law—Greece, Asia, up and down the coasts. All those places outside Judea, outside of Israel. They didn't have the same foundation as the Jews in Israel who have accepted Jeshua as the Messiah. So they had to plant their own roots before the tree could grow. And in many cases, the branches of the trees are coming out differently.

J: What else would you like us to know about your thinking right now?

P: I think that Jeshua's messages of love and being at one with God—recognizing that part of God that is within all of us, and allowing it to nurture itself—are the ones that will prevail, as long as the spirit of men continue, no matter what hardships they are exposed to. For it is so simple, yet so beautiful. So I'm pleased with the role that I've had to play in being a part of that.

J: All right. Thank you. What's concerning me is that in writing your story, Paul, we want to be certain we are asking about the most important of your journeys and the most important of your adventures.

P: Most important?

J: Things that happened to you.

P: The most important journey I ever took was from Jerusalem to Damascus when I was, I believe, thirty-five years old, when Jeshua appeared to me. It was outside of Damascus. That was my most important journey.

       I believe my second most important journey was the first long journey I took when I went from Jerusalem to Antioch and around Laodicea. I established the first series of appointments, of individuals who would then become the leaders of the church in those areas. I made some major decisions regarding the profile of the leaders and began to establish the foundation of how we were going to move ahead in these areas in sharing the Good News.

317

Chapter 19

PAUL'S FINAL DAYS

Our final session took place on August 26, 1991. Once we had proceeded beyond the traumatic and intense period representing the incarceration and crucifixion of Jesus, we had returned to weekly sessions. In the last session, representing the later years, we now had come full circle in the lifetime of Paul. From the young, enthusiastic, bright nine-year-old whom we met in the April 11 session, we find ourselves four-and-a-half months later hearing the words of wisdom of a philosophical, loving and humorous Paul, approximately at age sixty-two.

J: And, as you get your bearings, look around and see with your eyes, hear with your ears, feel and know. And now tell us what's going on today.
P: Just a quiet day. I'm in my little garden, the little house I live in, sitting on a bench.
J: Do you spend much time here, in your garden?
P: I spend a lot of time. Yes.
J: Do you spend it here alone, or do others come and sit with you here, too?

P: Oh, I have many people, many friends visit me and sit with me here when the weather is nice.

J: And what are you thinking about today?

P: I think of the past. They say that when most of your thoughts are of the past that means you do not have very much future left. And my thoughts are mostly of the past. Places I've been. Things that I did.

J: Are you expecting any visitors today?

P: I'm sure that I'll have some visitors. It's very informal. My friends come and go as they choose, which is the way I like it, too. So I always am pleasantly surprised when they show up.

J: Is the organization still called the Witnesses, or has it been renamed now?

P: We're now called Christians.

J: Who came up with that idea?

P: When we decided to allow gentiles to become Witnesses for Jeshua, a lot of our new Witnesses were non-Jews. We decided to call them by a name which would encompass both the Jews and the non-Jews.

  The name "Christos" evolved to "Christians"— the Christ name. That was probably, maybe about twenty years ago. No, maybe about fifteen years ago.

J: I remember that difficult period of time when you were deciding about forgoing the need to convert to Judaism first in order to become a follower.

P: Yes. That happened when I was on one of my journeys. I think it was towards the end of my second journey. I went back to Jerusalem to participate in that decision, and it was after that we began calling our followers Christians.

J: And do you consider yourself a Christian?

P: I consider everybody that has accepted Jeshua as their savior a Christian, whether they are Jews or whether they previously were gentiles.

J: Have you forgone your Jewish traditions then?

P: Oh, no. I'm still a Jew. The Jews that have accepted Jeshua are Christian Jews. And then you have those who are Christians who are not Jews.

J: Have there been problems with that?

P: Not among the Christians. Just among those Jews who didn't accept Jeshua as the Messiah.

J: So there were many who were very critical and even called Jeshua a blasphemer. Have those attitudes changed, or are there still some who say that?

P: If they have accusations now, they don't have them against Jeshua. They have them against those of us who have gone out and taught the Word and brought the Good News to other people. Jeshua has been gone now for almost thirty years. So the criticism is towards those of us who continued his work rather than to him. And they don't call us blasphemers.

J: What do they call you?

P: (Paul laughs.) When you say "they," who do you mean?

J: The critics.

P: The fundamental Jews who didn't accept Jeshua feel we have wronged Judaism by allowing non-Jews to participate in some of the rituals when we've tried to take them into the temples. We had many problems there. The places where we came under attack were where we were a threat to the authorities, in the beliefs that existed there. It might not have been only in Judea. You see, we also traveled to places where Judaism wasn't prevalent. Other belief systems were being challenged and threatened. Belief in idols. And some of the places we went to, they believed in a number of different gods and goddesses. So it wasn't just some of the Judaic people [who] were not in agreement with what we are doing. It depended on where we were. But I haven't been home for a long time now. I haven't been in Jerusalem for quite a few years now.

J: Where's the seat of the Christian movement now, headquartered if you will?

P: It's still in Jerusalem, but it's scattered now. Phillip has been very, very strong in the area north of Jerusalem, the regions north. And we are strong, based on our leadership there. John spends a lot of his time now in Ephesus. So it's scattered, depending on the strength of the people who are in charge in those areas.

J: I have some general questions for you today as you are sitting here in your garden.

P: Yes.

J: Some of the stories that were handed down say that you have ... How do I put this? Are you familiar with the story of the Garden of Eden and the concept of original sin regarding Adam and Eve?

P: Yes.

J: All right. Some say that you have said that only the woman was guilty, and that the man was innocent.

P: You're asking for my interpretation of Adam and Eve?

J: Yes.

P: I've never taken them literally. Most educated people don't.

J: I see.

P: So that's not accurate. I don't recall ever ... well, how do you make judgment on a myth?

J: What do you think the purpose of the fairy tale was? The myth taught some kind of lesson?

P: First of all, we don't know who made up those myths. They were probably by many different people throughout the ages, and to ascribe one motive to all of those fairy tales would not make sense. You would have to talk about a specific fairy tale and even then, you'd be guessing, unless you knew the motive of the person who wrote it and the time that it was written.

We don't have that information. It's an accumulation of stories over many, many years. And the stories of evil versus good usually are found in almost all the religious writings.

J: Yes.

P: Which they've told through anecdotes. So, in Adam and Eve, I would assume the message is [that] we are responsible for our actions. And the parable there is—they disobeyed the word of God and as a result of that they were punished. They had to experience the consequences of their acts.

J: The lesson that you would have us consider here is that we're responsible for the decisions which we make? We're responsible for our actions?

P: I believe that is accurate. And I believe that is true regarding all activities, whether they be ones in which the participants received rewards or whether they received punishments. They are actual stories telling us how we're affected by our actions. That every action has a future response from it.

J: In this story, Eve is characterized as having tempted Adam, and you are attributed with having interpreted that as women tempt men—that men have to be strong and ward off that temptation.

P: You're saying I'm attributed to that? In reference specifically to the Adam and Eve story, or just in general?

J: Well, in reference to the Adam and Eve story and in general. Yes, both.

P: Well, let's forget the Adam and Eve story. (Paul says this in good humor.)

J: All right.

P: There's no truth to that. I believe that personalities of individuals and the strength of their character will determine who is the influencer and who is the one being influenced, and it has nothing to do with gender. I've met many strong women and men in my lifetime. And I've never separated their strengths or weaknesses by gender, as opposed to their individual personalities. The only exception to that is that, traditionally speaking, there are certain positions that men have done better in our society and certain positions that women have been better. I would imagine that is more of a function of tradition rather than because of their having an advantage as a result of their gender.

J: I see.

P: Certain positions women can't hold because of the laws of nature, which gave them less physical strength and require them to carry a newborn. So society has adjusted itself, taking the laws of nature into consideration.

J: It has also been claimed that you disliked women. Now you're saying that isn't true at all. Can you name some of the women you've known through the years who have been your friends or whom you've admired?

P: Well, there are many women I've admired during my lifetime, and, if you're talking platonically, I have just as many women friends as I do men.

J: You have just as many women friends as men?

P: Yes. As I traveled throughout the lands in my journeys, many of the friends I left behind are women as well as men. No. Perhaps, that's not true. I was exposed to more men than I was women in those travels. But I did not separate their ability to become friends with me based on their gender. And I never sided with a man over a woman based on gender. Such as in a case with Vesta and the disagreements there that were happening. But anyway, in my private life, when I was younger, there were a number of women that I was close in heart to. And as I got older and traveled, I wasn't able to be in one place long enough, or wanted to be involved to where there became bonds. The woman that I came closest to marrying was Leah, when I was living in Jerusalem, prior to my conversion, when I was in my middle thirties. Does that answer your question? (It should be explained that Paul is talking about his conversion to becoming a member of the Witnesses, and not a change in his belief system.)

J: Yes. I think we'll have more questions about men and women because this has become a very important issue. I'd love to hear more about Leah if you would care to tell me more.

P: Well, that was so many years ago. There's nothing to tell. I just was saying she was the one that I came closest to being contracted to.

J: And the decision not to marry was yours, was it?

P: Yes.

J: And why was that?

P: I didn't feel a strong enough commitment towards her. And it was the right decision.

J: Why is that?

P: I could not have been a good husband to her all these years while I've been traveling so much. All the marriages of those of us who were apostles, who did a lot of traveling, were fragile at best because of the traveling we did.

J: Yes, I can imagine, if the husband is gone for weeks and months at a time.

P: There was a danger, too.

J: Danger?

P: Some of my colleagues were in danger, and some of them lost their lives.

J: Yes. We've talked some about that. One of the other stories is that you admired certain Roman gods that had voluntarily castrated themselves.

P: Roman gods that have castrated themselves?

J: Yes.

P: (Paul laughs.)

J: Now, I've not been able to find this in writing, but someone has said that Jesus recommended castration as a way to get to the higher kingdom of God.

P: Recommended castration? That is totally absurd. How could Roman gods, fictitious gods, castrate themselves? The Roman gods weren't taken seriously. Well, I guess they might have been by some of the Romans, but, even then I'm not sure. Roman gods castrating themselves? Are you under the impression that the gods were mortals?

J: No. I'm not under that impression. I also think they're stories.

P: Did I understand you to ask did Jeshua believe that men could castrate themselves and become closer to God?

J: One story is that he recommended that one volunteer become castrated for the kingdom of heaven's sake.

P: No. There would be jokes sometimes about individuals who are doing circumcision that were not very adept with their tools. But, I've never heard of anybody suggesting castration brings you closer to God. (Paul is laughing.)

J: Well, as you can see, things can become quite distorted over the years. Thank you for clearing that up. We talked much earlier about the difficulties the early Church experienced with women holding positions and that the sexual affairs were a problem. And you explained that your decision was that women would not hold offices, to avoid that complication.

P: Yes.

J: I think that's been misinterpreted as your hating women or your not wanting women in the Church, or your being against women.

P: Well, that's not accurate. My decision was based on prudence. We had too many incidents those first few years. And I made the decision based on what I felt was in the best interests of what we were trying to accomplish. It wasn't designed to discriminate against the women. It was just being practical in trying to solve some problems that had arisen.

J: So we'll be certain that is very clear as we retell this.

P: Some sects of the Jewish religion allowed women to hold higher positions than other sects did. My personal religious training had women having certain roles and men having other roles, and the women had lesser roles. But that was part of my religious training. That was the way the situation existed in the hierarchy, when I originally became part of the spreading of the Good News, and bringing people into our belief system, with Jeshua providing them salvation through their belief and love in him. I did not have any preconceived ideas that women should have a lesser role than men. It was only as a result of a number of incidents that I concluded it would be best to do it that way.

J: Are we now calling the Christians a religion?

P: Yes. And some of the Christians are Jews, and some (of the Christians) are gentiles. And as a result of that, they also practice the religion somewhat differently. But they have two common beliefs, which are that there is but one God, and that Jeshua is the Messiah, and through him we can receive salvation.

J: Does that feel comfortable to you that the practice of Christianity can be through one's own culture, and that it still works? For instance, if you converted someone who was ...

P: I understand your question.

J: OK.

P: And the answer to your question is no. I have strong dissent with those cultures which I consider immoral or unclean. And it would have been my preference, if

336

it had been possible, to allow all Christians to also accept Judaism. And for all the men to be circumcised, and for people to eat clean food. But it didn't happen that way, and it couldn't happen. But I still prefer, that even in the absence of their being Jews, that the gentile Christians would still honor some of the laws regarding cleanliness as well as high morals that are inbred in the Judaic religion.

J: OK. Were there then areas of the world to which you decided not to go to teach?

P: Well, when I was younger there were some areas that we felt were a waste of time trying to teach the Good Word and have the people accept it. So, there were some areas, yes, in which we were not successful, and so we decided to spend our time elsewhere. And of course in every area that we did go, we experienced different degrees of success and different degrees of acceptance.

J: Did you ever get to Asia?

P: Can you be more specific when you say Asia?

J: I'll try to give you a name: Bisnia, or Mycea, or Anatolia, or Byzantium? Are any of those familiar names to you?

P: I believe they are. I know the names. I can't recall if I personally, or some of my colleagues, have been there. But I know the names of two or three of those places. When we traveled, sometimes the hostility would be so strong we would immediately leave a place without stopping and staying. Other places, it might have been language barriers or custom barriers that influenced our staying or not staying. A lot of times it was influenced by the strength of the individual who was doing the missionary work.

J: The reason I'm asking is that some of the writing that Luke did indicates that you went through the regions of Phrygia and Galatia.

P: Galatia, yes.

J: That the spirit of Jesus asked you not to go farther.

P: Well ...

J: Would you interpret what you think Luke meant?

P: And as I indicated a little while ago, Galatia was one of them. If we went to places where we felt that we were not going to be well-received, then we would move on, feeling our time could be better spent elsewhere. And that area that you're referring to was one which we did not feel we were going to receive any kind of reception to justify our stopping there. So we decided not to go any further into that area, which would have been north. I believe northeast of the area that we'd already established ourselves.

J: All right. That clarifies that. Thank you. Then, was Luke editorializing when he wrote that the spirit of Jesus ordered you not to go any farther?

P: If one were to say that everything we do is inspired by God, then one could also say the things we do not do were as a result of lacking inspiration from God. I think that's just a matter of how one wishes to philosophize actions and motivations. There were physical and intellectual reasons at the time that prompted us to travel one place as opposed to another.

J: All right. Thank you. That's all the questions I have today. I'm wondering if we can then move forward to the next events in your life?

P: Well, my life is pretty uneventful at this stage. I spend a good deal of my time writing, which has become more difficult for me as a result of my eyesight not being as good as it used to be, and with friends visiting me. I don't go out anymore. There is, in Rome, a lot of anger in some circles towards the Christians, for they are being very critical of the lifestyle of the Romans. There are some members of our beliefs who are very extreme, and feel that if you haven't accepted our beliefs you cannot be received by God when you pass over from this lifetime. Of course many of those who do not accept our belief system don't have the same religious foundations we do regarding being reborn. And I think there's danger in being too critical about the Romans, particularly when you are living in their environment, in their society. But the ones who do that are the ones that are at the other end of the social spectrum and who resent the lifestyle and the wealth that some of those in Rome enjoy.

J: So, there's animosity created as a result of this?

P: Yes, a tremendous amount of animosity. The Romans, those who were in Judea as well as in Rome, are usually tolerant towards others. They don't ask you to believe in what they believe in. Of course, their beliefs are very surface beliefs, too. I mean, they're more interested in material life, and they're not as philosophical as the Greeks. Although, they have some wonderful writers and poets. The Romans, though, are very tolerant. But I believe there are some of the new Christians who are pushing them very hard and creating some animosities towards us as a result of their actions and behavior.

J: Can you tell us of an incident?

P: There are many incidents. There's a tremendous freedom of expression here, much more so than there was in Judea. And you must be careful taunting people in power, for every person has their limits. When they taunt these people and demonstrate against them, they're creating a serious situation. For it then has repercussions towards all the Christians. For years the Romans tolerated Jews living in Rome, and there wasn't any problem. But there are some problems now with the Christians as a result of those who are so vocal, who are being so critical of Roman lifestyle and Roman beliefs.

J: Has anyone been hurt or killed as a result? Or you just feel the tension growing here?

P: There's tension growing. I don't know of anyone who's been killed, although [there have been] some cases where the soldiers were sent to control, or to remove some of the people who were demonstrating. And when they have resisted, there have been cases of people getting injured during the resistance. I believe you should try to influence people to accept your beliefs. But don't be critical of them if they don't.

J: Please go on.

P: Whether they believe in our God or not, doesn't alter the fact that the law of nature was created by the laws of God. They are just as much a part of it. And they will be judged based on how they live their lives, even if they choose to accept some other belief system. It will be much more difficult for them than otherwise. But that is their choice, just as we must realize there are many Jews who haven't accepted Jeshua. They still are good Jews and lead a good life. They would have received salvation easier through Jeshua. But it does not mean that they won't still receive salvation.

J: This is a very important message you have here. It seems very hard for people to understand that or to practice it.

P: It has always been that way. Prior to Jeshua there were those who claimed that you could only have God through their teachings. Of course, that's one of the things that Jeshua objected to, the way Judaism was being taught in the temples. So now you have the other situation where there are those who are saying that you can only have God through Jeshua. And I believe that's also an extreme position.

J: You're saying it makes it easier?

P: Yes. It makes it tremendously easier. Just as i̶
      sick. To be given the appropriate medicines to heal
      them, they will be healed faster as opposed to not
      having those medicines. But it doesn't mean that they
      still cannot be healed. Perhaps the healing process
      will just take much longer.

J: Thank you. That makes it easier to understand when
      you teach it that way. Some people in my day would
      probably be in a category similar to the type you were
      describing, who would tell people how to live their
      lives and judge them harshly when they don't change.

P: My belief is that of Jeshua's. We don't have the right
      to judge others. We all judge ourselves at the proper
      time when we pass through this plane to the other.
      There will be others that will help us evaluate our-
      selves. Jeshua was very, very careful in believing that
      we should not judge others, that we should concern
      ourselves with our own lives. For he believed that
      how you conduct yourself in your life is how others
      will conduct themselves towards you. A person who
      acts in anger towards one person may act with love
      towards another, both as a result of how that other
      person has portrayed himself to that individual. Did
      you understand what I just said?

J: Yes. Yes. Let me say it back to you and you see if I do
      understand it. And that is that I receive back the kind
      of treatment that I give to others?

P: But I'm saying, let us speak of the other person. The
      other may act differently towards [us or another indi-
      vidual] because of the love, or lack of love, that indi-
      vidual is giving to the other. And it doesn't mean that
      the other is either good or bad. It means that he or she
      is just reacting to that which is given to them by us.

J: Which means we're not able to judge their behavior
      because we don't know how they have been treated.

P: It means that we can't judge their behavior because *we're* responsible for their behavior. They're responding to us.

J: They're responding to us.

P: Therefore we should judge ourselves and not them.

J: All right. Now I see. If someone responds to me in anger, I need to look at what I did to create that anger coming towards me?

P: Yes.

J: All right. So I'm accountable for the way I'm treated?

P: Yes. That's right.

J: Thank you. Are your eyes a problem now for you? Have your eyes been injured?

P: No.

J: Or is this a result of your getting older?

P: (Paul laughs.) I am old. And my eyes can't see things up close like they used to. So I have trouble writing like I used to. And reading. I need help if what I'm reading is small. I have to have someone else read it for me.

J: Is there one particular person who reads to you?

P: Oh, I don't discriminate. I'll let anybody read for me.

J: And people also write for you, or are you writing?

P: No. I do my own writing. I write to a lot of people, to places that I've been in the past.

J: You're keeping in touch?

P: If they respond to me, then I'll continue to write to them. But it takes so much time to have it sent from one place to the other, and then sometimes it may not have been successful in getting there at all. It creates certain voids in your life and in your heart. And you try to make up for it by filling them with those that you can stay in contact with.

J: One of the things I've noticed as I've gotten to know you, is that you have a very big heart. A very warm heart. My sense is, it's gotten bigger and warmer over

332

the years. Has that surprised you? That's not the right word. (Paul looks contemplative.)

P: I think that there were many times in my life when my priorities and my goals were not to be loved or be popular, as opposed to trying to accomplish certain things, even if they were unpopular. But I think now I'm at the stage in my life where I just am around friends, and therefore can relax. I do not have to put up certain guards and concerns that I had when I had other priorities.

J: We've talked about the injuries you sustained over the years. Do you have problems in your body as a result of those injuries?

P: Well, not as a result of those injuries. I think my problem is having gotten out of bed too many times. I don't believe any of my pains that I feel are as a result of previous injuries. I believe it's just from many years that I've spent. My body's just getting old, that's all.

J: OK. Thank you. We're looking at the last years of your life and moving forward with an eye towards that time of your death. Please let us know if you are ever arrested again.

P: I've never been arrested again. I'm living in Rome. Since I got here I have lived in a small house on a hillside with a little garden. And I'm not bothered by the authorities, and I do not do anything to incite them. (Paul is now speaking quietly. He seems weak, tired. It's an effort for him to talk.)

J: All right. Thank you. I'm going to ask you now to move forward to the day before you die in this incarnation and suggest that you do not have to feel pain. Just report the events. Moving forward now to the day before, tell us where you are and who you're with.

P: I'm in my house... lying in bed... Benjamin is with me.

J: Benjamin?

P: And Sophia.

J: Sophia? Who is Sophia?

P: Friend... and... there's another person. And I... realize that I'm going to be leaving here soon... I'm prepared to go.

J: You are prepared?

P: Yes. I can... my body is feeling ready... and I serve no further purpose here. I feel a wonderful excitement... deep inside that I will be with Jeshua soon.

J: Anything else that you'd like us to know at this moment?

P: No. I know I'm going.

J: All right. Please then move forward into the death, and describe the experience of the spirit separating from the body.

P: (Long pause.) I feel like I'm traveling. My spirit has left... the body remains on its bed, and I feel like I'm floating... and I'm floating... I see Jeshua, and I... his arms are outstretched... open... wearing a white robe... and I float into his arms, and we embrace... and Josie and Phillip... I feel that I'm filled with the love of God and Jeshua.

J: Continue. (Long pause.) I know it's difficult to find the right words. (Paul does not answer me.)

It was apparent that Paul was now in spirit. He would not respond to my questions. It was obvious to me, as I looked at his face, that he was experiencing tremendous peace and harmony. It was an extremely moving experience for both of us.

Over the next few weeks I was aware of how much I missed talking to Paul, sharing his life and his adventures.

Grief, such as one feels when losing a friend, nagged at me. I became increasingly aware, as I read and reread the transcripts, of God's presence in this work. I'm grateful I have had this opportunity to meet Paul and learn about Jesus firsthand. It is with that same gratitude we share all this with you.

EPILOGUE

As the weeks passed, Nick prayed for more guidance, reassurance, and support as he began to put into place the necessary commitments, along with Abe, Thomas, and Boris, to finance the exposure of the manuscript, as well as set up other projects aimed at bringing us a new tomorrow.

Though Nick had been plagued with concerns about going public in the past, he now was committed to doing whatever was necessary to return to Jesus' original messages. It was as if Christmas were starting all over again. Perhaps, this time, we, as a people, could get it right. Everything seemed to be in place, ready to go. He had Abe, Thomas, and Boris as faithful friends and compatriots. Julia was fully behind him, ready to champion her professional role in the thirteen sessions. The angels had seen to it that the financial resources, as well as the spiritual resources, were available. Certainly, it was time to begin.

The next day Nick pulled out notes he had once written at one of his most questioning moments. He slowly read the missive he had written to himself. It seemed to echo a growing inner voice, which repeatedly spoke to him: *Now is the time.*

> *For many years I have been reluctant to accept or acknowledge the information I was receiving that I had lived a previous lifetime as Paul of Tarsus. I had been concerned about the impact it would have on my life. After I had completed the hypnotic regressions and agreed to have them transcribed into a manuscript, I first decided I would use an alias rather than my own name, for I was concerned of being embarrassed by criticism and ridicule.*

> *When the angelic events occurred to my friends and me, they contributed in convincing me to step forward with the truth and use my own name, regardless of the consequences. I am disclosing these supernatural phenomena at this time but do not want them to distract people from the importance of the Messages contained in the manuscript.*

> *I am prepared to defend the truth found in the manuscript. There will be those who will reject as false the events and information that the witnesses and I have experienced ... because it will conflict with their belief systems. I shall not use the messages of Jesus and Paul to argue against any position. Belief systems are a personal right. They are a gift from God to each person to accept, that brings each person happiness.*

> *For I say we are all on the same journey, which is like that on an ocean. The destination of our journey is to become one with God. Each spiritual belief system and the way we conduct our lives is the vessel we are traveling in, on this journey. There are some of us who find the journey filled with great joy. Our vessel is secure and we have confidence in ourselves. We are engulfed in love to and from others. The waters are calm, and our course is steady.*

There are others who find themselves in stormy waters. They often go astray. Their journey is filled with fear, hostility, and distrust. Although they seek the same destiny, their journey shall be much longer as they travel in troubled waters. As Jesus told Paul, God's love is like sunshine, but there are many who choose to stand in the shade.

If the quality of the journey does not bring harmony and enjoyment each of us is entitled to, then we have the right and obligation to ourselves to challenge the religious and spiritual beliefs that are affecting us. Jesus told Paul that within every one of us is a part of God. It is that which gives us life, and it is that which is everlasting—if we center ourselves, look within, and become at one with that part of God within us.

I am not sure where the Messages of Jesus will once again take us, just as Paul often did not know his next travel itinerary. I am not a body possessing a new spirit and soul. I am a spirit and soul that is possessing a new body. I speak of Paul as a separate person although I know I have the spirit and mind that was once that of Paul. Yet, I am not comfortable as to how to separate or integrate the two, or, if you prefer, the one. I am sure I will be shown in time how to handle this duality.

I am currently visiting cities across the country and spending time speaking to large groups.

Nick Bunick
Christmas 1995

A Note from Nick Bunick

The Messengers was originally introduced in the Seattle/Portland markets in December of 1996, and immediately became a regional bestseller. Because of the overwhelming amount of mail that we have received just from the Pacific Northwest, it is apparent to us that it will be impossible to respond to all the letters that we shall receive nationally. We do love hearing from everyone, but apologize for not being able to give personal written responses.

However, we have decided to create a monthly newsletter which will include events that are taking place surrounding the continued work of Nick Bunick and his colleagues, including the telling of healings people have experienced, human interest stories, notable 444 experiences happening to many people who have read *The Messengers,* as well as dates for symposiums that we will be having around the country.

If you would like to receive this newsletter, we are hopeful that you are able to make a voluntary contribution of $20 or more, representing 12 months of the newsletter, in order to cover the expenses and defray costs. If you cannot afford to make a donation, we will still place your name on the mailing list, and perhaps those who can afford a larger donation can assist us in helping those who cannot contribute. Donations should be made to The Great Tomorrow, and any excess income will be used for spiritual and humanitarian programs.

Your letters, as well as your request to be placed on our subscription list, should be sent to:

The Great Tomorrow
P.O. Box 2222
Lake Oswego, OR 97035

God bless you all as you continue on your journey.

Nick Bunick

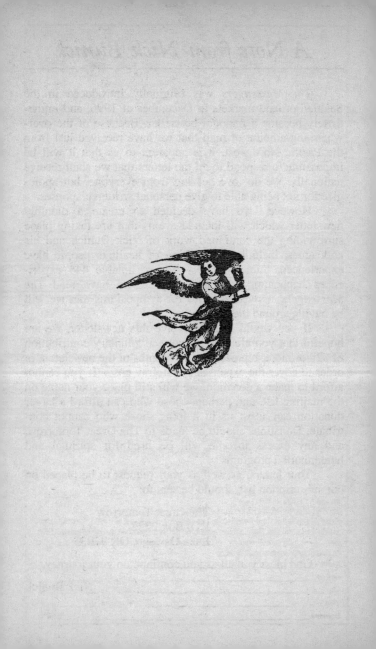